FITNESS FIESTA!

FITNESS FIESTA!

SELLING LATINX CULTURE THROUGH ZUMBA

PETRA R.
RIVERA-RIDEAU

DUKE UNIVERSITY PRESS   DURHAM AND LONDON   2024

© 2024 DUKE UNIVERSITY PRESS
All rights reserved
Printed in the United States of America on acid-free paper ∞
Project Editor: Michael Trudeau
Designed by Matthew Tauch
Typeset in Merlo by Westchester Publishing Services

Library of Congress Cataloging-in-Publication Data
Names: Rivera-Rideau, Petra R., [date] author.
Title: Fitness fiesta! : selling Latinx culture through Zumba /
Petra R. Rivera-Rideau.
Description: Durham : Duke University Press, 2024. | Includes
bibliographical references and index.
Identifiers: LCCN 2023049891 (print)
LCCN 2023049892 (ebook)
ISBN 9781478030812 (paperback)
ISBN 9781478026570 (hardcover)
ISBN 9781478059806 (ebook)
Subjects: LCSH: Zumba Fitness, LLC. | Hispanic Americans in popular
culture. | Hispanic Americans—Music. | Popular music—United
States—Latin American influences. | Popular music—Social aspects—
United States. | Dance—Social aspects—United States. | Stereotypes
(Social psychology) in mass media. | BISAC: SOCIAL SCIENCE / Ethnic
Studies / American / Hispanic American Studies | SOCIAL SCIENCE /
Ethnic Studies / General
Classification: LCC E184.S75 R59 2024 (print) | LCC E184.S75 (ebook) |
DDC 781.62/68—DC23/ENG/20240403
LC record available at https://lccn.loc.gov/2023049891
LC ebook record available at https://lccn.loc.gov/2023049892

Cover art: Photo by Igor Mojzes / Alamy Stock Photo.

FOR MY PARENTS, MEG AND GENE

FOR MY PARTNER, RYAN

AND FOR MY CHILDREN, ADRIAN AND RAFAEL

CONTENTS

ACKNOWLEDGMENTS

~~~~~~

IT TAKES A VILLAGE TO MAKE AN ACADEMIC BOOK. I could never have written this book without the support of friends, colleagues, and, above all, my family.

The first group I must thank are the Zumba instructors who generously shared their thoughts and their time with me. Many of them allowed me free access to at least one of their classes. I cannot name them to protect their anonymity, but if they read the book, I hope that they are pleased with it, even if they might not always agree with it. There is no book without them, and I am forever indebted to them for helping this project come to life. On another note, I also want to thank K. B., whose Zumba Fitness classes kept me going throughout the research and writing of this book—and through a global pandemic!

The second group is my family. I love reading book acknowledgments, and I'm struck by how we all usually put our families last. But without my family, too, this book would never have happened. I dedicate this book to them for all of their love and support. My parents, Gene Rivera and Meg Weiss-Rivera, have always supported and encouraged me. I am grateful to them for all the love they have given me through this process and, really, through my whole life. And, yes, I also thank them for a lot of free babysitting, without which academic mom life would not be possible.

Thank you to my partner, Ryan Rideau, for doing everything he does that I can't even begin to capture in words and for tolerating my Zumba Fitness obsessions. Thank you to my children, Adrian and Rafael, who were tiny when I started this project. They keep me grounded, remind me what's important, and make me laugh with their funny Zumba impressions. They are my everything.

Thanks also to the rest of our extended family. My sister Carmen is a constant source of support, love, laughs, and realness. Thanks to Nico for tolerating me all these years and for the friendship and solidarity. Thanks to Nalini for the funny jokes and dances and all the high fives. Thanks to all my aunts and uncles and cousins. Thanks to my in-laws, Brenda and Kevin Rideau, who have also supported me and cheered me on throughout this wacky academic career. I must give them, too, special thanks for child-care! Thanks to my sister-in-law Ashley Rideau and to the rest of the Rideau and Lacroix families.

I am so fortunate to teach at Wellesley College, where many colleagues and friends have supported me throughout the research and writing of this book. My American Studies department colleagues Genevieve Clutario, Elena Creef, Michael Jeffries, and Yoon Sun Lee have made working at Wellesley fun and easy. Special thanks to Paul Fisher for his mentorship and leadership over the years. Special thanks also to Irene Mata for all of her mentorship and friendship, and for making Wellesley feel more like home. Special thanks to Susan Ellison for her friendship, writing dates, venting, laughs, and porch hangouts. Thanks to Paula Johnson and Andy Shennan for their support of me and my work. Thanks to Olga Shurchkov, former director of the Knapp Center for Social Sciences, and Eve Zimmerman, former director for the Newhouse Center for the Humanities, for offering resources to support my research and writing. A very special thanks to the Women of Color Faculty Mentoring Group—I adore our little community. I have wonderful colleagues across the college, including Soo Hong, Sabriya Fisher, Tavi Gonzalez, Smitha Radhakrishnan, Kellie Carter Jackson, Julie Walsh, Eve Zimmerman, Adam Van Arsdale, Liza Oliver, Nikki Greene, Brenna Greer, Jennifer Chudy, Baafra Abeberese, Chipo Dendere, Koichi Hagimoto, and Mared Alicea-Westort. I would be remiss if I did not also mention my students, who continue to amaze me with their thoughtfulness, smarts, inquisitiveness, and amazing questions. My students in AMST 235 deserve special mention here for their insights that helped me hone some of my thinking on this project as well as the students in the TZE House who invited me to share my work with them. A very special thanks to Stephanie Cobas, class of 2022, who served as my research assistant at various times over the course of this project.

I am also blessed to work with many great colleagues, friends, and mentors across the country who have supported me over the course of my career. A very special thank you to Frances Aparicio for all of her support and mentorship, and for reading early versions of this manuscript. Thanks also to María Elena Cepeda, Jennifer Rudolph, Susan Ellison, and Sabriya Fisher for offering insightful feedback on chapters of the book. Thanks to Jossianna Arroyo at the University of Texas and to the CORE workshop at the Stanford Humanities Center for the opportunity to present this work (virtually) at your colloquia. Special thanks to my colleagues and friends Vanessa Díaz, Marisol Lebrón, Omaris Zamora, Deb Vargas, Yomaira Figueroa, and Lázaro Lima. As always, a super special thanks to Jennifer Jones and Tianna Paschel, without whom I am pretty sure I would have never survived academia. I would also like to thank the members of the New England Consortium for Latina/o Studies (NECLS) for all of their support since I moved back up to the area.

Thanks to everyone at Duke University Press for their help. I am completely indebted to Gisela Fosado, who believed in this project when it was just a kernel of an idea. Thank you so much for listening to me brainstorm, for talking me through really rough ideas and drafts, and for all of your encouragement over the years. I couldn't ask for a better editor. Thanks also to Alejandra Mejia for helping to manage all of the logistics and shepherding me through this process.

I want to thank my friends for the fun, laughter, and much-needed breaks. I am so lucky to have moved back up to the Northeast so I can see many of my old buddies more regularly, including Charisse Padilla, Maryclaire Capetta, Carla Martin, and Danielle Robles. Thanks also to those who are farther away, including Jamie Lawrence (special thanks to Jamie for reading!), Melanie Kiechle and Dennis Halpin, Sarah Ovink, Anthony Peguero, Taj Frazier, and Arya Soman. Thanks to our new Wayland crew for welcoming us into the fold.

Finally, I want to say something about how this book came about. The last time I saw one of my mentors, Juan Flores, was just about six weeks before he passed away very unexpectedly. We were at a conference that I had co-organized with Jennifer Jones and Tianna Paschel at the University of Notre Dame. Somehow the topic of Zumba Fitness came up, and Juan teased me about my love of Zumba Fitness classes. I mentioned to him how I was waiting for someone to write about all the contradictions in Zumba Fitness. "Well," he said, "why don't you write it?" But I knew this time he wasn't joking. I never got to tell him how much that one conversation gave me the final push to commit to this research project at a time when I really struggled to figure out the next steps on my academic journey. Wherever he is, I hope he gets a kick out of this book.

WARM-UP

THERE ARE FEW THINGS I HATE MORE than waking up early or exercising. Imagine my friends' surprise, then, when as a graduate student, I started getting up early to get to the gym by 8 a.m. *three* times a week. The culprit? Zumba Fitness. Zumba Fitness is a dance-fitness program that uses mostly Latin music, along with other genres like Bollywood, soca, dancehall, and Afropop. An instructor leads routines that range in intensity and musical style during the one-hour class. The Zumba Fitness program offers a variety of class formats, including Zumba Basic (what most people think of as a "regular" Zumba class) and variations like Aqua Zumba, Zumba Gold, Zumba Toning, Zumba Sentao, Zumba Step, Zumba Kids, Zumbini (for babies), and the company's HIIT program,[1] STRONG by Zumba.

Zumba Fitness was the best stress relief. I felt rejuvenated after each class. With early morning Zumba, I didn't need five cups of coffee to get over my writers' block. And my experience confirmed what several medical studies have since demonstrated: that frequent participation in Zumba Fitness reduces anxiety and depression.[2] Zumba Fitness classes helped alleviate the anxiety of job applications, academic competition, and dissertation deadlines. What's more, Zumba Fitness featured music I loved. My dissertation examined the racial politics of reggaetón in Puerto Rico, and reggaetón just happened to be one of Zumba Fitness's four core "rhythms" featured in its classes. The class flew by. It did not feel like I was working out—I had embraced Zumba's tagline, "Ditch the workout, join the party!" I was hooked.

But Zumba Fitness also made me uncomfortable. As this book demonstrates, Zumba Fitness's marketing strategy promotes many stereotypical images of the exotic, tropical, foreign Latin other. I loved exercising to my favorite songs, but I wondered how other students who were less familiar with the music interpreted these routines. I was bothered by the idea that Zumba Fitness called salsa, merengue, reggaetón, and cumbia "rhythms" when they are, in fact, vibrant and diverse genres of music that each incorporate a variety of rhythmic structures. I loved singing along to my favorite songs and doing the body rolls and booty pops. Still, I questioned if, for other people, these moves offered evidence for what they already considered a hypersexual and loose "Latin culture." I heard women in the locker room talk about how they envied their Latina instructor's supposedly "natural" hip-shaking moves. I attended a class taught by the same instructor that attracted Asian and Latin American immigrants who shared their challenges acclimating to life in the United States. I participated in classes where students shouted "¡Olé!" and waved around maracas off beat, and other classes where students proudly sang along to the Spanish lyrics of Daddy Yankee and Victor Manuelle. I heard stories from some white women about how Zumba Fitness gave them an opportunity to express their sexy side, and stories from some Black, Latina, and Afro-Latina women about how they tried to be more reserved with their moves so that they wouldn't be seen as hypersexual vixens.

This book is my attempt to grapple with the contradictions I have experienced in my own Zumba Fitness journey. And I am not alone. I have heard similar conflicting feelings from friends, relatives, and Zumba instructors, including many of the instructors I interviewed for this book. To get at the heart of these contradictions, I've attended Zumba Fitness classes in New England and the South, from California to Maine. I've taken Zumba Fitness classes in schools and community centers, corporate gyms and dance studios, college campuses and children's museums, and even on a cruise ship. I've danced to different Zumba rhythms[3] like reggaetón, tango, soca, salsa, Bollywood, dancehall, belly dance, cumbia, quebradita, flamenco, merengue, hip-hop, bachata, azonto, and more. All of this has taught me that there is no one way to do Zumba Fitness. Zumba Fitness means a lot of different things to different people, and it can get messy sometimes.

Fitness Fiesta! explores these contradictions through close analyses of videos, advertisements, memes, and newspaper coverage along with interviews that I conducted with Zumba instructors and presenters. Taken together, these sources tell a complex story about how Zumba Fitness represents and commodifies "Latin culture." This happens as much in the everyday space of the gym as it does in the marketing materials produced by Zumba's Home Office, the company's corporate headquarters in Florida. I will demonstrate how multiple, and often conflicting, ideas about Latinx identities and cultures circulate simultaneously in the Zumba Fitness world.[4] Some might question why it matters what Zumba Fitness says about Latinx culture. The program has been ridiculed for being a fad, tacky or cheesy, not real exercise, or on its way out. Regardless of its future (and, to be clear, I don't see Zumba Fitness going anywhere anytime soon), the reality is it is a tremendously popular fitness program that, for many, is their main point of contact—if not their only one—with "Latin" culture. For this reason, it is critical to unpack the lessons, images, and ideas about Latin(x) American cultures that circulate in the Zumba Fitness universe. Doing so unearths deeply entrenched understandings of the relationship between race, belonging, citizenship, and Latinidad in the contemporary United States.

THE THREE ALBERTOS

In Zumba Fitness circles, the company's origin story has taken on almost mythical status. It begins with the "Three Albertos." First is Alberto "Beto" Pérez, the creator and face of Zumba Fitness. The story begins when Beto forgot to bring his music to an aerobics class he taught in his native Cali, Colombia. So, he substituted a tape with his favorite salsa and merengue hits instead. The students loved it, and he continued building a dance-fitness following with this new formula in Colombia.

Eventually, Beto made it to Miami where he began to teach his special brand of aerobics that he called "Rumbacize." One day, a Colombian woman in his class named Raquel Perlman asked him to meet with her son, (the second) Alberto. Alberto Perlman had enjoyed some success promoting Latin American internet start-ups, but once the dot-com bubble burst, he found himself unemployed and living at his mother's house. He met Pérez and saw potential to expand Rumbacize. Together they linked up with the third Alberto, Alberto Aghion, Perlman's childhood friend and former business partner. The three Albertos created a business plan that merged Pérez's dance background with Aghion and Perlman's business savvy. They named their new program "Zumba," what Pérez later described as "an invented word, a fusion of samba, the lively Brazilian dance form, and rumba, meaning 'party.'"[5]

In 2002, they produced their own workout video set of Beto's classes to peddle nationally on television. Perlman obtained funding for the infomercials from investors in Ohio. The infomercials grew popular, and the three Albertos began receiving other opportunities, including the chance to partner with Kellogg's who put Zumba Fitness DVDs in their Special K cereal boxes. Infomercials expanded to the Spanish-language market in 2004. Eventually people began calling Alberto Aghion to find out how they could become instructors. The Albertos had done a few local trainings that licensed instructors to teach Zumba Fitness, and in 2005, they created the Zumba Educational Division. They began producing music, choreography, and marketing support. In 2006, they created the Zumba Instructor Network (zin), which is fundamental to their business operations. Instructors pay monthly dues to join zin in exchange for new music and choreography to use in their classes. The fitness craze continued to take off, gyms became more interested, more zin members joined, and the brand became a global phenomenon.[6]

Zumba Fitness now boasts a global audience.[7] Potential instructors attend a one-day training taught by a Zumba Education Specialist (zes), which is the highest level of Zumba Fitness professional. Upon completion, instructors earn a license that permits them to teach Zumba Fitness; however, they also have to pay the Zumba Home Office monthly dues to keep their licenses in good standing and to join the Zumba Instructor Network. In return, instructors receive music recordings to use in their classes on "zin volumes" or, increasingly, the zin Play app. The company also provides zin members with marketing tips, choreography, a website domain, and exclusive access to discounts and the Zumba Convention (among other things). In this way, Zumba Fitness's primary customers are its own instructors who dutifully give the company their monthly dues and, often, purchase Zumba products from vacations to clothing. The Zumba Home Office does not release revenue figures, but in 2012, Perlman suggested that the company was worth "nine figures"[8]— and since then, even if its popularity is said to have peaked, Zumba Fitness has only grown.[9] Zumba Fitness's business model thus revolves around an idea that the company produces entrepreneurs, giving instructors all the tools that they need to be successful. What instructors do with that information is up to them. As we will see later, many Zumba instructors encounter significant challenges with this business model; however, some also see it as a way to achieve individual success and, in some cases, the American dream.

The serendipitous story of Zumba Fitness's creation and ultimate success foregrounds many of the critical values and ideologies embedded within the Zumba Fitness brand. The frequent mentioning of the three Albertos' Colombian roots, and in particular Beto's history teaching dance-fitness classes in Colombia, represents Zumba Fitness as authentically rooted in Latin American culture. This authenticity forms a critical part of the Zumba Fitness brand and how instructors on the ground view their own relationships to the exercise program. In addition, the story is fully steeped in the ideals of the American dream. Persistence, endurance, innovation, and sacrifice all take center stage in the story of Zumba Fitness's beginnings. This ethos aligns the program with hegemonic ideologies of neoliberalism and postracialism in the United States. In so doing, Zumba Fitness capitalizes on the marketing of ethnic difference—in this case what I term *tropicalized Latinness*—without troubling the racial status quo. Instead, Zumba Fitness couches its narrative within the rhetoric of cultural appreciation, honoring diversity, and meritocracy that ultimately masks the continued salience of racial hierarchies in the United States.

FIT CITIZENS

I often get funny looks from people when I explain that I am researching Zumba Fitness and what it tells us about Latinx identity and citizenship. Many people understand Zumba Fitness to be something that is tied to Latin culture, but the issue of citizenship throws some people off. Perhaps this is because of the common attitude in the United States that one's fitness is a result of their individual choices to consume healthy foods, exercise regularly, and avoid habits like smoking or drinking alcohol. However, it is precisely this assumption that one's health and fitness stem exclusively from their lifestyle choices that obscures how physical ability is central to our conceptions of citizenship. Many scholars of disability studies have made this argument in relation to the ways that judgments of an individual's or group's capacity for rational thought and physical strength have been used to restrict their citizenship rights and exclude them from important civic spaces.[10] Kathleen LeBesco argues that disability and weight gain are often depicted as fundamentally distinct due to assumptions that one does not *choose* to live with a disability, but one *can* modify their lifestyle in order to avoid the unhealthy consequences of being overweight. Nevertheless, she argues that both disability rights activists and fat activists strive to combat similar structural inequalities like the lack of access to services or the negative impact of social stigmas. Despite being construed as a choice, LeBesco shows that the weight and shape of the body are essential to hegemonic definitions of citizenship that determine who belongs in the United States.[11]

Because healthy habits are considered matters of choice, engaging in fitness demonstrates a commitment to neoliberal ideologies that link citizenship to one's self-sufficiency and productivity. Historian Shelly McKenzie argues that, since the 1950s, fitness became tied with patriotism and productivity; to be fit was to be a good citizen, a hard worker, and an impactful contributor to society.[12] At the same time, to have fit citizens in the wakes of several major wars also assured that the military would have ample able-bodied men to fight if the need arose.[13] This intimately linked patriotism to physical fitness.

As time wore on, though, ideas about physical fitness began to stress *individual* fitness outcomes rather than national security, although still in the context of civic duty. Beginning in the 1960s, media and policy discourses shifted to endorsing fitness as a way to achieve ideal health and beauty.[14] Promoters of fitness argued that it could also lead to other emotional and personal enhancements like increased happiness and professional competence.[15] Physical fitness increasingly became a marker of not only health, but also the type of morality and self-discipline consistent with hegemonic expectations of "proper" citizens.[16] "Maintaining a fit body," write sociologists Shari L. Dworkin and Faye Linda Wachs, "is no longer viewed as a personal choice, but as an obligation to the public good and a requirement for good citizenry. The once narcissistic body obsession has not only become a marker of individual health, but a form of social responsibility and civic participation."[17] Jennifer Smith Maguire argues that the notion that individuals either choose to be fit or to be "inactive" rendered fitness "an ethical and moral choice affiliated with connotations of status, virtuousness, and self-responsibility."[18] Even with increased attention to beauty or personality enhancements, the relationship between physical fitness and citizenship never disappeared.

This coupling of physical fitness and citizenship ramped up in the 1980s.[19] The fitness industry mushroomed during this time with the advent of more private fitness clubs and the popularity of fitness celebrities like Jane Fonda, whose aerobics videos made exercise possible whenever and wherever the consumer chose to do it.[20] It is no accident that these ideas about fitness and individual accountability grew in earnest during President Ronald Reagan's administration, which emphasized toughness and self-reliance. Indeed, McKenzie writes that Reagan used exercise to demonstrate his own ruggedness and fitness for office.[21] The widespread availability of fitness options furthered the assumption that fitness was always a personal choice. Physical fitness conjoined health, patriotism, and morality by making individual self-sufficiency central to being a productive, industrious, and valued citizen.

During this time, the Reagan administration dismantled social welfare programs. To do so, the federal government perpetuated the stereotype of the so-called welfare queen, or the Black single mother who allegedly preferred to live off state assistance rather than work.[22] The pernicious image of the "welfare queen" reproduced racist depictions of Black women as lazy and sneaky people who actively chose to reap the benefits of other people's labor. Around the same time, anxieties about immigrants, especially Latin American ones, arriving in the United States increased. Although Reagan's Immigration Reform and Control Act of 1986 offered a path to legal status for some undocumented immigrants, it also sought to curb undocumented immigration through punitive policies targeting laborers, employers, and others. This revealed the profound anxiety that immigrants, especially Mexican immigrants, would unfairly take advantage of the benefits of US citizenship (e.g., social welfare benefits, public schools) without contributing to society or the economy (despite the fact that undocumented immigrants *do* pay taxes in the United States). All of these criticisms of social welfare programs targeted Black and Latinx communities assumed to be slothful and cunning "freeloaders" who aimed to take advantage of others' work.

These stereotypes conjure up very specific images of racialized and gendered bodies. For instance, the unruly Black woman's body is a controlling image in the Global North that has long signified racist ideas about Black women's hypersexuality and excess. This excess—being too much, too big, too flashy—is then used to depict Black and Latinx bodies as the opposite of the morals and ideals of modern, rational subjects imagined as white.[23] Weight exemplifies this excess. As Amy Ferrell notes, when increased numbers of immigrants and African Americans arrived in the northern United States in the mid-twentieth century, "fatness became yet another signifier of inferiority, a line demarcating the divide between civilization and primitive cultures, whiteness and blackness, sexual restraint and sexual promiscuity, beauty and ugliness, progress and past."[24] Overweight Black and Latinx bodies seemingly confirmed stereotypes of Black and Latinx people's alleged lack of restraint.

Present-day rhetoric about the obesity epidemic in the United States continues these racialized assumptions that it is the poor, the immigrant, and the person of color who is most at risk. It is true that Black and Latinx communities are disproportionately more likely to be obese than their white counterparts. And yet, several scholars have pointed out that this anxiety about obesity often pathologizes individual behavior rather than addressing structural inequalities that prevent these communities from accessing healthy food, safe exercise spaces, or adequate healthcare.[25] Instead, the obesity epidemic in Black and Latinx communities is considered the result of cultural deficiency. For example, Natalie Boero analyzes the prevalence of "mother blame" in discussions of the childhood obesity epidemic. Mother blame faults mothers for teaching their children unhealthy habits and feeding them junk food. Boero points out that African American and Latinx mothers are especially targeted by discourses of mother blame.[26] In this way, mother blame can be directly related to the stereotypes of the so-called welfare queen whose selfish attitude prevents her from parenting properly.

Cultural deficiencies are also mobilized in depictions of immigrants' eating habits. Anthropologists Laura-Anne Minkoff-Zern and Megan A. Carney find that Latinx farm laborers *do* know what healthy food is, and *do* value healthy eating. However, the prevailing logic for "food assistance programs" targeting these populations "focus[es] on Latino clients' lack of diet-related knowledge, while overlooking im/migrant food-related knowledge and income-related limitations."[27] Such programs depict US approaches to food and behavior as more informed and "civilized" while Latinxs' "habits" are understood to be "primitive" and faulty. This is no surprise given that, historically, public health officials have often painted Latin American and other immigrant populations as culturally suspect, filthy, and carriers of rampant disease—in other words, immigrants allegedly posed serious threats to the health and well-being of the (white) American public due, in part, to their presumably deficient approaches to health.[28]

That obesity—the contemporary marker of the lack of fitness—is associated with the poor, the immigrant, and the person of color is not surprising. These are the same groups already deemed "failed citizens," or those who do not conform to hegemonic values and ideals associated with citizenship.[29] Catherine Ramírez reminds us that people of color, whether immigrant or not, are often depicted as failed citizens given the historical emphasis on whiteness as a marker of Americanness, which persists despite claims that the United States has now become postracial.[30] Although obesity absolutely impacts an individual's health outcomes, the point here is that *who* is fit and what fit *looks like* is intrinsically racialized and, as such, firmly linked to ideas about who can be a productive and self-sufficient citizen. As Cathy Zanker and Michael Gard put it, "From preventing obesity, cancer, and diabetes to improving school results, giving direction to the lives of disaffected youth, and rebuilding dysfunctional communities, it is hard to think of a problem for which physical activity is not seen as a cure."[31] Foregrounding individuals' physical fitness and lifestyle choices obscures the structural inequality that causes health problems for racially and economically marginalized groups.

In this context, the fact that Zumba Fitness is a *Latin* dance-fitness program might seem like an opportunity to reformulate "Latin culture" as something capable of making the body healthy and fit rather than a culturally deficient approach to food and wellness. For example, Beto Pérez, the face of Zumba Fitness, conforms to the ideal male fit body while also foregrounding his experiences and identity as a Colombian immigrant to the United States. However, Zumba Fitness's popularity has not led to a perception that Latinx people are more physically fit or healthy. Instead, as I show in this book, Zumba Fitness has embraced the neoliberal approach to health and wellness that stresses individual commitments to maintaining a healthy lifestyle. Zumba Fitness might be Latin-based, but it still reproduces hegemonic standards of citizenship. Zumba Fitness thus becomes an avenue to produce fit citizens, but not necessarily a space for confirming Latinx citizenship despite being widely recognized for being uniquely "Latin." This contradiction is further amplified in the social and historical context in which Zumba Fitness developed, one steeped in anti-immigrant and anti-Latinx sentiment, but also one where Latinx stars made significant inroads in mainstream US popular culture.

LATINX STARS AND LATINX THREATS

Zumba Fitness emerged at a time of rampant and growing xenophobic and anti-Latinx sentiment in the United States. By the time Zumba Fitness released its infomercials in 2002, the United States had witnessed the passing of myriad laws and propositions meant to restrict an imagined "wave" of Latin American immigrants into the United States. In the 1990s, state policies like California's Prop 187 in 1994 and federal laws such as the Illegal Immigration Reform and Immigrant Responsibility Act of 1996 created increasingly difficult hurdles for immigrants to settle and earn a living in the United States.[32] After the terrorist attacks of September 11,

2001, anti-immigrant sentiment increased as pundits and politicians warned of a potential national security threat posed by undocumented immigrants who arrived to the United States. They depicted the US border with Mexico as an especially dangerous place where terrorists, drug dealers, and other violent criminals could arrive into the United States undetected. Despite the fact that Mexicans had nothing to do with 9/11, and that 9/11 attackers arrived in the United States with visas, undocumented Mexicans embodied the threat posed by this new "flood" of immigrants into the country. Concerns about terrorism dovetailed with long-standing stereotypes of undocumented immigrants as criminals, disease-ridden, and uneducated individuals seeking to take advantage of social welfare programs in the United States.

The unfounded link between terrorism and immigration emerged not only in policies targeting immigrants and the increased militarization of the border, but also in mainstream media when pundits such as Lou Dobbs (CNN) and Bill O'Reilly (Fox News) stoked nativist fears of an immigrant takeover.[33] This discourse escalated throughout the mid-2000s. In 2006, a national wave of protests supporting immigrants' rights and demanding a pathway to citizenship for the undocumented was met with escalating rhetoric about how an influx of Latin American immigrants would not only impact the US economy but fundamentally transform the social order and culture of the United States more generally. In this context, which flags people waved at demonstrations or what languages they spoke in public allegedly symbolized where their loyalties lay—the United States or somewhere else.[34] Even a 2006 Absolut Vodka ad that targeted consumers within Mexico became a flashpoint for nativist rhetoric about the alleged Mexican takeover of the southwestern United States.[35] In this context, several states passed increasingly punitive anti-immigrant legislation, such as the notoriously draconian bills SB1070 of Arizona and HB56 of Alabama. Federal courts struck down many aspects of these bills, but the message was clear: Latin American immigrants (especially Mexicans) threatened life as we knew it in the United States.

Leo Chávez terms such discourses the "Latino Threat Narrative." He writes:

> The Latino Threat Narrative posits that Latinos are not like previous immigrant groups, who ultimately became part of the nation. According to the assumptions and taken-for-granted "truths" inherent in this narrative, Latinos are unwilling or incapable of integrating, of becoming part

of the national community. Rather, they are part of an invading force from south of the border that is bent on reconquering land that was formerly theirs (the US Southwest) and destroying the American way of life. Although Mexicans are often the focus of the Latino Threat Narrative, public discourse . . . often includes immigration from Latin America in general, as well as US-born Americans of Latin American descent.[36]

Although the Latino Threat Narrative may have surfaced with a vengeance in the mid-2000s, the assumption of Latin American immigrants as potentially dangerous foreigners has long circulated in the United States. As Lee Bebout points out in relation to Mexicans in particular, these discourses have been integral to racializing Mexicans and Latinx people more broadly as distinct from whiteness, and thus Americanness, in the United States.[37] In other words, discourses like the Latino Threat Narrative do more than portray Latinx populations as dangerous and undesirable; they also shore up the associations between whiteness, citizenship, and Americanness in the United States.

Ironically, though, the 1990s and 2000s were also a time of growing Latinx representation in US mainstream media. By the time Zumba Fitness released its infomercials in 2002, the US mainstream had witnessed the so-called Latin boom in popular music, a moment when Latin artists dominated the top of the charts. Many of these artists, such as Ricky Martin, Shakira, Enrique Iglesias, and Marc Anthony, crossed over into the US mainstream market after having incredibly successful careers in the Spanish-language Latin music industry. The result was a frequent portrayal of these artists as foreign despite the reality that most were from, or had strong ties to, the United States. Latin boom artists were continually framed via long-standing tropes of hypersexuality and exoticism that further marked them as racialized others. But these stereotypes became packaged in such a way that rendered these artists as nonthreatening. That is, instead of the hypersexuality of the Latina immigrant mother that threatens the demographic and cultural dynamics of the United States, the hypersexuality performed by crossover stars like Shakira and Ricky Martin became something exotic, titillating, and appropriate for mainstream consumption.[38]

Another characteristic that enabled Latin boom stars' entrance into the mainstream is what María Elena Cepeda calls their *"appearance* of whiteness."[39] In other words, as I have argued elsewhere, these stars embodied a "Latino whiteness" that racially marked them as other vis-à-vis

Anglo whites in the United States but that also distinguished them from nonwhite Latinx people and African Americans.[40] Media representations of Latinxs have historically prioritized those with the so-called Latin look—lightly tan skin, Eurocentric features, and straight or wavy hair. The ubiquity of these images implies that the authentic Latinx person embodies Latino whiteness. Frequent stories and analyses of the systemic exclusion of Afro-Latinx and Indigenous Latinx populations reveal just how common the affiliation between Latino whiteness and Latinidad is in hegemonic depictions of Latinx communities. At the same time, Latino whiteness distanced these Latin pop stars from the "browning of America" associated with the Latino Threat Narrative. Images of the dark-skinned clandestine Latino man dodging authorities on the border accompanied this idea of a "brown wave" or "flood of immigrants" taking over the United States.[41] In contrast, the Latin boom stars' Latino whiteness presented them as assimilable Latin American immigrants whose exoticism and foreignness added a spiciness to US culture that marked them as racialized others. Although they were not fully assimilated as white Americans, these crossover artists' nonthreatening otherness enabled their incorporation into the mainstream. Through performing and embodying this otherness, Latin boom stars could serve as a foil against which normative, mainstream, white Americanness was defined. Their crossover did not necessarily indicate a greater acceptance of these stars as equals to white Americans but, rather, as representatives of a racial and ethnic difference that could be safely and easily consumed by all.

In addition to their Latino whiteness, many of these stars also embodied the so-called American dream. If the Latino Threat Narrative assumed that Latin American immigrants arriving into the United States would eventually drain state resources, the Latin boom artists portrayed a different sort of immigrant who instead would contribute to the US economy. In fact, their embodiment of the American dream conformed to other media depictions of Latinx and Latin American communities as hardworking immigrants. For example, Leah Perry notes, mainstream media routinely depicted 1990s artists Selena Quintanilla and Jennifer Lopez as people marked by immigration despite the fact that Quintanilla was born and raised in Texas and Lopez in New York. This not only reiterated the depiction of Latinx people as always foreign, but it also made achieving the American dream a condition for citizenship.[42] Hector Amaya analyzes the incorporation of immigrant narratives in popular television shows like *Ugly Betty*, which aired from 2006 to 2010 and told the story of a daughter of Mexican immigrants in Queens, New York, trying to make it in the fashion industry. As one of very few representations of Latinx life on mainstream television, *Ugly Betty* helped reinforce the perception that "good" immigrants become self-reliant and economically successful. Amaya argues that *Ugly Betty*'s success reveals "some of the key conditions Latinas/os have to fulfill to be incorporated in mainstream English-language media, conditions that include fitting into neoliberal definitions of diversity that further devalue the political and cultural capital associated with Latino narratives and Latino labor."[43] This emphasis on the American dream as integral to US citizenship represents those people who do not "make it" as failures due to their own personal faults and supposedly subpar work ethic rather than systemic inequality.

The idea that some Latinx people could achieve the American dream aligned with a representation of Latinx immigrants as hardworking and traditional. This narrative portrayed Latinx communities as people who could potentially embody the values of hard work and moral conservatism of the mainstream United States. Notably, Latinx communities were desired primarily for their purchasing power or voting habits, thus centering neoliberal justifications for their potential inclusion into US society. In this vein, broader policy discussions again stressed the potential economic contributions of Latinx communities while maintaining their ethnic difference. Still, as Arlene Dávila notes, this more "positive" representation of Latinxs did not remove the understanding of them as a cultural and social threat. Instead, these contradictory discourses circulated simultaneously.[44]

Many of the contradictions inherent to Zumba Fitness become less surprising when understood as part of a broader context of contradictory representations of Latinx communities as simultaneously desirable and threatening, assimilable and foreign. The hyperemphasis on Latinxs' foreignness furthered the historically rooted understanding that citizenship and whiteness were intrinsically linked. The success of cultural phenomena like the Latin boom and *Ugly Betty* proved that mainstream audiences had an appetite for "Latin" culture provided it did not threaten the status quo. Similarly, Zumba Fitness manages these contradictions by peddling stereotypes of Latinx people and culture as fun, musical, sexy, prone to partying, and exotic while simultaneously marshaling these stereotypes into consumable products that could become pathways toward upward mobility and multicultural inclusion. Thus, Zumba Fitness can be a symbol of an appealing and consumable cultural, racial, and ethnic difference that suggests the end of systemic racism even as it promotes racist stereotypes.

. . . .

ZUMBA IS LIKE STARBUCKS

I met Miriam at Starbucks during her break between teaching fitness classes.[45] At the time, Miriam taught five Zumba Fitness classes a week, including Zumba Basic, Zumba Gold, and Aqua Zumba. Although Miriam enjoyed Zumba Fitness for many of the same reasons that other instructors did—she liked the music, the sense of community—she also thought Zumba Fitness had a brilliant marketing scheme. While sipping on our lattes, Miriam explained, "Zumba has amazing marketing. It's a brand. It's a sense of belonging. It's like, you know, people that drink Starbucks. It puts you in a category of people that do this, and the great thing about this is that you actually connect with people around the world. You find people alike. . . . It's a sense of belonging to a brand. It's catchy. It's colorful. It's energetic. It's really great. But it's the best marketing." Miriam's comments point to a critical aspect of Zumba Fitness's business model cooked up by Alberto Perlman and Alberto Aghion—an enthusiastic dedication to the brand. In fact, CNBC called Zumba the "world's largest branded fitness program" of 2018, indicating just how effective this dedication is.[46]

Zumba Fitness's business model offers a fair amount of autonomy to Zumba instructors. Besides ensuring instructors pay their monthly dues, there is no centralized oversight of instructors' classes. Instructors can include whichever songs they like from a variety of genres, and they can utilize the choreography provided by the company or create their own. Instructors are supposed to follow what they refer to as the "Zumba formula" when organizing their classes. Many instructors described the Zumba formula as "70/30," meaning 70 percent Latin music and 30 percent something else, be it Top 40, hip-hop, or some other "world rhythm" like belly dance or Bollywood. The Zumba formula provides some degree of standardization across Zumba Fitness classes, as do the ZIN volumes and the ZIN Play app. Since many instructors rely on the choreography provided by Zumba Fitness, a student can attend different Zumba classes and encounter the same routine. For example, my mother-in-law brought me to her regular Zumba Fitness class in California. Although I live in Massachusetts, I already knew several routines in the California class since they all consisted of choreography created and distributed by Zumba's Home Office.

Still, not everyone follows the formula. Some instructors prefer to create their own choreography or to include songs they find outside of ZIN volumes. Even when different instructors might use some of the same choreography, no two classes are the same. Instructors have their own personality and flair, and they organize their playlists in different ways. Some incorporate a lot of US popular music in English. Others rely more heavily on popular "world" rhythms like Bollywood, soca, Afropop, or dancehall than on the four Latin core rhythms. They might modify their playlists based on the tastes and abilities of their students. Regardless of how faithful the instructors I interviewed were to the Zumba formula, they all agreed that Zumba Fitness classes should have diverse music with very limited US American pop, routines that are easy to follow, and a pace that varies in intensity.

Most people in Zumba Fitness classes are not privy to the instructions provided to their instructors about the Zumba formula. Based on my informal conversations with friends, family, and fellow students in my own Zumba classes, the vast majority of the students in Zumba Fitness classes have no idea that a formula exists. With all of the variety in Zumba Fitness classes, and with no one to guarantee that the instructors follow the Zumba formula, what is it that actually makes the brand that Miriam described so identifiable?

The answer is tropicalized Latinness. Many people often point to the Latin music that dominates Zumba Fitness classes as the primary evidence of the fitness program's "Latin" identity. But I would argue that Zumba Fitness's Latinness extends beyond its soundtrack. Instead, *Fitness Fiesta!* shows how Zumba Fitness manufactures a specific brand of "Latinness" that draws from and informs a wider set of values and assumptions about Latinx people and cultures in the United States. I define Latinidad and Latinness as distinct entities. *Latinidad* is a term that scholars use to describe the state of being Latinx in the United States. Latinidad often foregrounds the panethnic nature of the Latinx experience by exploring the similarities and differences between distinct national origin groups (e.g., Salvadorans, Puerto Ricans, Colombians). Many scholars stress that Latinidad emerges from the ground up as different Latinx groups respond to institutionalized forms of ethnoracial discrimination they encounter in the United States that are rooted in the ongoing (neo)colonial relations between the United States and Latin America.[47] Of course, there is no guarantee that Latinx communities would all align under this umbrella category. G. Cristina Mora shows how a panethnic "Hispanic" category emerged out of a marriage between different institutions—US government agencies, Latinx activists, and Spanish-language media—that convinced people to coalesce behind the category in the 1970s.[48] Corporate entities have also been invested in bringing together groups of Latin American descent in the United States into one consumer market.[49] While such top-down, institutionally driven efforts to create a panethnic category might make some skeptical of its power, Latinidad has still been useful for groups of Latin American descent to organize and push for civil rights. This is never a completely smooth or seamless process. Rather, as Frances Aparicio argues, groups must engage across differences related to race, national origin, language, and other social categories in order to come together. For this reason, she proposes *Latinidad/es* as a term that "allows us to document, analyze, and theorize the processes by which diverse Latina/os interact, subordinate, and transculturate each other while reaffirming the plural and heterogeneous sites that constitute Latinidad."[50] Latinidad is thus not a natural or inherent category, but one that is always in flux and always negotiated. Despite the various institutions and corporations with vested interests in a panethnic category, I see Latinidad as something that is of particular importance to descendants of Latin Americans in the United States who, despite their differences, share some common ground, especially in terms of their ethnoracialization.

On the other hand, I define *Latinness* as a top-down definition of Latinx identities and cultures that emerges from *outside* Latinx communities. Rather than a panethnic identity that recognizes difference, tropicalized Latinness primarily serves as a site of consumption by audiences who may or may not identify as Latinx. Moreover, tropicalized Latinness centers homogeneity. Drawing from the work of scholars like Alberto Sandoval-Sánchez, Brian Eugenio Herrera, Isabel Molina-Guzmán, and Frances Aparicio and Susana Chávez-Silverman, I use tropicalized Latinness to refer to the dominant racist assumptions and stereotypes that inform commodified, hegemonic tropes of Latin(x) American cultures and people. Brian Eugenio Herrera writes that Latinness and its corollaries like *Latin* or *Latinization* "describe cultural mechanisms of appropriation and, just as often, misunderstanding." Herrera argues that these terms point out the "very constructedness . . . inaccuracies and inauthenticities" of performances and representations of Latinx cultures and identities that depart from "actual Latina/o peoples, communities, and audiences."[51] Such representations become normalized by what Isabel Molina-Guzmán calls "symbolic colonization," or the "storytelling mechanism through which ethnic and racial differences are hegemonically tamed and incorporated through the media." In her analysis of mainstream media representations of Latinas, Molina-Guzmán argues that this symbolic colonization reproduces stereotypes of Latinx people as "foreign, exotic, and consumable."[52] Ultimately, then, the process of symbolic colonization reinforces stereotypes of Latinx cultures and communities in the construction of Latinness, but it does so in ways that render them safe for consumption even as they further entrench structural forms of racial inequality.

Tropicalization is at the heart of Zumba Fitness's Latinness. Frances Aparicio and Susana Chávez-Silverman define tropicalization as a process that "imbue[s] a particular space, geography, group or nation with a set of traits, images, and values" that creates a "mythic idea of Latinidad based on Anglo (or dominant) projections of fear."[53] Hegemonic tropicalizations stem from "instances in a long history of Western representations of the exotic, primitive Other."[54] We see these hegemonic tropicalizations in images of hypersexual Latina performers whose foreignness might be amplified by their exotic places of origin, or their spoken accents. Their curvaceous bodies often signal racial difference that depicts them as close to but distinct from Blackness. Tropicalized Latinness is thus marked by an exotic, foreign, racialized otherness that is fundamentally distinct from allegedly more white, respectable, and civilized US Americanness.

Tropicalization also signals an attachment to place. The exotic, sexual figures who embody tropicalization are assumed to arrive in the United States from an undifferentiated tropical zone of sunshine, beaches, and sea breezes, where anything goes and one can live out their most basic and unfettered desires. The residents of the tropics—in this case Latin Americans and their US Latinx diasporas—are depicted as *naturally* prone to primitive behavior as a result of having come from a supposedly unrestrained environment that exists both metaphorically and geographically outside of the boundaries of US modernity. The tropical signals both cultural and geographic—and therefore foreign—difference.

More than inaccurate or problematic representations, the circulation of tropicalized Latinness actually does ideological work that provides fodder for the continued marginalization of Latinx and Latin American communities by the United States. Hegemonic tropicalizations seemingly confirm ethnoracial hierarchies that depict Latin Americans and US Latinxs as racially suspect and inferior to Anglo whites. Representations of Latin Americans as childlike, unintelligent, and unable to govern themselves have been used to justify US interventions in Latin America, from the literal takeover of Latin American governments (as in the ongoing colonial relationship with Puerto Rico) to creating the conditions for US companies to profit from the labor and natural resources of Latin American nation-states (like the interventions of the United Fruit Company across much of Central America). As Nelson Maldonado-Torres points out, the very same assumption that Latin America requires US aid to become more civilized or modern extends to Latinx communities in the United States who are similarly understood as distinct from the rest of the allegedly more modern and civilized US body politic.[55] In this context, representation is more than a reflection of social conditions; it actively aids in the creation of those conditions in the first place. Disseminating images of Latinxs as the antithesis to the standards associated with the modern respectability of US mainstream (white) culture shapes people's understandings of what and who Latinxs are, and allegedly "justifies" their ongoing exclusion from full civic rights in the United States. Tropicalized Latinness is thus integral to the marking of Latinx people as unfit for citizenship.

Several scholars have analyzed and critiqued the prevalence of these stereotypes in film, television, popular music, literature, and theater.[56] Zumba Fitness differs from many of these other forms of mass-mediated representation in that it is an exercise program in which Latinness is actively experienced rather than passively consumed. Whereas representations of Latinx bodies take center stage in analyses of popular media, Latinx bodies are not necessarily visible or even present within Zumba Fitness classes. Instead, more abstract cues from gestures, sounds, dance moves, or aesthetics make Latinness legible to participants regardless of whether or not they are Latinx themselves. This does not mean that Zumba Fitness enthusiasts who are not Latinx envision themselves as taking on a Latinx identity in Zumba Fitness class. Instead, they *experience* tropicalized Latinness in their one-hour Zumba Fitness class. Ironically, this experience can actually mark non-Latinx Zumba Fitness enthusiasts as distinct from the cultural practices they encounter in their classes. On the other hand, those who identify with Latinx music and dance might view participating in Zumba Fitness as something that allows them to celebrate their cultural pride and traditions. Although individuals may have very different interpretations of what happens in a Zumba Fitness class based on their own backgrounds and life experiences, the overall Zumba Fitness brand thrives on tropical-ized Latinness, often in very problematic ways, to distinguish itself in the fitness world. It is this dominant construction of tropicalized Latin-ness promoted by the Zumba Home Office, and how this becomes inter-preted, mediated, and occasionally contested on the ground, that is the focus of this book.

Despite trafficking in racial stereotypes, the Zumba Fitness brand is depicted as a place that values racial difference and inclusivity. For exam-ple, Alberto Perlman told the *Miami Herald* that the "inclusivity is what is special. Everyone is welcome. People in wheelchairs, people from all walks of life, all countries, all ages—that is very unique to Zumba."[57] At her 2019 Zumba Convention Fitness Concert, singer Becky G explained, "That's what I love about Zumba is it brings us all together. Doesn't matter where you from, what color you are, what you stand for, we all come together and we share a beautiful moment."[58] And many instruc-tors I spoke with for this project routinely celebrated Zumba Fitness as a space for understanding and celebrating other cultures. On the surface, such proclamations seem positive. However, as I mentioned earlier, only those who conform to the image of the exotic Latin foreign other can become stand-ins for the integration of Latinx people as a whole. Those Latinx people who do not or cannot become framed within tropes of tropicalized Latinness are depicted as undesirable, problematic popu-lations. It is this contradiction—the incorporation of some ideas about Latin culture and the firm exclusion of others—that enables the coexis-tence of structural racism and multicultural tolerance.

For this reason, dominant ideologies of neoliberal multiculturalism can easily incorporate tropicalized Latinness without dismantling struc-tural inequality. Neoliberal multiculturalism enables the integration of certain racialized subjects into a multicultural society while continuing to maintain white supremacy and stigmatize others.[59] Despite rhetoric that praises inclusion, access to the Other actually allows for those in power to affirm their own position.[60] Tropicalized Latinness thus offers people the opportunity to engage with and dabble in something "Latin" without disrupting the structural racism and xenophobia that preclude Latinxs' full access to citizenship rights. And so, the overwhelming anti-Latinx and anti-immigrant sentiment that paints Latinxs as fundamen-tally unfit for citizenship does not actually present a barrier to the growth and popularity of a Latin dance-fitness program like Zumba Fitness.

Throughout the course of this project, I have heard many detractors' reasons for why they hate Zumba Fitness. It is bad exercise, just a fad. It fosters an irrational, almost cult-like dedication. It isn't authentic, but rather another egregious form of cultural appropriation. It is similar to a multilevel marketing scheme, full of false promises of success. It is just annoying. But I would argue that Zumba Fitness *is* in fact worth taking seriously. For many people who I have met, Zumba Fitness is their introduction to "Latin" culture. This means that tropicalized Latinness shapes many people's understanding of what being Latinx is. And it is precisely because of this dedication to the brand that Zumba Fitness has such a big impact on how people understand themselves in relation to Latinness in the United States. Ultimately, Zumba Fitness's circulation of tropicalized Latinness disseminates racist stereotypes of the Latin foreign other while simultaneously dismissing the continued impact of systemic racism.

ZUMBA, NEW ENGLAND STYLE

This book analyzes how Zumba Fitness creates and sells tropicalized Latinness. I use a variety of sources to make my argument: marketing materials from the Zumba Home Office; Zumba Fitness exercise videos and video games; memes and other representations of Zumba Fitness that circulate online; reviews and discussions of Zumba Fitness in popular publications; and my own ethnographic experiences in classes and interviews with Zumba instructors. Since I am not a dues-paying ZIN member, I do not have access to materials that Zumba Fitness exclusively produces for its instructors, like full-length choreography videos or Zumba-produced music.[61] However, I still had a wealth of material to choose from. For instance, for many years, the Zumba Home Office published a monthly online newsletter called *Z-Life* that chronicled Zumba Fitness trends like new clothes, "hot tracks," and individuals' inspirational "Zumba Stories." Snippets of choreography are available on Zumba Fitness's official YouTube channel and on the public social media accounts of popular Zumba Fitness presenters. Zumba Fitness sells many exercise videos and video games available for home use regardless of ZIN status. Online advertisements enticing students to enroll in a Zumba class or to become instructors are regularly available. Zumba's products, like Zumba Wear or the now defunct "Shake Shake Shake" vegan shakes, are advertised and sold on the company's website. These public materials are crucial to the Zumba Fitness brand, perhaps even more so than exclusive content given to instructors, because they attract students who could potentially become dues-paying ZIN members. These public materials are also critical for my purposes since they shape the view of Zumba Fitness in the popular imagination for both detractors and enthusiasts. I combine these sources with other online sources, such as blog posts or memes, produced about Zumba Fitness by practitioners and detractors. Altogether, these sources uncover how Zumba Fitness sells tropicalized Latinness, and to what effect.

I combine my cultural studies analyses of these products and media with ethnographic research and interviews completed from 2016 to 2019 in New England, especially the Boston metropolitan area. The Zumba Home Office divides different areas into "districts," of which New England is District 45. Many Zumba instructors explained to me that District 45 is especially active—one even called it a "saturated market." There are countless Zumba Fitness classes in the area, as well as a plethora of professional development opportunities for Zumba instructors.[62] Over the course of my project, I attended not only Zumba Basic classes conducted by the instructors whom I interviewed, but also several special events organized by local instructors like charity "Zumbathons" or "Master Classes" taught by Zumba International Presenters from around the world. Therefore, despite my geographic limitations, I had the opportunity to experience a variety of Zumba Fitness styles and programs in diverse settings and taught by different levels of instructors. Focusing on one particular location allows for a more in-depth look at how experiences on the ground at times confirm and at other times counter what is presented by the Zumba Home Office.

On the other hand, collecting ethnographic data in District 45 has some limitations. Although some men teach Zumba Fitness, this area is dominated by women instructors, and all of my interviews are with women. About two-thirds of my interlocutors are also white. The white women I interviewed had very different experiences from the Black and Latina women who spoke with me, a point I have tried to highlight in the book. Since the Zumba Home Office does not release statistics about who their instructors are, it is impossible to know if the women I spoke with are representative of all Zumba instructors worldwide. Moreover, virtually all of the instructors taught predominantly white students. Had I conducted research in a different place with a more diverse clientele, their relationships to tropicalized Latinness might be different.

For instance, one Black instructor related to me her experience visiting a Zumba Fitness class in Atlanta, Georgia. She recalled, "I went there, and it was like one white person in the whole class, and I was like, 'Oh my God!' There are all these other networks . . . it's really different from being up here in New England." I have similarly heard about different types of classes from friends and family members, such as ones taught by Latinx instructors in New York City with a distinctly Spanish Caribbean clientele, or ones that cater to predominantly Black communities by featuring more funk or hip-hop music. Every class is different. *Fitness Fiesta!* analyzes a very small slice of the Zumba Fitness world, one that is primarily populated by white Americans, but with some racial and ethnic diversity.

Regardless of their racial background, many instructors whom I spoke with said they knew little, if anything, about Latin music or dance prior to starting Zumba Fitness. While this might limit some aspects of my research, in other ways, focusing on this population offered important insights into how the Zumba Home Office's selling of tropicalized Latinness was received on the ground by people with relatively little exposure to Latinx culture and life in the first place. At the same time, it is important to note that Zumba instructors did not all agree with the ways that the Zumba Home Office marketed Latin culture. Many instructors, including white ones, criticized the exotifying nature of Zumba Fitness's marketing, and they were skeptical of Zumba Fitness's potential impact on fostering greater cultural understanding. More research on other Zumba Fitness scenes will almost certainly reveal different interpretations of Zumba Fitness and tropicalized Latinness, including ways it might serve a different purpose, one that allows for alternative ideas and expressions of Latinx life to flourish. But, for this book, I focus on the dominant tropes that Zumba Fitness peddles to the wider public. My goal is not to provide a holistic or all-encompassing analysis of the various Zumba Fitness scenes and interpretations that exist in the United States or globally—and, in fact, I believe such a wide-ranging analysis of Zumba Fitness is virtually impossible given the amorphous nature of the company's business model. Instead, I aim to show how Zumba Fitness sells tropicalized Latinness and how instructors who are otherwise unfamiliar with Latin music respond to it. This is the story of one Zumba Fitness scene in one time and place, but it is also a story that reveals much about the relationship between popular culture, citizenship, and belonging in our contemporary "postracial" moment.

OUTLINE OF THE BOOK

Fitness Fiesta! centers on five key tropes that Zumba Fitness uses to construct and market tropicalized Latinness: authenticity, fun, fiesta, dreams, and love. One of the contradictions of Zumba Fitness's constructions of "Latin" culture is how it centers ideas about cultural authenticity in Latin America while simultaneously homogenizing Latinx culture as a "south of the border" style vacation. The first three chapters focus on how the tropes of authenticity, fiesta, and fun foster this contradiction. The first chapter, "Selling Authenticity," analyzes the trope of authenticity. Authenticity surfaces in Zumba Fitness via discourses that present their "rhythms" (i.e., the musical genres they utilize) as historical traditions unchanged by movement across space and time. I explore items such as the 2009 book *Zumba: Ditch the Workout, Join the Party! The Zumba Weight Loss Program*, written by Zumba Fitness founder Beto Pérez, and Boston-area instructors' recollections of Zumba Fitness "Jam Sessions" (educational programs for instructors) to consider the types of music origin stories that circulate in the Zumba Fitness world. I contrast these with examples of major global pop stars who collaborate with Zumba Fitness to show how the company's narrative of ancient, unchanged, and, therefore, "authentic" musical traditions conflicts with the reality of Zumba Fitness's modern pop soundtrack. The chapter ends with a discussion of how Zumba instructors interpret these origin stories, and their conflicting ideas of what counts as authentic. Overall, I argue that authenticity is a social construction that reproduces long-standing racist and colonial ideologies that present Latin America as more primitive and exotic than the United States.

Despite the trope of authenticity's emphasis on specificity, this embrace of stereotypes of Latin American primitivity lends itself to generalizations about Latinx life and culture. Chapter 2, "Selling Fiesta," explores how the trope of fiesta paints all the aforementioned authentic rhythms as part of a nonstop, exotic, and sexy fiesta. The Spanish word *fiesta* translates to *party*. More than just a word, though, fiesta has become an abstract trope that incorporates a host of stereotypes of Latinx communities as loud, fun-loving, and, especially, hypersexual people. Fiestas exist outside of the normative structures and behaviors associated with modernity and the Global North. As such, the trope of fiesta works together with authenticity to naturalize racial hierarchies that equate whiteness with reason, while simultaneously obscuring the systemic inequalities inherent to these same racial hierarchies. "Selling Fiesta" explores the role of sexuality and the exotic tropics in constructing the trope of fiesta. I analyze how stereotypes of Latinx sexuality in particular permeate the Zumba Wear clothing line and internet memes about the fitness program. I combine my own reading of these materials with Zumba instructors' explanations of how they manage expressions of sexuality in their classes, with special attention to how race and gender impact their experiences. Ultimately, "Selling Fiesta" shows how the trope of fiesta produces a homogenized and hypersexualized tropicalized Latinness that both conflicts with and conjoins with the trope of authenticity to render Zumba Fitness foreign, exotic, sexy, and racially distinct from US Americanness.

Fiesta operates alongside fun, another trope that reproduces modern racial hierarchies. Zumba Fitness distinguishes itself from other exercise programs by de-emphasizing discipline and prioritizing fun. Fun implies an uninhibited freedom that only exists within the fiesta space, one that affords Zumba participants an opportunity to disregard the behavioral constraints associated with modern, respectable US Americanness. Descriptions of Zumba Fitness stress fun as a natural outcome derived from the program's roots in Latin dance. I analyze the trope of fun through a close reading of Zumba Fitness advertisements and publications such as their online newsletter *Z-Life*. I pair this with ethnographic data that reveals how hard Zumba Fitness instructors work to plan their classes and to curate fun. Still, many participants in Zumba Fitness classes are unaware of the level of preparation that their instructors go through, which is essential in order for fun to be perceived as an effortless, innate aspect of Zumba Fitness. I argue that the trope of fun works with that of fiesta to render tropicalized Latinness nonthreatening to the racial status quo, reframing potentially threatening qualities into desirable ones. Overall, authenticity, fiesta, and fun create a tropicalized Latinness that can be incorporated into the multicultural fabric of the United States, giving an illusion of equality but in actuality reinforcing the mechanisms of Latinx exclusion.

The final two chapters analyze how the tropes of dreams and love transform tropicalized Latinness into an ideal representation of hegemonic ideologies of postracialism and neoliberalism. In so doing, dreams and love further neutralize the potential threat posed by stereotypes like hypersexuality and primitivity embedded in tropicalized Latinness. Instead of presenting these qualities as suspicious or dangerous, love and dreams situate tropicalized Latinness as something that can be incorporated into the United States even as Latinx people remain excluded from US citizenship rights. Here, I follow Catherine Ramírez's assertion that some subjects are simultaneously included and excluded from the state. She notes that not all groups in the United States are understood to be assimilable into the mainstream. Instead, Ramírez posits that for some groups, "their simultaneous inclusion and exclusion underscore that assimilation is not only the process whereby outsiders are turned into insiders; it is also the process whereby certain social actors and groups are rendered outsiders on the inside."[63] In this case, tropicalized Latinness represents "outsiders on the inside" by continuously signifying Latinxs' perceived otherness in ways that do not threaten, but actually *reinforce* the racial status quo in the United States. The tropes of dreams and love accomplish this by infusing tropicalized Latinness with neoliberal and postracial ideals that maintain hegemonic norms and systemic inequalities.

The trope of dreams centers stories of the ideal Latinx immigrant who capitalizes on the marketability of tropicalized Latinness to achieve the American dream. The American dream serves as the quintessential neoliberal symbol that prioritizes individuals' economic contributions and market viability as a condition of normative citizenship. Zumba Fitness frequently celebrates Beto Pérez for his rags to riches story, moving from an impoverished child in Colombia, to a scrappy immigrant in Miami, to a global fitness star. In "Selling Dreams," I analyze the recounting of Pérez's ascent in his own writings alongside stories of other Zumba International Presenters with similar testimonials about how Zumba Fitness enabled them to live out the American dream.[64] Like the Latin boom before it, these stories portray Zumba Fitness as an effective avenue for financial success while identifying certain Latinx bodies as assimilable into the multicultural United States. But Zumba Fitness is not so lucrative for everyone. I use ethnographic data to show that Zumba instructors of all racial backgrounds often struggle to achieve the financial stability promised by the program. This critique of the American dream exposes the failure of neoliberal multiculturalism to address systemic inequalities that disenfranchise Latinx people.

Similarly, "Selling Love" addresses yet another problem with the neoliberal multicultural thrust behind Zumba Fitness: the circulation of racist stereotypes alongside discourses of love, cultural tolerance, and diversity. Zumba Fitness promotes a "spread love" philosophy that centers positivity and acceptance and avoids any discussion of structural racism.

This makes the program a quintessential example of postracialism in the United States. Zumba Fitness only creates opportunities to address social problems about which there is little controversy, such as health issues like cancer or current events like natural disasters. This furthers the idea of selling love by emphasizing charity and neoliberal approaches to solving social problems without questioning, let alone acknowledging, the structural inequalities that are at the root of these problems. To demonstrate how this works on the ground, I analyze the Zumba Fitness brand's emphasis on individual charitable giving alongside discussions with local Zumba instructors about whether they see Zumba Fitness as an effective space in which to address social problems locally or nationally. I argue that the trope of love either ignores systemic racism or renders it a thing of the past. However, the contradictions embedded within Zumba Fitness enable some instructors to use their Zumba Fitness classes to highlight and educate students about issues impacting Latinx and Black populations.

Overall, *Fitness Fiesta!* considers the complex and often contradictory images of tropicalized Latinness that circulate in the Zumba universe. In general, I am very critical of the Zumba brand, even though I remain a dedicated Zumba Fitness participant who does indeed find Zumba fun. My ambivalence is similar to many of the other Zumba instructors and participants whom I have met over the course of my research. I hope to dwell in this contradiction. My goal is not to catalog the stereotypes embedded in Zumba Fitness but, more importantly, to show how they operate in ways that further enable systemic racial discrimination against Latinxs and other people of color in the United States. I aim to demonstrate how something that appears to wholeheartedly embrace cultural difference can ultimately reproduce the very same stereotypes it claims to refute. These seemingly positive forms of representation can have very insidious consequences. It is for this reason that Zumba Fitness matters. Many of the people I talk to generally think of Zumba Fitness as a positive platform for promoting good lifestyle habits such as health, self-care, happiness, and acceptance of others. But for all of the benefits many individuals (including myself) have experienced, the fitness program provides an important case study for understanding why even the most "positive" representations can actually reproduce unequal structures of power and further racial exclusion. This contradiction reflects one of the primary ways that race operates in the United States. Only by understanding this process can we move forward with imagining more egalitarian and emancipatory futures.

SELLING
AUTHEN-
TICITY

〰〰〰

IN 2013, ZUMBA FITNESS ENCOURAGED CONSUMERS to "Escape on a Fitness Adventure" with their new video game, *Zumba Fitness World Party*. And that is just what I did. I followed along as virtual avatars of popular Zumba International Presenters such as Kass Martin, Loretta Bates, Gina Grant, and Beto Pérez himself taught me new routines. They beamed in from different locations. I followed Loretta and Gina's Puerto Rican–inspired routines from the courtyard of a colonial-style building in Old San Juan. Heidi Torres instructed us how to hula in front of a Hawaiian volcano. Beto sometimes directed routines from the streets of Rio de Janeiro, or at other times on a dock floating somewhere in the Caribbean Sea. I danced along with my Nintendo Wii remote attached to my hip. Each time I hit a move just right, I earned more and more points. Eventually, I reached "euphoria" and the sites came alive. The Hawaiian volcano erupted, dolphins jumped through the pristine Caribbean waters, and the lights in the balconies of the colonial outpost in Old San Juan began to shimmer.

With each song I mastered, I unlocked new opportunities to learn about the countries where this music comes from. These came in the form of brief video clips that showed how the International Presenters featured in the game learned their particular routines. It is notable that the video game features avatars of real people rather than fictional characters as most dance-fitness games do. Many Zumba enthusiasts whom I've met see these presenters as authorities who choreograph routines based on extensive knowledge of both fitness and Latin music and dance. Viewing presenters' bodies on the screen gives the impression of taking an actual Zumba Fitness class with an expert, rather than mimicking the movements of a faceless or nameless avatar who lives in a virtual world. In other words, the Zumba International Presenters' participation in the game already gave it an aura of authenticity, even before these present- ers revealed how and where they learned these routines. Melissa Chiz and Nick Logrea talked about training in step dancing in Ireland and flamenco in Spain. Gina Grant and Loretta Bates practiced bomba, salsa, and reggaetón in Puerto Rico, and Armando Salcedo and Heidi Torres traveled to Hawai'i to learn hula and Polynesian dance. We learned about other routines from dancers native to the region. Beto Pérez brought us to a small hut where a Colombian band performed a traditional style of cumbia (interestingly included in the Caribbean part of the game). Dr. B., who was our guide through India, talked about the Bollywood films and Indian wedding traditions that informed her dance routines. These videos show that the routines I learned in *Zumba Fitness World Party* are not just any routines—they were *authentic*. These routines came from the "source." The Zumba International Presenters traveled to far-off lands, they explained, to learn the dances and the histories behind them from, as Gina Grant put it, "the masters themselves." The implication is that video game players experience routines informed by multiple levels of expertise—that of the Zumba International Presenters and that of the choreographers and cultural workers they engaged with on their travels.

Zumba Fitness World Party thus transports consumers around the world to encounter "real" dances directed by Zumba Fitness experts. This is evi- dent in the game's commercial as well. It begins by focusing on a young, blond, white woman in black leggings and a light blue tank top dancing in a lush green landscape alongside traditional Polynesian dancers clad in feathered headdresses. She then transports to a Carnaval in Brazil, and finally a DJ dance party led by Beto Pérez. The voiceover says, "Escape to Hawai'i, Brazil, and beyond in the ultimate Zumba video game workout that takes you around the world." We then see the woman exercising in her living room to the "hot new soundtrack," indicating that playing the video game moves her body to lose weight, and moves her body from place to place.[1] Similarly, the product description for the video game on Amazon claims to offer consumers "a cultural joyride around the world" where "you immerse yourself in the movement and music of ex- otic global destinations" for a "fun, freeing fitness journey that expands your horizons."[2] Words like "exotic," "escape," "freeing," and "cultural joy- ride" imply both physical and cultural distance between the consumer,

1.1 Still from the commercial for the 2013 *Zumba Fitness World Party* video game featuring the white protagonist surrounded by Hawaiian dancers after she gets "transported" to Hawai'i while playing the game.

1.2 Still from the commercial for the 2013 *Zumba Fitness World Party* video game featuring the white protagonist in the midst of a Brazilian Carnaval crowd. Along with figure 1.1, these images convey the video game's emphasis that gamers could travel the world and experience authentic culture and dance from their points of origin.

imagined as a white American woman, and the dances that come from the tropics.[3]

Reinforcing the distinction between the video game player's identity and the origins of the choreography included in the games they play is par for the course in many dance video games. Kiri Miller argues that dance games provide a safe space for individuals to experiment with different dance styles from the isolation of their own home. In so doing, participants can engage in "experimental forms of repetition in which practitioners engage *with* difference, trying on unfamiliar kinesthetic styles."[4] Perceptions of authenticity are critical to the marketing of the average dance video game. Miller notes that dance games contain within them "ideas about how certain kinds of bodies are supposed to move."[5] Dance game choreographers strive to create routines that match players' expectations and knowledge of a given singer or genre.[6] Thus, whether or not players consider what they are doing in a game to be authentic depends in part on what they already know about the dance styles in the game, even if what they know is primarily grounded in stereotypes. *Zumba Fitness World Party* was the fourth video game released by the Zumba Fitness company, whose foray into dance video games happened at a time when dance games were some of the most lucrative games on the market.[7] Prior Zumba-related video games did so well that in 2011 the *Zumba Fitness* game was the top selling dance game in the United States and much of Europe.[8] *Zumba Fitness World Party* comes on the heels of established interest in dance games, but it also differs from many dance games because it makes explicit the origins of the choreography included in them. In fact, origins are so critical to the game that learning about them is one of the prizes that players can get—the more you master routines, the more points you unlock, the more videos you can access to teach you about these dances. At the same time, the overall marketing scheme around the video game and the kitschy imagery of the places where these dances come from reproduce recognizable stereotypes of the exotic tropics.

In this way, *Zumba Fitness World Party* makes explicit one of the central contradictions of the Zumba Fitness brand: the promotion of a homogeneous tropicalized Latinness (indicated here by the exotic and fun "joyride" of the game) alongside an acknowledgment of the cultural specificities and accuracy of Zumba Fitness's "rhythms" and choreography (evidenced by the Zumba International Presenters' travels to find "real" dance forms). The trope of authenticity depicts Zumba Fitness's dance and musical elements as drawn from specific historical cultural traditions. What makes it possible for a discourse of authenticity so firmly rooted in ideas of place and cultural specificity to bolster tropicalized Latinness, a construct that actively homogenizes groups? This chapter seeks to answer this question by considering the cultural work of authenticity. I approach authenticity as a discursive trope that reveals how preconceived notions of what counts as "Latin" inform whether or not a given cultural practice is understood to be authentic. In other words, when we think something is authentic, it is often because it matches what we already think to be true. Arlene Dávila notes that authenticity is ultimately about "differentiation and evaluation" that can reproduce social hierarchies along racial, gender, linguistic, and national origin lines.[9] As such, determining authenticity is intimately connected to much larger questions of citizenship, belonging, and value.

The Zumba Fitness corporation takes great pains to paint their products and services as rooted in authentic Latin dance and music traditions. Authenticity becomes paramount to the brand both for the company as a whole, and for individual instructors who must present themselves as knowledgeable in order to attract and maintain their student base. Both Zumba Fitness and many instructors sell their brand as not just exercise but also as a form of cultural appreciation. Indeed, many instructors I talked to saw themselves as cultural educators and mediators as much as (and sometimes more than) fitness professionals. In this context, authenticity becomes an important marketing tool for both instructors and the Zumba Fitness corporation more broadly.

To create its routines, Zumba Fitness claims to seek out the most "authentic" music and dance grounded in "ancient" traditions. This quest depicts authentic Latin music and dance as traditional, static, and, above all, foreign. Dabbling in authenticity means leaving behind the modern trappings and globalized cultural trends that define the contemporary world for exposure to allegedly more "real" cultures from far-off lands. Defining authenticity as something from distant places and times reproduces modern racial hierarchies that equate the Global North with civilization, modernity, and reason, and the Global South with primitivity and instinct. Analyzing authenticity not as something to be discovered and preserved but rather as a concept deeply intertwined with larger structures of colonialism, racism, and capitalist exploitation redirects our view toward how authenticity contributes to the creation and reproduction of tropicalized Latinness. Zumba Fitness's overall commitment to authenticity across all levels—from the marketing in the Zumba

Fitness Home Office to the choices individual instructors make in their classes—reveals authenticity at work.

FINDING THE REAL RHYTHM

Few people enter a Zumba class expecting to receive a lesson about the histories or cultural significance of Latin music. Nevertheless, many of the people that I have met in Zumba Fitness classes feel that they are experiencing something grounded in culturally authentic practices. Zumba Fitness spends considerable time connecting the music it uses to ideas like tradition, "local" culture, and heritage. This strategy is not unique to Zumba Fitness. Restaurants, tourist sites, art dealers, music makers, and others who peddle "Latin"—and more broadly "foreign"—cultures similarly rely on tropes that tie their products to "authentic" places. For example, scholars of world music note that the classification of something as "world music" assumes that the music was created without access to modern technology or musical trends, even though this is almost never the case. In so doing, the world music industry represents its music as especially traditional, static, and foreign in order to attract consumers interested in "authentic" music from around the globe.[10] In the food industry, chefs such as Rick Bayless and Diana Taylor have ascended the Mexican food scene by presenting themselves as students and cultural translators of authentic food preparation in Mexico.[11] Similarly, art dealers seek out artists from Latin America rather than US Latinxs because they see Latin American art as more "authentic" and thus more marketable.[12] Across all of these industries, authenticity is defined as historical, traditional, and distant both in terms of space and time—critical qualities that determine the marketability of "Latin" culture.

Zumba Fitness relies on similar strategies. Despite drawing from hugely popular and transnational genres of music like reggaetón and salsa, Zumba Fitness depicts Latin music as a historical tradition unchanged by migration, technology, or globalization. In 2009, Zumba founder Beto Pérez published his exercise book titled *Zumba: Ditch the Workout, Join the Party! The Zumba Weight Loss Program*. The book offers detailed instructions about Zumba Fitness steps, sample routines, and a weight loss diet. It includes an extensive chapter about the history of each of Zumba Fitness's four core rhythms: merengue, cumbia, salsa, and reggaetón. Pérez explains: "I feel very strongly that people need to know where the music comes from, to talk about the path from Africa to Latin America and the parallel developments in the US. Knowledge of dance history makes a difference in how you hear the music, hear the beats, and ultimately in how you dance. Everything just sinks in better when you understand the origin of these wonderful dances. So first, let's go back in time and discover the rich, fascinating heritage of these dances."[13] Pérez is absolutely correct that the foundations of these core rhythms come from the African diaspora. In fact, much of what is widely recognized as "Latin music" in the United States would not exist without the essential contributions of Afro–Latin American and Afro-Latinx artists and communities. Moreover, many Latin American countries point to music and dance as symbols of their African heritage, which they often represent as folkloric and historical. For example, dominant definitions of Puerto Rican national identity often present bomba, one of the dances included on *Zumba Fitness World Party*, as a quintessential example of enduring African culture in Puerto Rico. Isar Godreau argues that, in this context, Blackness is filtered through a temporal distancing, meaning that it is acknowledged as part of an ancestral or historical influence in contemporary Puerto Rico.[14] *Zumba Fitness World Party* replicates this discourse in a video about bomba titled "Tradition." As we watch Gina Grant and Loretta Bates learn bomba on a patio overlooking the sea, Bates explains that "the bomba and the plena, they go back so far and they go into the roots of who Puerto Ricans are. When you're dancing, you feel the Puerto Rico of today but you also feel the Puerto Rico of yesterday." We witness the class where Grant and Bates learned bomba accompanied by live drums, and one drummer explains the role of the primo in following the steps of the dancer. Several women in traditional dress—long skirts and headwraps—dance alongside them. The lead plena dancer in the segment reiterates Bates's emphasis on tradition by stating that "when you hear the plena, the music tells you about Puerto Rican history." Although bomba and plena are technically two different types of music and dance, the video game represents them as almost interchangeable examples of historical Afro–Puerto Rican folklore. In contrast, *Zumba Fitness World Party* depicts salsa and reggaetón as more modern dances marked by hypersexuality and currently enjoyed by Puerto Ricans everywhere. This comparison reiterates the positioning of Afro–Puerto Rican music and dance, especially bomba, as an "ancient tradition" unchanged by modern life, and thus a critical symbol of Puerto Rico's national heritage and history. Puerto Rico is not unique in this regard. Other Latin American countries have embraced similar narratives that utilize "authentic" music from Black communities as emblematic of the African heritage of their populations, such as Brazilian samba or Cuban rumba. Like with Puerto Rican bomba, these narratives rely on very rigid and narrow definitions of authenticity that present Blackness and Black culture as historical. In this context, Pérez's embrace of the African origins of Zumba Fitness's four core rhythms jibes with common assumptions about African culture as a historical influence in Latin American music and culture. His imperative to "go back in time and discover the rich, fascinating heritage of these dances" defines this authenticity using similar practices of temporal distancing evident in Puerto Rico and elsewhere.

On the surface, highlighting the influences of groups that have been marginalized from state projects, as is the case with Indigenous and Black communities in Latin America, is laudable. However, in this instance, both *Zumba Fitness World Party* and Pérez's book reference African dance using enduring racist stereotypes of Blackness as primitive and premodern. In *Listening for Africa*, David Garcia argues that audiences across the Americas have long incorporated stereotypes about Blackness into their listening practices. He writes, "The geographic places where Black music and dance were believed to have originated (Africa) and still survived (Caribbean and South America) were separate in every possible way—socially, economically, and temporally included—from the modern city or metropolis. . . . It was the act of and belief in listening to and analyzing the African past that reinscribed one's belonging in the modern world."[15] In other words, consumers could access African cultures via listening to popular music. This exemplifies what Roshanak Kheshti has termed the "aural imaginary" in which the practice of listening reproduces images of a racialized other, however abstract.[16] In this context, the Afro-Latinx genres that comprise Zumba Fitness's four core rhythms can conjure up a host of stereotypes consistent with modern racial hierarchies for consumers. At the same time, as Garcia observes about representations of the mambo, Afro-Latin music could be "unmistakably primitive, of African origins, and unhealthy, while at the same time be revitalizing, pleasurable, and modern."[17] Zumba Fitness thus follows the long-standing depiction of Afro-Latin rhythms in the US popular music scene as indicative of a marketable racial, ethnic, and foreign difference that also seemingly confirms stereotypes of primitive Blackness.

Pérez's focus on the past as the site of authentic dance steps unsullied by modern techniques exemplifies Garcia's argument that tropes of primitivity, instinct, and sexuality link African-based music and dance to a premodern, ambiguous, and imagined "Africa." In *Zumba*, Pérez frequently invokes nineteenth-century origins of contemporary dances. Readers are encouraged to imagine enslaved African women and men performing a courtship dance in the Colombian countryside that became the basis of Zumba Fitness's basic cumbia moves. Another description of cumbia's origins states, "One story has it that the dance originated with slaves who were chained together and, of necessity, were forced to drag one leg as they cut sugar cane to the beat of the drums. This is why today we drag our feet as part of the cumbia dance steps."[18] Pérez similarly ties merengue to the nineteenth century by crediting Dominican soldiers with originating popular merengue dance moves during celebrations of the end of the Haitian occupation in 1844. He writes, "Most men carried guns or rifles at all times, even in the dance floor. With a carbine hanging from your shoulder, it is hard to move your back, so they did not, and today you don't, either."[19] In these descriptions, the dances associated with Zumba Fitness's core rhythms stem directly from nineteenth-century ways of life—an interpretation that ignores the many transnational exchanges and historical shifts that impacted the development of these musical genres, not to mention their tremendous popularity in our present day. Moreover, unsettled debates about the precise temporal and geographic origins of each of these four core rhythms persist, discrediting any attempts to tie them to precise moments and places.[20] *Zumba* acknowledges how radio networks fostered the transnational movement of artists and sounds across the Americas, such as when Pérez describes the growing popularity of merengue around the world.[21] But, technology here is not understood to have transformed merengue's sound or the process of music *making*; instead, technology helps to disseminate authentic rhythms around the globe. In this way, *Zumba* privileges historical continuity. Regardless of their accuracy, *Zumba*'s assertions attempt to authenticate Zumba Fitness's routines as unadulterated, "pure" forms of Latin dance.

The temporal distancing that occurs by exclusively focusing on the nineteenth century is accompanied by a similarly exclusive focus on Latin America as the birthplace of these musical traditions. What movement does occur in *Zumba*'s retelling of the four core rhythms' origins generally happens within Latin America and the Caribbean, such as with the migration of Jamaican laborers to Panama whose descendants helped create reggaetón.[22] More commonly, though, *Zumba* states that the four core rhythms were created in Latin America, even if in some cases they became popularized in the United States or distributed through global networks. For example, Pérez writes that the origins of salsa are undetermined, but could be in Cuba, Colombia, or Puerto Rico.[23] Indeed, several scholars have long debated the origins of salsa, but they often point to Cuba, Puerto Rico, and New York City as potential places of origin.[24] Although Pérez acknowledges that salsa's origins are difficult to pinpoint, his listing of only Latin American countries in the development of salsa ignores the critical role that New York Latinxs played in the music's development and globalization. New York City is widely recognized as a critical site for the development of salsa, especially as the headquarters of the famed Fania Records, arguably the most important salsa label of all time. Scholars such as Juan Flores and Wilson Valentín-Escobar have argued that salsa is a major expression of Nuyorican, or New York Puerto Rican, identity shaped by life in the United States.[25] However, in *Zumba*, New York Puerto Ricans are responsible for popularizing the dance, not innovating the music. The book states, "Salsa was basically a street dance, made popular by Puerto Rican immigrants in New York City in the 1950s and danced in the ghettos."[26] Among the many problems with this statement is the implication that Latin Americans created salsa, and US Latinx people merely danced to it.[27] This assertion erases the contributions of musicians like Eddie Palmieri or Willie Colón, New York Puerto Ricans who were integral to the development of the music itself. The emphasis on Latin American music makers over US Latinx ones mirrors some of the exclusions inherent to the Latin music industry, which also privileges Latin America. For example, María Elena Cepeda and Deborah Pacini Hernandez both argue that the prioritizing of the Spanish language in common definitions of Latin music reinforces the perception that Latin music comes from Latin America, and leaves out the many US Latinxs who grow up bilingual or as monolingual English speakers.[28] In fact, US Latinx communities have long contributed to Latin music, from creating popular record labels to producing iconic artists such as Selena, Marc Anthony, or Romeo Santos (to name a small few). By locating Latin music exclusively within Latin America, *Zumba* reinforces this perception that Latin music is intrinsically foreign. This foreignness is critical to the Zumba Fitness brand's construction of authenticity.

Zumba's origin stories exemplify the rigid ideas about culture, time, and place that inform constructions of authenticity. Here, the purpose of authenticity is not so much about recounting "accurate" or "true" histories of these cultural phenomena. Instead, authenticity serves as a marketing tool to attract consumers interested in exploring other cultures to the Zumba Fitness program. Authenticity must therefore be sutured to foreignness in order to be legible to these consumers. The trope of authenticity also legitimates tropicalized Latinness. That is, if these cultural practices are, above all, authentic, then the stereotypes associated with tropicalized Latinness can be perceived as true, too. Authenticity thus plays a critical role in making tropicalized Latinness attractive and nonthreatening to the average consumer while simultaneously reinforcing global racial hierarchies that depict Latin America as less civilized than the United States.

"PITBULL ISN'T ZUMBA"

Despite relying so heavily on ideas about ancient tradition to define authenticity, Zumba Fitness utilizes contemporary popular music as its soundtrack. The four core rhythms all are part of the Latin pop machine. In fact, in the 2010s, reggaetón became one of the highest grossing music genres worldwide and is arguably the backbone of contemporary Latin pop (and, to a certain extent, US mainstream pop). Incorporating popular songs into its repertoire allows Zumba Fitness to capitalize on the global consumption of Latin music. Latin music is what attracts people like me who are familiar with it. But Latin music also presents something exciting, foreign, and different to consumers who seek a type of Latin authenticity that dovetails with their perceptions of authentic and traditional Latin American cultures. This tension reveals the very constructedness of authenticity, a concept that emphasizes accuracy but actually manipulates representations of cultural practices to fit hegemonic discourses of modernity.

The relationship between Cuban-American artist Pitbull and Zumba Fitness brings this contradiction into stark relief. Armando Christian Pérez, or Pitbull, began his career in his hometown of Miami, Florida. His music combines rap, Miami bass, and pop sung predominantly in English, with some Spanish thrown in. Since the early 2000s, Pitbull's music has shifted from the Miami bass and US southern crunk of his early years to a more global pop sound evidenced by his nickname "Mr. Worldwide," which he adopted with the release of his 2011 album, *Planet Pit*. That album included a song called "Pause" that Pitbull recorded specifically for the Zumba Fitness program. With English-language lyrics, a repeated sax riff, light congas, and a house beat, the song is quintessential Pitbull. It also sounds like something one might hear in a dance club, on the radio, or in fitness classes of all types, not just in a Zumba Fitness class.

Still, Amanda explained to me, "Pitbull is not Zumba. It's a misconception. Yes, he sings songs we might teach in Zumba, but Pitbull himself is not Zumba." Many instructors agreed with her. Several warned me that a class with too much Pitbull was bad. A true Zumba Fitness class, they assured me, included more diverse music. Besides, many said, Pitbull's music is not Latin music, or at least not the *only* Latin music out there. Leah explained, "I think it's partly because people don't have access to the variety of music. Pitbull has some lyrics in Spanish where everyone's like, oh yeah, that's Spanish music, because they *think* it's Spanish music, and a lot of it is Spanish music, but a lot of it isn't. But the thing about Spanish music is that there are a lot of varieties of Spanish music, and they sound really different, but to an untrained ear, it's the exact same thing. And that defaults to Pitbull, because it's the popular, mainstream thing." According to Leah, Americans' familiarity with Pitbull makes him appear representative of Latin music. However, Zumba instructors (should) know better. They are familiar with a "variety of music," including different rhythms and artists associated with "Spanish music." In other words, when done correctly, Zumba Fitness offers participants the opportunity to learn different types of "real" Latin music as opposed to mistaking it for Pitbull.

On one hand, Pitbull's combination of predominantly English lyrics, unique mixtures of different genres, and upbeat tempo exudes the sort of fiesta-like atmosphere of Zumba Fitness. His music is familiar enough to not be *too* foreign, but different enough to signal something exotic. Although this might irritate some instructors, many realize that their students often want something that sounds somewhat familiar so as not to feel intimidated by the music or dance steps used in class. Miriam mentioned that her classes include Pitbull along with other Latin music stars, such as Shakira or Enrique Iglesias, who are similarly familiar to US mainstream audiences: "You have to think about popular songs, popular artists, that in the end people want to move to." Likewise, Amanda said, "I think when people have familiarity with stuff, that's when they're like, 'Oh, I love that song!'"

Familiarity includes people's knowledge about both the artists and the songs. Some popular songs in Zumba Fitness classes sample mainstream US pop songs. For example, soca group Red Eye Crew's song "Jack and Rose" integrates the iconic flute melody and chorus of Céline Dion's hit "My Heart Will Go On" into its refrain (it's worth noting that "My Heart Will Go On" came from the blockbuster film *Titanic*, whose two main characters are named Jack and Rose). Bacall and Malo's remake of Toto's "Africa" featuring Prince Osorio also blends "foreign" sounds with a recognizable US pop classic. In addition, Zumba Fitness produces its own remixes, like the samba version of a-ha's "Take on Me" and a reggaetón beat mashed up with Bruno Mars's "That's What I Like," that balance familiarity with "foreign" sounds.

US pop songs have also made their way into Zumba Fitness classes. Zumba Fitness now includes genres like hip-hop, country, or Broadway into their "rhythms." And like Latin artists, mainstream pop stars collaborate with Zumba Fitness. In March of 2018, pop star Meghan Trainor and Zumba Fitness released a joint Zumba choreography video for her single "No Excuses." The video featured Trainor performing the choreography with popular International Presenters Loretta Bates and Gina Grant. Trainor wanted to collaborate with Zumba Fitness because she heard her songs regularly in the Zumba Fitness class at her local gym, and because she thought the brand as a whole celebrated women's "empowerment," which she said was central to the message of "No Excuses." Indeed, the press release accompanying the song stated that the decision to release the video on March 5, which was just a few days before International Women's Day, was because of the importance of promoting women's empowerment.[29]

Still, despite the infiltration of mainstream pop into the Zumba Fitness scene, many instructors I met said that they intentionally foreground Latin music in their classes. Stephanie explained, "You know, you always get those folks that are like, 'Can we do more Top 40s? Can we do more pop music?' And I look them dead in the face, and I say, 'That's not Zumba. That's not what we're here for. I'm taking you on a trip around the world.'" Virtually every instructor I talked with mentioned the "trip around the world" as a central part of what they called the "Zumba formula." Leah described the formula this way:

> During your training, they tell you 70/30. And that is the ratio. You should have 70 percent international rhythms, and then 30 percent whatever else. In every Zumba class, you should see four core rhythms. There should always be a salsa. There should always be a merengue. There should always be a cumbia, and there should always be a reggaetón. And they should

always happen somewhere in the first four songs. Most of the time, it should be like that. . . . And then they say, you know, throw something else in there. So, you might do a belly dance, a flamenco, a dancehall.

Leah's description reveals not only the centrality of the four Latin core rhythms in Zumba Fitness, but also other "foreign" genres like dancehall, flamenco, or belly dance assumed to come from outside the United States. By focusing on world music or Latin music genres, Zumba Fitness emphasizes that the most authentic rhythms come from "foreign" lands.

However, Latin music is big business. In 2018, Latin music made headlines when it overtook country to become the fifth most consumed genre in the United States.[30] Latin music is not made up of isolated, unchanged musical traditions but instead is, and always has been, massively popular, mass-marketed, and global pop music. In fact, it is worth mentioning that while many instructors I spoke with shunned Pitbull, they regularly relied on his Sirius xm radio station "Globalization" to find new songs to play in their classes. Pitbull is not the only major Spanish-language singer to affiliate himself with Zumba Fitness. Latin music stars Don Omar, Gente de Zona, Daddy Yankee, Oro Sólido, and Becky G have all collaborated with Zumba Fitness in different ways, from recording songs for the company's Zumba Instructor Network (zin) volumes to performing at the Zumba Convention. Caribbean artists like Jamaican dancehall singer Shaggy, Trinidadian soca legend Machel Montano, and Haitian American hip-hop artist Wyclef Jean have also worked with Zumba Fitness. Each of these artists has their own global fan base. None of them would be considered folkloric or traditional. Instead, these artists are popular precisely because they sound "modern." Moreover, many of them integrate influences from US pop and hip-hop, and some, like Wyclef Jean, are particularly known for combining different genres. What's more, Becky G, Wyclef Jean, and Raúl Acosta (founder of Oro Sólido) grew up in the United States. Ultimately, what makes these artists perfect fits for Zumba Fitness is that their music does not sound *too* foreign, save for non-English-language lyrics (or, in the case of some Caribbean stars, non-US American Standard English). Still, they are unfamiliar enough to many US mainstream audiences to appear authentic.

In fact, Zumba Fitness itself has developed a reputation as an effective crossover mechanism for Latin artists seeking to gain traction in US mainstream markets. Zumba Fitness makes different kinds of licensing deals that enable the company to use music from popular artists.

For example, Zumba Fitness paid licensing fees for Wyclef Jean's song "Historic"; however, the company did not pay any "sponsorship fees" to Wyclef because, as Alberto Perlman explained, Zumba is a "promotional platform."[31] When Pitbull released "Pause" in 2011, Zumba Fitness distributed the song on its ZIN networks for instructors, and Beto Pérez created a special music video with a Zumba routine that circulated on YouTube.[32] Similarly, reggaetón artist Don Omar released the song "Zumba" in 2012, which he penned specifically for the fitness program. He also included the song on his album *MTO2*. In this instance, Zumba Fitness licensed the song from Universal Music and then promoted it through its ZIN network, social media, and classes. For his part, Don Omar retained the rights to the song and received significant promotion for his album around the world.[33] Don Omar told *Billboard*, "I'm going to have 12 million hits weekly if I post a song with [Zumba Fitness]. It is a great moment for me and for all the artists out there to start to look into these kinds of platforms to promote our music, because it is the business of the future."[34] These major artists are willing to forgo direct payment from Zumba Fitness with the assumption that their music will reach audiences hitherto unfamiliar with them.

Perlman made the case for Zumba Fitness's crossover potential when he told *Billboard*, "All of a sudden Sweden is dancing to [Don Omar's] 'Hasta que salga el sol.' I have people in Kansas City who suddenly know [Colombian singer] Carlos Vives. So we can offer exposure to markets that usually don't know who these artists are."[35] Given the associations between places like Sweden or Kansas City and whiteness in the popular imagination, Perlman's comments imply that it is a non-Latinx white audience who is exposed to Latin music for the first time through Zumba Fitness. An Afro-Latina instructor confirmed this assumption when she told me that Latin music stars like Carlos Vives and Maluma were "sort of becoming more mainstream. Like my very, very, very white friends from the suburbs are like 'Maluma! Gente de Zona!' It's weird." Another instructor thought Zumba Fitness "opens up a barrier [for Latin music] because [Latin artists] are leaking into radio stations for a regular audience who doesn't do Zumba."

At the time of these interviews, "Despacito" had become the third Spanish-language song to reach number one on the US charts, and media hyped up possibilities of other Spanish-language hits crossing over into the US mainstream market. It is difficult to determine whether or not Zumba Fitness can take credit for these trends on a broader scale, although it is the case that many Latin music industry executives see Zumba Fitness as an important space to market songs.[36] Still, most of these artists already had their own committed audiences and successful careers prior to involving themselves with Zumba Fitness. For Zumba instructors who are otherwise unfamiliar with Latin music, it is Zumba Fitness that seems to be the trendsetter.

Most of the instructors I spoke with had very limited exposure, if any, to Latin music prior to their participation in Zumba Fitness. They relied primarily on the materials and programs promoted by the Zumba Home Office for information about the music and artists that they use in class. Unfortunately, this often results in casting these popular artists within the same rigid definitions of authenticity used to describe Zumba Fitness's four core rhythms. One example is Daddy Yankee, one of the biggest music stars in the world who is credited with mainstreaming reggaetón with his 2004 hit "Gasolina." He began his career when reggaetón was called "underground," circulating informally on the streets of Puerto Rico. In fact, as Yankee's profile rose, he could not get a record company to sponsor his work given reggaetón's reputation as a music of the lower classes. So, he started his own Cartel Records, and to this day remains an independent artist who owns all of his masters. Over the past thirty years, Daddy Yankee has been a profound force in the Latin music industry. Yankee is arguably one of the most important and successful reggaetón artists in history with the most number one singles on *Billboard*'s Latin Rhythm Airplay chart, and he was the first Latin artist to reach number one on Spotify (which he accomplished in 2017).[37]

In addition to being a world-renowned artist, Daddy Yankee is also a shrewd businessman. He has collaborated with Zumba Fitness on several songs. His song "Limbo," from his sixth album *Prestige*, was featured on the *Zumba Fitness World Party* video game, and Gina Grant appeared as a dancer in Daddy Yankee's music video directed by Jessy Terrero. "Limbo" reached the Top 10 on the Hot Latin Songs chart. By the time he released "Limbo" in 2012, Daddy Yankee really did not need to rely on Zumba Fitness to promote his work or to maintain his fan base. Still, in 2013, Perlman recalled, "Daddy Yankee texted me five days ago and said, 'I wanted you to know that "Limbo" is as much your hit as it is my hit.' It was perfect for Zumba. When he showed it to us, he said, 'I said Zumba nine times in the song and it's because you guys have inspired me.'"[38] Since then, Daddy Yankee has created several other songs for Zumba

Fitness as well. For example, his 2017 hit "Hula Hoop" responded to fans' requests for a remixed version of his previous song "Shaky Shaky." Allegedly, many of those fans were Zumba instructors. "Hula Hoop" was the first in a "global partnership" between Yankee and Zumba Fitness.[39] Other songs like "Azukita," "Con Calma," "Dura," and "Firehouse" regularly make their way onto Zumba Fitness playlists.

Daddy Yankee is as much of a global pop star, if not more so, than Pitbull. And their music does not always sound that different. Still, for some instructors I spoke with, Daddy Yankee appeared more "authentically" Latin than Pitbull. This could be in part because Daddy Yankee comes from Puerto Rico, which, despite being a territory of the United States, is depicted as a foreign place in the Zumba Fitness world. Alternatively, this could be because Daddy Yankee exclusively sings in Spanish whereas Pitbull often has English-language lyrics in his songs. However, Zumba Fitness's narratives of authenticity and origins also shape how instructors view stars like Daddy Yankee. Despite his popularity, some instructors I spoke with credited Zumba Fitness for Daddy Yankee's success. One instructor relayed to me that she saw Daddy Yankee's success as a direct result of his collaborations with Zumba Fitness.

> Daddy Yankee's not stupid. He got in there early, and I think his success is due in large part to his partnership with Zumba. . . . I heard "Hula Hoop" on the radio recently. I thought, the guy is amazing. He went from being this popular guy in his own country, and then he's worldwide. He's a global star. And that's what "Shaky Shaky" basically showed. He had crowds all over the world doing this stupid dance, and it was super popular. The look on his face was like, "Can you believe this is going on, this is happening to me?" He was just cracking up through the whole thing. It was great.

These comments demonstrate just how much Zumba Fitness's discourses of "tradition" and "authenticity" shape some people's interpretation of these global stars. In this instance, one of the world's biggest global stars becomes reframed as a local artist who emerged on the pop music scene *because* of Zumba Fitness. Given how salient the trope of authenticity is in Zumba Fitness, it is hardly surprising that those unfamiliar with Latin music would see Zumba Fitness as integral to the success of someone like Daddy Yankee, however established he might have already been.

A similar misconception is evident in *Zumba*'s history of reggaetón, the genre that Daddy Yankee helped to create. One would be hard pressed to describe reggaetón as "ancient" since it emerged in the late 1980s and 1990s. However, Pérez's *Zumba* book attempts to date reggaetón's origins to the early twentieth century when "Jamaican laborers who came to help build the Panama Canal" brought it with them.[40] Of course, descendants of West Indian laborers in Panama played a critical role in the development of reggaetón; however, their contributions emerged in the 1970s and 1980s with reggae en español, which did not exist during the Panama Canal's construction in the early 1900s.[41] *Zumba*'s dubious origin story of reggaetón goes on to portray reggaetón as "a defining symbol of urban youth in Latin America, specifically Puerto Rico."[42] The awkward rhetorical moves in *Zumba*'s account of reggaetón history mirrors the frequent depiction of Daddy Yankee as a relatively unknown and foreign musician. Such descriptions do not match the reality of reggaetón's position as one of the most popular music genres in the world.

Part of Daddy Yankee's success and longevity comes from his ability to capitalize on different trends and to control his own business deals (along with his obvious talent). It is clear from interviews[43] that Daddy Yankee does see a benefit to collaborating with Zumba Fitness, but he does not *need* Zumba Fitness to be successful. I would argue that Yankee and Zumba Fitness benefit from each other, and in many ways Yankee's participation in the program benefits Zumba Fitness far more than it benefits him. Collaborations between Daddy Yankee and Zumba Fitness legitimize the company's claims to using both the hottest and the most authentic Latin music. On one hand, Daddy Yankee's connection to Zumba Fitness attracts people like me—established reggaetón fans who are looking for a fun exercise program. Stephanie explained to me that she "grew up with Daddy Yankee" and was thrilled to see him perform at the Zumba Convention: "I wanted to die, I was so excited!" On the other, framing Daddy Yankee as an authentic Puerto Rican reggaetón singer attracts people who see him as a culturally authentic newcomer to the pop scene. The different and conflicting message that Zumba Fitness uses music that is unchanged, exotic, and "traditional" while it simultaneously foregrounds the hottest global pop makes it possible for Zumba Fitness to appeal to audiences with very different levels of exposure to Latin music. Ultimately, this renders the trope of authenticity central to Zumba Fitness's marketing to consumers with diverse experiences and understandings of Latin music while still conforming to problematic stereotypes.

HOW TO LEARN AUTHENTIC
LATIN RHYTHMS

Regardless of instructors' feelings about Zumba Fitness's claims to authenticity, many consider their own knowledge about "authentic" Latin music and dance as vital to their success as instructors. Presenting herself as knowledgeable helps the instructor with her own business, in part because it attracts a loyal student following that then allows for increased revenue and potential opportunities to teach at other gyms, rec centers, and elsewhere. Still, most instructors I spoke with discussed teaching authentic Latin music and dance to their students as more of a moral imperative than a business strategy. It is worth mentioning that, once they paid their dues, bought their Zumba Wear, took extra classes to learn new choreography, and acquired additional fitness certifications, many instructors just broke even or, at best, earned a few thousand dollars per year. Most did not rely on Zumba Fitness for their primary income. Thus, instructors were often motivated equally, if not more, by the belief that Zumba Fitness's benefits extended beyond fitness to greater tolerance and appreciation for other cultures. Since many instructors became exposed to Latin dance and music for the first time via Zumba Fitness, they saw a personal responsibility to accurately represent "Latin" cultures.

A good example is Erin, a white instructor in her thirties. Although Erin took dance classes as a child, she never learned Latin dance until attending her first Zumba Fitness class. After that, she felt an obligation to learn more. Like many instructors unfamiliar with Latin music, Erin first struggled with identifying distinct rhythms. She decided to educate herself more about them, stating, "I started to listen a lot more to Latin music after I got licensed, because I knew I needed to work on that skill for myself." Now, Erin describes Latin music as "my heart, it's part of my life." She almost exclusively listens to Latin music for fun, not just for Zumba Fitness. Moreover, Erin continuously tries to learn more about the genres and dance moves she teaches. She said, "It's sort of like background knowledge so that I feel like I'm representing the culture in the most authentic way. 'Cause I am not Latina, right? I only have a love for Latin culture, that I feel like I want to represent and know what I'm doing."

I heard many stories like Erin's from several non-Latinx instructors who previously had limited exposure to Latin music. Demonstrating that an instructor "knows what [she's] doing" here is important not only to ensure the accuracy of her choreography but also to show a deep appreciation of "Latin culture." Other instructors shared similar sentiments with me. Julia mentioned, "I feel like a kizomba or a samba or even African, it's such a rhythm that you have to really dwell and discover it. If I'm going to teach it to someone else, I kind of need to know my shit, right? So, I feel like I need to educate myself so that I can be a better instructor."[44] Stephanie talked about the importance of instructors who teach predominantly Caribbean and Latinx students to "come correct." She said, "With the whole cultural appropriation thing, there is a big judgment. So, we either need to come correct and do it right, if you're not of that culture, or be ready to be run out of the gym." These comments reveal that instructors see knowledge about "authentic" cultures as important to their abilities to be good instructors, their connections to students, and their opportunities to cultivate a loyal clientele base—all crucial to their success as fitness instructors.

So how do instructors with no prior knowledge of Latin music and dance learn about these dances? Zumba Fitness maintains a robust offering of workshops about Zumba Fitness choreography and music. After becoming a licensed instructor, or ZIN member, one can attend classes like ZIN Jam Sessions. These special classes are taught by Zumba Jammers (also called ZJs), who try out for the job and then complete extra training that allows them to create and teach choreography to ZINs. Some areas have Zumba Jammers who regularly teach the local instructor base. Zumba Jammers also travel to different parts of the country, or even internationally, to conduct Jam Sessions or Master Classes.[45] Several instructors I spoke with described themselves as "jam junkies." Some attend Jam Sessions once a month, and others attend once a week. The appeal of Jam Sessions is not only the convenience of getting new choreography, but also the opportunity to learn authentic dance and rhythms from Zumba-certified experts. Each Jam Session lasts three hours, and instructors told me they leave with about four to five new "choreos," or routines. ZINs often receive "notes" and other materials to help them implement these routines in their classes. Angela called what she learns in Jam Sessions "the real Zumba," or the official choreography associated with the program.

Zumba Jammers can be generalists, or they can be "Rhythm Jammers" with a specialization in a particular "rhythm" like cumbia, salsa, reggaetón, or samba. Many instructors told me that Jam Sessions were especially useful for learning the histories and cultural significance of different dance styles. "Jam Sessions are amazing because they give you a history for the particular rhythm you're there for," Rebecca said. "The salsa jammer in this area gives a really strong history of the predominant instruments that are used. You know, every Rhythm Session that you go to, they will give you a really wonderful handout. They used to spend time actually doing it as a lecture, but they get right down to business now so they just give you the material. It's fascinating." Julia described her experience learning "authentic African dance" at a Jam Session: "First they teach you the history of the dance or the rhythm, where it came from. They put on a song. So, you listen to like an African song. So, you listen to the drums. They'll have actual drums in class, and they'll do live drumming to the music. It makes the experience so much more unique. And in those particular sessions, the songs that you get are African rhythm or kizomba rhythm. And the moves will be specific to that. So it's very unique."

The incorporation of historical background and live drums in Julia's "African" Jam Session gives the class an aura of authenticity. Angela described a similar experience when she attended Rony Gratereaut's popular workshop "Puerto Rican Flow" at the Zumba Convention one year:

> Rony decided to do just one song to teach us, and it was actually a Ricky Martin song. But he had a whole cultural aspect to the session. You walked in and he had flags up. He had a video going explaining a little bit of the history of Puerto Rico, and then he had a traditional dancer with traditional costumes. He had a live band. It was a plena band. They came and they were singing and playing instruments, and the way he presented the rhythms he was going to break down, he was breaking down bomba y plena, and the way he was breaking it down, the way he was talking about his country, it was like, it was moving. Puerto Ricans left crying. I almost cried.

Angela interpreted Gratereaut's presentation as a lesson in authentic Puerto Rican musical traditions. Her mention of bomba and plena is especially important given that these genres are often represented as the most authentic and traditional Puerto Rican dance practices. However, the same tension of balancing the traditional with the contemporary remains. Angela notes that the song they learned was by Ricky Martin, a global pop star who began his career with the 1980s boyband Menudo, and whose music reflects global pop trends much more than it does bomba or plena. In fact, Licia Fiol-Matta notes that it was not until Martin began eyeing the US crossover market that he started to incorporate "Afro-Latin" sounds such as bomba into his music in order to mark his authenticity as a Latin artist within the US mainstream market. However, Fiol-Matta also remarks that despite Martin's professed attachment to traditional Puerto Rican bomba and plena, his songs have very little to do with Puerto Rican music.[46] Likewise, although I do not know which kizomba song Julia learned in her Jam Session, the genre kizomba is a relatively modern phenomenon, developed in Angola in the 1980s and popular in places like Portugal and Cape Verde. In these instances, the Jam Session reproduces the contradiction of situating modern pop music within rigid definitions of authentic Latin music as traditional, historical, and static.[47]

Regardless of whether or not the information instructors receive in Jam Sessions is accurate, what is important here is that many instructors trust Zumba Fitness to provide them with accurate information. Many instructors perceive Jam Sessions to be taught by experts and authorities who know about "real" Latin music. Julia mentioned, "I think it's safe to trust [Zumba Jammers and International Presenters], because they are hired to do this. They know what they're talking about."

A second place where ZINs can learn "real" Zumba is the annual Zumba Convention. Each July, thousands of Zumba instructors from around the globe descend onto Orlando, Florida, for one week. Erin described Convention as "summer camp for Zumba instructors." Convention includes motivational talks, themed parties, and the highly anticipated Fitness Concert, which features performances by popular Zumba International Presenters and famous musical acts (past performers include Daddy Yankee, Gente de Zona, Becky G, Sean Paul, and Pitbull). Attendees can also learn new business strategies or earn certifications in various Zumba Fitness formats. For many instructors I spoke with, the Zumba Convention is worth the cost because it is a one-stop shop for professional development about all aspects of their fitness careers.

A highlight of Convention is the coveted "Flavor Sessions." These sessions focus on a specific rhythm, genre, or dance tradition. The Zumba instructors I've talked with have attended a variety of Flavor Sessions about dance styles like belly dance, hip-hop, twerking, Latin Urban, "Central American," kizomba, "African," or "tropical urban." They told me about Flavor Sessions called Puerto Rican Flow, Asian Invasion (K-Pop and other East Asian pop styles), Welcome to the Jungle (African dance), Mandarin Mayhem (Chinese pop), Reggaeton Rebellion, and Dominican Explosion.[48] The names of the Flavor Sessions are notable. Titles like "Asian Invasion" or "Welcome to the Jungle" reference deeply troubling stereotypes in the United States that mark Asian and African cultures, respectively, as exotic, potentially threatening, foreign, and fundamentally different from modern US life. Titling these Flavor Sessions with such problematic language naturalizes these stereotypes by linking them to the presumably authentic cultural routines that instructors learn during the workshops.

Popular Zumba Presenters—both Zumba Jammers and Zumba Education Specialists—teach most of the Flavor Sessions at Convention. Some of them are originally from the regions of the world that their sessions represent. For example, Rony Gratereaut of Puerto Rican Flow is from San Juan; Zumba International Presenter Ricardo Marmitte, who teaches African dance, is a native of Mauritius; and Dominican Explosion's creator, Zumba Jammer Carlos Henriquez, grew up in the Dominican Republic. The pairing of a particular Flavor Session with someone from that region of the world further underscores the perceived authenticity of that class. Indeed, many instructors prioritized attending sessions by Zumba Jammers, Zumba Education Specialists, and International Presenters whom they do not normally have access to. Angela attended many belly dance workshops one year in order to better cater to her "Middle Eastern" students. Julia makes it a point to attend sessions taught by "jammers who don't travel to Boston ... at a jam, not only will I bring home choreography, but I'll also bring new techniques and new moves that we here would never have thought of because they are not ethnic or local to us." Convention thus becomes a way for instructors to learn a variety of dance moves from people whom they perceive as authentic performers of a particular "ethnic" dance practice.

Still, many popular International Presenters teach Flavor Sessions even if they are not from the place where the dance style originated. In these instances, workshops sometimes incorporate other strategies to mark them as authentic. Popular Zumba International Presenters Loretta Bates and Marcie Benavides (both from the United States) teach Reggaeton Rebellion. The Zumba Home Office invited them to create a reggaetón-themed workshop in 2010, and it has become a staple of the Zumba Convention. Loretta Bates's journey into Zumba Fitness was similar to that of many of the other instructors I talked to: her Zumba instructor identified her as particularly talented and encouraged her to earn her license. Bates was initially reluctant because she did not have previous exposure to Latin music. But she decided to teach, and she quickly rose through the Zumba ranks to become a Zumba Education Specialist. When the Home Office asked Bates to take on the reggaetón Convention workshop, she told me that learning the history of reggaetón was a critical part of the process: "Because my [college] degree was international studies, I want to know the why behind everything. I don't want to just do a class where you're going to learn steps. Where does this rhythm come from? What's the history behind it? How did it grow? How did it spread? So I did a lot of research." Marcie's husband, DJ Francis (himself a Zumba Celebrity DJ), attended the session, too. He played clips of songs to illustrate Bates's and Benavides's brief history of reggaetón that they discussed before teaching the routines. Many of the instructors I spoke with appreciated this approach to Reggaeton Rebellion, although most noted that this background information is not necessarily useful for their own classes where students want to exercise, not learn the history of Latin music. Nevertheless, many instructors believed that learning the histories of various dance and music traditions through programs like Reggaeton Rebellion made them a better instructor.

However, not all instructors see Zumba Fitness's materials as authentic. Some are ambivalent or even actively critical of Zumba Fitness's claims to authenticity. For instance, Kathy thinks that Zumba Fitness does not provide enough background information about their routines—a sentiment echoed by several other instructors. As a white American woman, Kathy feels that it is important for her to know the most accurate and authentic information about these dances as a way to pay respect to other cultures and traditions. So, she spends considerable time researching on her own. Kathy makes it a point to "investigate" the background of individual artists and the original meanings of choreography. She has even contacted choreographers unaffiliated with Zumba Fitness to ensure that she is doing dances properly. These personal investigations supplement Zumba Fitness's informational materials, which she wished were more detailed and more prevalent in the spaces available to ZINS for learning choreography.

Kathy regularly watches online videos of specific dance steps so that she can incorporate more authentic moves into her choreography. One example is quebradita, a partner dance from the US-Mexico border region that is now a Zumba Fitness "rhythm." Quebradita is typically danced to banda music, which originated in Sinaloa, Mexico, but has taken on new forms as technobanda in Los Angeles, California, since the 1990s. Both technobanda and quebradita served as markers of Mexican American youth identity in the context of increasing anti-immigrant sentiment with the passage of Proposition 187 in 1994.[49] In fact, some of the most famous banda stars like Gerardo Ortiz or the late Jenni Rivera grew up near Los Angeles. Quebradita's popularity at one point brought it into the mainstream with use in national commercials and international dance competitions. Sydney Hutchinson notes that the integration of quebradita into Zumba Fitness is part of the dance's mainstreaming within Latinx communities.[50]

Quebradita usually involves acrobatic moves, jumps, twists, and lifts. After exposure to quebradita in Zumba Fitness, Kathy looked up dances on YouTube to learn more.

> When you see the real quebradita, you know when they're throwing [the girl] up? You know how they go on the side, the leg is going out? And the leg comes out and back down, and it's so gorgeous. So, I did a quebradita last Sunday. I found myself just doing some really basic moves. You know, a lot of belt-holding and skirt-pretending. So, I look [online]. I saw a bunch of non-Latinas try to do quebradita, and they're inserting all sorts of non-quebradita moves into the song, and I'm like, oh, this is the saddest thing. The moves of this dance are so beautiful. You don't want to salsify it or anything. You don't want to hip-hoppify it. So, I finally found a Mexican instructor doing it in Mexico, in a plaza, you know, with the country in the background, and said, we need to use that one.

Kathy's quest for authentic quebradita inadvertently reinforces the same rigid definitions of Latin music and dance as Pérez's book Zumba does. Kathy's concerns that dancers' "hip-hoppifying" quebradita might make it inauthentic align with the assertions from materials like Pérez's Zumba book that depict Latin dance as a static cultural tradition. In fact, many Mexican American youth have combined banda with rap for over twenty years. Josh Kun argues that such fusions often reflect young Mexican Americans' lives in Los Angeles, including connections to African American communities, rather than a bastardization of "real" Mexican music.[51] Indeed, the quebradita referenced in Zumba Fitness is rooted not in unchanged tradition, but the histories of migration and expressions of Mexican Americanness in the United States. It is likely that some of the quebradita dances that Kathy encountered online were actually filmed in the United States, given quebradita's popularity in the US-Mexico border region. However, her choice to prioritize what she saw as a performance in a "Mexican plaza" demonstrates just how entrenched assumptions that authentic Latin dance must be foreign are. It is important to stress that a profound respect for other cultures informs Kathy's investment in authenticity. Her tremendous concern about "cultural appropriation" is what motivates her to seek out her own information when she thinks Zumba Fitness has not provided enough. But the metrics of evaluation for authentic Latin culture in the Zumba Fitness world continuously stress the static, the traditional, and, above all, the foreign. Kathy's efforts reveal that one can prioritize cultural appreciation and authenticity while still, even inadvertently, replicating reductive, stereotypical assumptions about Latin music.

Kathy was not alone in seeking out more authentic music and choreography for her classes. Instructors already familiar with Latin music often criticized the songs that Zumba Fitness produced. Andrea grew up in a West Indian household where she heard salsa, reggae, soca, and other types of Caribbean music. She told me she uses her own music in her classes because Zumba Fitness songs are "watered down, because they have to have it for people who teach at the Y [YMCA] and for people who teach at senior centers. They have to have it for everybody, so it does have to be watered down. I understand that. But if folks want the original, if they're able to use the original songs, then I think that's good." Miriam also questioned the value of music produced by the Zumba Fitness corporation. She grew up in Latin America where she danced salsa frequently for fun—in fact, like me, her love of Latin music was one reason she started attending Zumba Fitness classes in the first place. As an instructor, Miriam sees Zumba Fitness as a great way to expose people to Latin music who might not otherwise hear it. But she admonished Zumba-produced music because "the quality is not good." Miriam continued, "The introduction to Latin music to a crowd that hasn't been exposed is great, and you want to bring the cultural aspect of it, and I myself wouldn't want them to think that this is what Latin music is, because I don't always think that Zumba's music is good quality music. And this is why sometimes I bring my own [music to class]." Miriam makes it a point to use original Spanish versions of songs rather than English translations or remixes. Introducing her students to authentic aspects of her own culture was really important to Miriam, even if she was not always convinced that her students actively wanted to learn about Latin music. She felt strongly that exposing students to her personal definition of authentic Latin music was a critical benefit of the Zumba Fitness program regardless of individual students' goals.

Leah, a young white woman, grew up "social dancing" with salsa and bachata. She struggled to learn Zumba Fitness steps to these "rhythms" because she saw them as completely different from her prior experience with social dancing. Leah compared learning the Zumba version of salsa to "learning another language." But, as a fitness instructor, she found Zumba Fitness's easily countable 4/4 beat and the pace of steps useful for teaching. In fact, instructors who regularly go out dancing in Latin nightclubs know that what they teach in Zumba Fitness classes is not what happens in "real life." Still, many of these instructors have separate full-time jobs, families, and other time constraints, so the choreography and music provided by Zumba Fitness make it possible for them to keep classes fresh and fun. These instructors don't necessarily see Zumba Fitness as a harbinger of authentic Latin dance. Instead, they prioritize efficiency and fitness—something that many claim their students are actually after, not a lesson in authenticity.

Ultimately, the different decisions by instructors like Andrea, Leah, Kathy, and Miriam reflect the diverse ways that instructors engage with discourses of authenticity provided by the Zumba Home Office. Not all instructors prioritize authenticity or see Zumba Fitness as especially authentic. Still, they all consider authenticity as critical to their own self-branding. Whether through Jam Sessions, Convention, materials provided by the Zumba Home Office, or through their own reconnaissance, these instructors view their ability to communicate their expertise in authentic Latin music and dance as both a moral obligation and an effective business strategy. No matter one's opinions about Zumba Fitness's accuracy, authenticity remains a critical currency for instructors seeking to build their own brand.

AUTHENTICITY IS IN THE EYE
OF THE BEHOLDER

Authenticity depends on who decides what counts as authentic, and what previous ideas they bring to their evaluations of authenticity. Despite claims to multicultural tolerance, many of the narratives around authenticity used in Zumba Fitness center the same problematic assumptions that govern definitions of Latin music in the music industry itself—that is, ideas that authentic Latin music comes from a traditional Latin America and is sung exclusively in Spanish. The framing of authentic Latin culture by the Zumba Home Office trickles down to the everyday space of the gym. Zumba Fitness informs many instructors' perceptions of authenticity. The trust that instructors place in Zumba Fitness to provide them with accurate information can ultimately backfire, enabling some of these instructors to reproduce stereotypes about Latin(x) American culture despite their commitment to diversity and inclusion.

Although not every instructor embraces Zumba Fitness's discourses around authenticity, this contradiction is hardly surprising. The concept of authenticity must be placed in a larger sociopolitical context, especially in a space like Zumba Fitness, where most participants see themselves as open-minded individuals who value diversity and equity. In many ways, this is what makes the trope of authenticity so troubling. At first blush, the effort that the Zumba Home Office claims they put into researching cultural traditions before creating their routines is admirable. It implies a measure of respect for cultural difference. And yet, in true multicultural fashion, incorporating these various traditions into Zumba Fitness winds up situating them within rigid parameters of authenticity that maintain colonial depictions of Latin America as foreign and primitive. Authenticity is not just about accuracy. Rather, it is a method of evaluation intimately connected to much bigger structures and ideologies about race, ethnicity, and national belonging.

SELLING FIESTA

THE THREE ALBERTOS HAD A BIG PROBLEM when they started making presentations to investors interested in Zumba Fitness: Beto Pérez did not speak English. Both Pérez and Alberto Perlman frequently bring this up when they recount Zumba Fitness's beginnings. Remember, Alberto Aghion and Perlman devised the business strategy, but Pérez was the creative mind behind the entire program. How could they explain what Zumba Fitness was all about to investors who did not understand Spanish? The solution: let Beto's dancing speak for itself. Pérez would do a Zumba Fitness demonstration for investors. When he finished, he would politely excuse himself from the meeting by shaking hands and saying "Nice to meet you, sorry I need to go." Then, Pérez waited in the parking lot while Perlman would negotiate. The two would meet afterward and head on their way.[1]

One outcome of this strategy is the "silent cuing" characteristic of Zumba Fitness classes. Zumba instructors do not talk in class—no motivational speeches, no "feel the burn" talk, no explanation of moves. Zumba Fitness claims that instructors' speaking would detract from the party music and atmosphere of the class. Zumba Fitness's tagline is, after all, "Ditch the Workout, Join the Party!" But speaking with the body instead of the voice also reinforces one of the most pervasive stereotypes of tropicalized Latinness: the always-dancing Latinx body. From Cinco de Mayo to "Livin' La Vida Loca," mainstream depictions of Latin culture center drinking, music, dance, revelry, and fiesta. Long-standing stereotypes in the United States have represented Latin Americans and their US diasporas as fun-loving party people whose Latinness becomes legible in part through a perceived natural ability and affinity for dance.

Fiesta, the Spanish word for "party," has become commonplace in US popular culture, found in everything from popular music (think Lionel Richie's "All Night Long," or the Pogues's "Fiesta") to the names of stores and restaurants (in my area a store called "Paper Fiesta" sells party supplies) and even a car (the Ford Fiesta). More than a mere translation of a Spanish word, though, I see *fiesta* as a far-reaching, abstract trope that signals the racial and cultural difference of tropicalized Latinness. A formal event almost never qualifies as a fiesta. Instead, the word *fiesta* conjures up images of a boisterous and loud party, one full of music, dancing, and bright colors, where inhibitions melt away. Fiestas come with sounds of "olé" or maybe some drums, with sombreros and Hawaiian shirts, with sexy music, dancing, and often a shot of tequila or a fizzy mojito. Not just any party can be a fiesta. Fiestas must be raucous, raunchy, and lively.

In this context, the trope of fiesta reproduces the mind-body divide intrinsic to Western modernity. The fiesta is a space where anything goes, a space governed by the supposedly more carefree and sexual cultures of places "south of the border." The figure of the dancing Latin body signals a kind of freedom and sexuality otherwise unavailable to modern Western subjects. In the US mainstream marketplace, Latin music and dance exemplifies not only the foreign, but also the exotic, erotic, and exciting. As Ignacio Corona writes, "From commercials to soundtracks, Latin music is stereotypically linked to the body and the senses, to hotness, passion, and sensuality."[2]

Key to this equation is the representation of Latin music as non-threatening. The fiesta alludes to some of the most common stereotypes of Latinx communities in the United States—laziness, substance abuse, hypersexuality, and potential danger. However, the trope of fiesta removes these more sinister characteristics, or at least reframes them as desirable. For example, the stereotype of Latina hyperfertility that provokes anxiety about demographic change becomes reconfigured as a hotness and sexiness unique to Latin culture that can be consumed by a mainstream, white audience. The trope of fiesta foregrounds the more enticing aspects of tropicalized Latinness—sexiness, happiness, fun, and parties—while ignoring more threatening stereotypes and obscuring structural inequalities facing Latinx communities.

If fiesta is abstract, though, then how does it work with the trope of authenticity that connects Zumba rhythms to specific places? The trope of fiesta homogenizes these different places and locates them in "the tropics." As an imagined geographical zone, the tropics links together places as diverse as South Africa and Colombia, Cuba and Hawai'i, by representing their distinct cultures through well-worn stereotypes of exotic and racialized others. The Zumba Fitness brand continuously oscillates between acknowledging place-based cultural traditions, and presenting these traditions as the products of an undifferentiated tropical zone marked by fun, sexy, and nonstop fiestas.

This imagined tropics is not new. The image of the tropical, exotic, foreign other has been central to depictions of "Latin" culture for decades. We see this in the performances of Carmen Miranda, for example, whose "tutti-frutti hat," exaggerated accent, and sexy dancing created the prototype for representing Latinas, and Latin America more broadly, as exotic, foreign, and sexual.[3] Her contemporary Desi Arnaz made a name for himself singing the Cuban "conga," and his 1950s performances as Ricky Ricardo in *I Love Lucy* often featured Arnaz beating his drum in a frenzy while flanked, in part, by tropical foliage.[4] Three decades later, Cuban American Gloria Estefan's music video "Rhythm Is Gonna Get You" depicted a face-painted Estefan surrounded by drums as she sang about a contagious rhythm that could not be stopped.[5] Almost twenty years after Estefan, Puerto Rican superstar Ricky Martin ushered in the so-called Latin boom of the late 1990s and early 2000s with a Grammy performance of "La Copa de La Vida" surrounded by drums, carnivalesque performers, and a lot of hip-thrusting. Nuyorican, Bronx-bred Jennifer Lopez's early music videos often featured tropical scenes that have now become iconic, like the palms enveloping her in "Waiting for Tonight" and the beach dance scene in "Love Don't Cost a Thing," and there are numerous music videos that showcase Lopez rolling around in sand and surf.[6] More recently, Luis Fonsi and Daddy Yankee reached number one on US pop charts with "Despacito," spurring a lot of media coverage that framed Fonsi, in particular, as a "Latin lover" who sang in front of a prototypical Caribbean backdrop of colorful homes, crashing waves, and seductive palms.[7] Over and over again, we see Latin stars metaphorically framed as tropical and literally framed by plants, beaches, sun, and sweat.

Each of these crossover acts also drew heavily from Afro-Latinx cultural practices and signifiers in their performances. They performed music created by Afro-Latin(x) American communities, be it samba, rumba, hip-hop, or reggaetón. However, these figures all embodied a whitened "Latin look" that suppressed any acknowledgment of their performances' African roots or even the mere existence of Black communities in their respective countries. Myriad scholars have discussed the invisibility of Afro-Latinx bodies in US mainstream and Spanish-language media. This happens in part because the specific Latin bodies deemed marketable are those that can be exotic, sexy, and ethnically othered without being too racially threatening, indicated by the whitened Latin look.[8] Thus, the Latin foreign other might perform Afro-Latinx dance or music but remains a decidedly non-Black figure in the US cultural imagination.

The trope of fiesta in the Zumba Fitness brand draws from the templates created by Latin stars like Carmen Miranda, Gloria Estefan, or Ricky Martin, but does so with more abstract cultural cues that do not rely on images of a "Latin" body. It is no accident that many people I meet in the Zumba Fitness world—instructors, International Presenters, fellow students in my classes—compare their classes to a "vacation" where they get temporary relief from the structures, norms, and rules of everyday life. To attend Zumba class is to be in fiesta, and to be in fiesta is to encounter, feel, and perform a sexy tropicalized Latinness. This chapter mines different aspects of the Zumba Fitness brand to identify the workings of the trope of fiesta in selling tropicalized Latinness. Fiesta shows up often in unexpected ways. I consider both products that Zumba Fitness sells, namely the company's popular Zumba Wear fashion line, and the vacation vibes of a Zumba Fitness class. Several characteristics link these two things together: loudness, color, and sexiness. All of these characteristics play a critical role in the trope of fiesta and, in turn, tropicalized Latinness. Although not necessarily embodied by Latinx people, these more abstract qualities signal a connection to an imagined tropics that allegedly unites the diverse musical and dance traditions that make up the Zumba Fitness world.

BRINGING THE TROPICS
TO NEW ENGLAND

I arrived to the studio just north of Boston on a hot, sunny afternoon in 2019. Inside the room was dark with low lighting, which gave the impression of being in a nightclub rather than a gym. I had come for a Master Class with Brazilian Zumba Jammer and International Presenter Allan Bapuru from Salvador da Bahia, Brazil. The online flyer had promised that Bapuru would "Bring Brazil to Boston" in "90 Minutes of Sweat." The image featured a smiling Bapuru in a yellow shirt and backward hat,

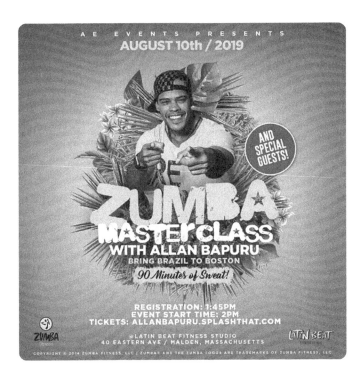

2.1 Flyer for 2019 Zumba Fitness Master Class with Zumba Jammer Allan Bapuru that promises to "Bring Brazil to Boston." The plants and bright colors are typical of the types of imagery associated with tropicalized Latinness.

surrounded by green palm leaves and pink hibiscus flowers, and pointing directly at the viewer. The flyer itself was very bright—greens, pinks, yellows, and a striking blue that reminded me of the ocean.

The flyer for Bapuru's class visually depicts many of the elements typically associated with fiesta and tropicalized Latinness. The focus on Bapuru's Brazilian heritage emphasizes his foreignness and authenticity as a Zumba Jammer who brings choreography directly from the source—Latin America. During the class, Bapuru taught typical Zumba Fitness choreography to a Brazilian soundtrack. Like most instructors, Bapuru wore Zumba Wear clothing, but his outfit was in the colors of the Brazilian flag—yellow, green, and blue—thus further emphasizing his Brazilianness. He did not talk much. Bapuru explained during the event, "My English is no good, *mas o meu corpo fala* [but my body speaks]." Once again, the dancing Latin body communicates to the audience to make up for limited English proficiency.

Although the class took place in Massachusetts, the flyer situates Bapuru and his class squarely within an imagined tropical place. Here, the tropics are not necessarily mapped onto a specific geographical site. Despite the specificity of the phrase "Bringing Brazil to Boston," the images, colors, and language on the flyer could have pertained to almost anywhere. The tropics are interchangeable, signaling a host of characteristics that reproduce distinctions between the allegedly more modern, civilized Global North and the licentious and primitive Global South.

The imagination of the tropics as a place of sexual freedom, adventure, passion, and fun is not new. Catherine Cocks argues that the tourism industry of the late nineteenth and early twentieth centuries depicted the tropics as sites of leisure that departed (but not too much) from the dictates of modern life in the Global North. Significantly, this entailed a shift from understanding the tropics as a place that was dangerous and savage to a place that fostered relaxation, consumption, and even health.[9] These historical representations of the tropics have persisted, as Juan León describes in his discussion of the tropics in the contemporary imagination:

> [The tropics] can be free of artificial structure and attuned to the environment. In these tropics storms and tropical breezes complement human excitement and languor. The allure of ripe fruit complements the pleasures and satiations of the uninhibited life of the tropical body. Distant from things modern, these fanciful tropics can be many related things: places of recreation rather than work, feeling rather than intellection, spontaneity rather than planning, indulgence rather than self-restraint, fecundity rather than sterility, community rather than alienation. Most broadly, these tropics represent surrender to human nature and the natural world rather than (perhaps stifling) control over both.[10]

In the tropics, an "anything goes" attitude is an acceptable and even expected approach to life. One does not need to regulate one's behavior in the same ways in the tropics, for the tropics disregard the individualism, hyperproductivity, and intellectualism so closely aligned with the Global North. This is precisely what makes the tropics the perfect place for a nonstop fiesta.

The environment, marked by hot weather and lush landscapes, is especially important in the imagination of the tropics. León's description of "tropical fruit" or "tropical breezes" stresses the warm climate that distinguishes tropical places from the colder temperatures and temperaments of Europe or the northern United States. But these tropics were not just pristine landscapes. People inhabit(ed) the tropics, and they were not always viewed in the same favorable light as the places in which they lived. The very same tropical climate that could prove relaxing for the hard-working US (white) American was considered to be an impediment for its inhabitants. Cocks argues that nineteenth-century racial ideologies often assumed that the tropics bred laziness and improper morals for the dark-skinned people who lived there. The tropics allegedly hampered civilization and progress.[11] As a result, tropical people, who are almost exclusively imagined as nonwhite, are racialized as primitive, hypersexual, and instinctual others who embody the opposite of the values, intelligence, and morality of modern white subjects. León writes that even if the tropics can be attractive and enticing, the residents of the tropics are contradictorily imagined as dangerous, "ferocious savages."[12] These tropical figures exist outside of the metaphorical and geographical boundaries of the United States.[13]

The contradictory reputation of the tropics as both a place of desire, freedom, and fun on one hand, and danger, violence, and savagery on the other mirrors two dominant stereotypes of US Latinxs (i.e., alluring and sexy versus dangerous and threatening). Alberto Sandoval-Sánchez identifies two figures who personify the "Latin other" in the US imagination: the "Latin foreign other," an immigrant to the United States who identifies with their homeland, and a "Latin domestic ethnic and racial other" who is born and raised in the United States.[14]

The figure of the Latin foreign other comes directly from the tropics and exists "to sing, dance, romance, be comical, and live from fiesta to siesta."[15] Because Latin foreign others are assumed to be immigrants, they are considered authentic representatives of their homelands even when they perform stereotypes of their cultures. Sandoval-Sánchez notes that this authenticity is also rooted in the Latin foreign other's performances of Afro-Latin(x) American music and dance.[16] The Latin music industry has just as much institutionalized anti-Black racism as any other global enterprise. The whitening of some of Latin music's most popular genres—from mambo to reggaetón—reveals the historical and ongoing racialization of Latin music and culture as non-Black, even if Afro-Latinx communities played an essential role in the creation of many popular Latin genres.[17] Performances by Latin foreign others reflect these systemic biases by the Latin music industry. Delia Poey succinctly describes this process in her definition of the "Latin@ Rhythmic Other" when she writes that "the Rhythmic Other alluded to in the songs may well have its roots in Africa, but by the time that Other is brought into play . . . it is reduced to sound and made present by a . . . body that is phenotypically white."[18] Latin music is also routinely depicted as foreign despite the role of US-based Latinx producers and musicians in its development; this is especially true of crossover Latin stars who are depicted as foreign newcomers onto the music scene regardless of their own backgrounds or previous successes.[19] Distance from Blackness makes this exotic and unique culture consumable because it does not threaten the US racial order, while tropicalized Latinness's reputation as perpetually foreign differentiates it from the presumably more civilized US mainstream. By embodying tropicalized Latinness, the Latin foreign other can enter mainstream US culture without disrupting the hegemony of respectable whiteness.

This Latin foreign other stands in stark contrast to what Alberto Sandoval-Sánchez terms the "Latin domestic ethnic and racial other" imagined as "illegal aliens, criminals, gangsters, and drug addicts" who reside in major US cities.[20] The Latin domestic ethnic and racial other represents the more threatening aspects of ethnoracial stereotypes associated with Latinx communities, especially ideas about illegality and violence. Sandoval-Sánchez focuses his comments on forms of representation such as *West Side Story*, the play and subsequent film that depicted the violent conflict between white and Puerto Rican gangs in New York City. Rather than African diasporic cultural roots, the Latin domestic and racial other is instead connected to stereotypes of working-class, urban, African American youth who, according to Murray Forman, have "been discursively constructed, from the outside, as a visible and troubling blight on American society."[21] Urban Latinx populations, especially Puerto Ricans in New York, have likewise been linked to such stereotypes of the "urban," but remain racialized as distinct from Blackness. Instead, these urban Latinx youth are racialized as *akin* to African Americans, if not Black themselves.[22] The result is a construction of Latinx identity as similarly racially othered, but in a more threatening way that is not easily consumable precisely because it is too domestic and too connected to urban Blackness.

Zumba Fitness's reliance on the Latin foreign other thus allows the company to market itself as exotic, foreign, and ethnic while distancing itself from the Latin domestic ethnic and racial other. This is not new. Numerous industries, from food to the fine art world, circulate these same tropes.[23] Perhaps one cultural arena most analogous to Zumba Fitness is Latin dance. Spanish Caribbean music and dance forms, especially salsa, dominate the perception of Latin dance in the popular imagination. Whether in salsa clubs or ballroom competitions, television shows or movies, Latin dance signifies something hot, tropical, sexy, and exotic. For example, Joanna Bosse finds that white ballroom dancers often see Latin categories like rhumba or salsa as inherently sexual.[24] Similarly, Cindy García notes that Latinas who conform to stereotypes of the exotic and hypersexual Latina salsa dancer have more cultural and social capital within Latin nightclub scenes. In addition, white Anglo women can "safely" explore their own sexuality in salsa nightclubs since these spaces are already assumed to be sexualized in the first place.[25] Carmela Muzio Dormani's analysis of rhetoric on the popular reality television competition show *So You Think You Can Dance* confirms García's and Bosse's ethnographic observations. Dormani found that convincingly performing hypersexuality was paramount to contestants' receiving high assessments from the show's judges.[26] Over and over again, Latin dance has become a metonym for Latinx, and especially Latina, sexuality. In turn, as Jane Desmond states, Latin dance subsequently becomes indicative of a supposedly more passionate, emotional, sexual, and irrational Latinx figure; Desmond writes, "The unstated equation is that Latins [*sic*] are how they dance, and dance how they are."[27]

In this context, the Latin foreign other performs "authentic" Latin music and dance that conforms neatly to the ideas about tropicalized Latinness so pervasive in the dominant US imagination. Music and sound play a critical role in the racialization of tropicalized Latinness. Jennifer Lynn Stoever terms this the "sonic color line," or "the process of racializing sound—how and why certain bodies are expected to produce, desire, and live among particular sounds—and its product, the hierarchical division sounded between 'whiteness' and 'blackness.'"[28] She argues that the "listening ear" is the "ideological filter" that imposes dominant ideologies of race, gender, and class onto how people listen to sounds of the "other."[29] Part of what heightens the fiesta feel of a Zumba Fitness class is not just the *sound* of Latin music but also all of the other ideas about "Latin culture" as sexy, fun, and exotic that are wrapped up in those sounds.[30]

Few Zumba instructors described themselves as "becoming" Latinx in Zumba class. For example, I have never met anyone in Zumba Fitness who dons "brownface," or skin-darkening makeup used by white performers in the ballroom scene.[31] Instead, many instructors describe Zumba Fitness classes as a "one-hour vacation," a time when they and their students can feel transported somewhere else. That place is the imagined tropics—sexy, warm, exotic, and carefree—populated by Latin foreign others whose movements and lifeways can be experienced briefly and safely in the space of a Zumba Fitness class. Of course, this is not always explicit. Juliet McMains argues that white ballroom dancers ironically re-affirm their own whiteness when performing in the Latin category; how-ever, she writes that this is not necessarily "a conscious or even a primary reason for Anglo-Americans' participation in Latin dance."[32] As I detail in a later chapter, most white Zumba instructors I have met actually be-lieve that they are doing the opposite—that is, creating a more tolerant and inclusive multicultural community. Moreover, for many women, in particular, Zumba Fitness classes present an opportunity to express their sexuality in a safe and supportive environment, more often than not in the company of other women and outside of the male gaze. The problem here is not that women can express their sexuality, but rather that this self-expression happens exclusively through an engagement with tropi-calized Latinness. In other words, crediting Zumba's "Latin" foundation as *the* aspect of the program that enables this temporary sexual expression ultimately reinforces stereotypes of Latinx hypersexuality. In turn, Zumba Fitness participants can access tropicalized Latinness just briefly, one hour at a time, in their local gym, rec center, campus, dance studio, or even in their home.

WELCOME TO THE JUNGLE

Tropicalized Latinness engulfs the entire Zumba Fitness brand, includ-ing its products and advertising. One of Zumba Fitness's most popular products is its clothing line, Zumba Wear, launched in 2008.[33] Zumba Wear sells everything from leggings and sports bras to jackets, hats, bracelets, sneakers, and even Swarovski crystal necklaces. There are other nonwearable accessories, too—water bottles, keychains, stickers, phone holders, and more. Zumba Fitness does not release profit numbers on its Zumba Wear lines (or any products, for that matter). In 2018, Perlman told the *Miami Herald* that Zumba earned "significant" revenue from its apparel.[34] Zumba Wear is a big moneymaker for the Zumba Home Office, and perhaps one of the company's more enduring products.

Most people I know who don Zumba Wear clothes are instructors. For some instructors, Zumba Wear is practical. Zumba Wear clearly identifies instructors for their students and other people they encounter in a gym, fitness club, or rec center. For example, Julia explained that Zumba Wear's bright colors make it more feasible for students to "find" her in a crowded class and just "follow the yellow shirt." Since instructors must market themselves and their classes, being identifiable in the gym alerts consumers who might not otherwise know about Zumba Fitness that it is available to them. Stephanie mentioned that she would field questions about the program in the women's locker room when health club members approached her to ask about the logo on her shirt. Such encounters outside of the gym expand instructors' business, as well. Leah recalled that when she wears Zumba Wear to places like the supermarket, people ask her about the brand and the program since they might have heard of it from a friend or relative but are not quite sure what it is. In this way, Zumba Wear both advertises the brand for the Zumba Home Office, but also benefits some instructors who can attract new students to their classes by wearing it when they are out and about.

Although Zumba Wear includes typical exercise gear—leggings, tank tops, and the like—it differs from the monotone black or dull colors usually found in other fitness clothing brands. Alberto Perlman told *Business Insider* that Zumba Wear deliberately departed from the typical black leggings so commonly found in the gym. He stated, "Everyone is wearing black yoga pants and then you see the Zumba people wearing colorful, cool cargo pants. It makes a statement that says 'I don't have to hide like everyone else. I can show a little bit of brightness, and not have to wear these black pants.'"[35] The colors mark Zumba Fitness as "brighter" and perhaps more fun. Stephanie explained to me,

> I just like being able to continue to be fashionable in my exercise class, and I like to get dressed up. I can look cooler in a Zumba class than I can going out now, because I have more crazy Zumba clothes. Other classes, it's like, you've got to wear all black, that's it. It's kind of boring. I like having fun. I feel like if you look good when you work out, you're going to feel good. Isn't that how we always think about clothes in general? You look good, you feel good. So, if they're going to let me do that in the Zumba class, then why not?

Stephanie's comments reflect Perlman's assertions that the clothing line differs from typical exercise clothing because, as Leah told me, "it's bright, it's fun, it's loud."

Leah's description of Zumba Wear as "bright," "fun," and "loud" reflects several key components of the trope of fiesta. One is loudness. On the most basic level, loudness refers to something that is played or articulated at a high volume. In Zumba Fitness, loud music helps to create the fiesta atmosphere of the class—the louder the music, the better the party. Of course, parties are generally meant to be loud, boisterous, and fun. But the issue of loudness has particular racial connotations for Latinx communities. On one hand, as Jennifer Lynn Stoever describes, loudness can be "fetishized as exotic or demonized as unassimilable, noise and loudness frequently function as aural substitutes for and markers of race."[36] Those sounds that cannot be easily tamed or controlled are rendered "noise" that offends and intrudes on an otherwise respectable or ordered space.[37] If Latin music provides the soundtrack to fiesta in a Zumba Fitness class, it can become noise when played loudly in the wrong place. This is what happened when a tourist complained on Reddit that loud "Spanish hip hop" kept him up all night when he rented an AirBnB in the Dominican neighborhood of Washington Heights in New York City in 2016. He wrote "What's wrong with these people? Don't they work? . . . People have no education, everybody here talks loud, loud music day and night ANYWHERE, even in the more secluded areas. . . . And let me tell you they talk about drugs and jail all the time."[38] For the Reddit user, loud music is far more than an annoyance. Instead, it indicates a host of racist stereotypes such as criminality, laziness, drug addiction, and stupidity often applied to Latinx communities. This is not an isolated incident. For example, media coverage of Puerto Rican migration to New York City in the 1950s included frequent references to loudness and noise as a sign that Puerto Ricans were unassimilable, unruly, and threatening.[39]

Of course, loud music plays a critical, and often welcomed, role in almost every type of cardio fitness class. No one wants to be in a quiet Zumba Fitness class. Despite being perceived positively by Zumba enthusiasts, though, loud music functions as a marker of racial otherness in the gym just as it does in criticisms of "loud" urban Latinx communities. In both cases, Latinness is characterized as distinct from the more orderly and muted sounds of whiteness and the Global North, whether as the threatening Latin domestic racial and ethnic other as in the case of New York Puerto Ricans and Dominicans, or as the exotic dancing Latin foreign other as in the case of Zumba Fitness. Loud music in Zumba Fitness is not just consistent with aerobics and dance-fitness formats in general. Loud music is one of the things that makes Zumba Fitness a Latin fiesta.

This connection between Latinness and loudness extends beyond the sonic. Loud also means something in poor taste that does not conform to the aesthetic standards of respectable or professional spaces. Latinas' self-stylings, including tight clothes, long nails, or bright patterns and colors, compose part of what Jillian Hernandez terms "sexual-aesthetic excess." Sexual-aesthetic excess underscores "modes of dress and comportment that are often considered 'too much': too sexy, too ethnic, too young, too cheap, too loud."[40] In turn, these stylistic choices become construed as expressions of Latinas' sexual and racial otherness.[41] Television characters like *Modern Family*'s Gloria Delgado-Pritchett exemplify how fashion choices like leopard print and high heels contribute to her stereotypical caricature of a hypersexualized Colombian woman in the United States.[42] Similarly, aesthetic and fashion choices, especially tight clothes or acrylic nails, have been used to depict Latinas as unfit mothers and improper women.[43] Even government officials like Supreme Court Justice Sonia Sotomayor or Congresswoman Alexandria Ocasio-Cortez have not escaped ridicule for wearing bright red nail polish or lipstick, respectively.[44] Such attention to what on the surface appear to be superficial details reveals how these sorts of fashion and aesthetic choices have become synonymous with stereotypes of Latinas as too loud and too unrefined to be successfully assimilated into respectable US Americanness.

In this context, Zumba Wear's bright colors and boisterous patterns conform to dominant images of Latinx excess and loudness. Color, argues Johana Londoño, plays a critical role in the racialization of Latinx communities. Whether in fashion, film, or the built environment, Londoño writes that, historically, "Latin America was produced as exceptionally colorful in contradistinction to the supposedly less colorful North." However, like notions of authenticity in popular music, color was not equally attributed to US Latinx populations. Londoño argues that instead there was "a sublimation of a US Latinx presence in a discourse of Latin American colorfulness that seemed more exotic and alluring, and perhaps safer in its distance, than the cultures of domestic racialized spaces."[45] Like Latin music, color distinguishes Latinness as something foreign and unassimilable, but also desirable and fun. Consequently, the very same stylistic choices demonized when adopted by US Latinas become celebrated and encouraged in other mainstream cultural spaces like Zumba Fitness.[46] Zumba Wear diffuses the threat of sexual-aesthetic excess by reframing these aesthetics as part of an exotic culture embodied by the Latin foreign other.

Zumba Wear collections vary, but they all generally connect to the trope of fiesta through their colors and patterns. Zumba Wear launched its new "Dance in Color" line in the fall of 2021. The name, "Dance in Color," implies something exciting or different. "In color" brings to mind its grayscale opposite, a contrast that is analogous with the stereotype of tropicalized Latinness as more boisterous and flashier than the muted aesthetics of the Global North.[47] The line featured clothing in oranges, pinks, yellows, and blues, often with distinctive geometric patterns. Some items were simply brightly colored leggings in hot pink or turquoise or a black cargo pant with fuchsia trim. Others had phrases like "Color Your Dancefloor" or "Dance Happy" printed on them to further connect Zumba Fitness to a sense of "aliveness" and fun. On one women's black open-backed tank top, "Girls Just Wanna Have Salsa," a play on Cyndi Lauper's 1983 hit, "Girls Just Wanna Have Fun," appears in multicolored lettering. Referencing a commonly recognized mainstream US pop phrase domesticates the perceived foreignness of salsa while also equating salsa with fun. A bright orange T-shirt available in both men's and women's sizes says "Red Hot Moves," alluding to the reputation of Zumba Fitness, and Latin dance more generally, being fun, popular, and sexy. While "Dance in Color" might not seem overtly linked to tropicalized Latinness, the combination of bright colors and references to sexiness and fun explicitly connect the clothing line to fiestas and tropicalized Latinness.

Other Zumba Wear collections are much less abstract, incorporating common stereotypes of the tropical and exotic Latin foreign other. In 2017, Zumba Wear released the "Rhythm of the Wild" collection pitched as the opportunity for consumers to unleash their "inner wild child" and "embrace [their] bolder side." Zumba Wear creative director Melanie Canevaro stated, "We pictured our Zumba Tribe going into the jungle to explore and party. Tropical aloha prints and Tahitian-inspired graphics in bright neon are the focus of this collection."[48] These descriptions of the fashion collection, in addition to the "Rhythm of the Wild" name itself, reproduce stereotypes of the "wild" as untamed, exotic, and tropical. The Rhythm of the Wild collection included bright colors, botanical themes, and phrases like "My Vibe, My Tribe," and "Jungle Queen" printed on the clothing. Terms like "rhythm," "tribe," and "jungle" all bring up the more salacious and potentially threatening aspects of the tropics. Importantly, these terms also reference long-standing stereotypes of a primitive racial other marked by infectious and unruly rhythms and wild landscapes.

However, Canevaro's comments stress that consumers, or the "Zumba Tribe," are only temporarily located in the "jungle." They are there to "explore and party" and thus cannot be confused with the Latin foreign other that inhabits the tropics. In this way, the bright colors, botanical patterns, and troubling word choices used in Rhythm of the Wild reproduce stereotypes of tropicalized Latinness that distinguish it from the Global North.

A second 2017 Zumba Wear collection, "Let's Get Loud," similarly featured bright colors and nature-themed patterns, most prominently leopard print. "Let's Get Loud" incorporated several words like "Gozadera" that directly tied the collection to Latin music and that would be familiar to most Zumba Fitness enthusiasts. In fact, the 2018 Zumba Convention performers Gente de Zona, an Afro-Cuban reggaetón duo, had a major hit titled "La Gozadera" popular with both general audiences and in Zumba Fitness classes. The clothing line's name is yet another song title, one of Jennifer Lopez's singles from her 1999 debut album, *On the Six*. Though sung in English, "Let's Get Loud" features piano riffs and brass commonly found in the "Miami sound" of Latin pop stars. The song is a party anthem, telling listeners, "Life's a party, make it hot / Dance, don't ever stop / Whatever rhythm" and "Let the music make you free / Be what you want to be / Make no excuses." Lopez's hit specifically signifies the trope of fiesta by linking loudness with partying, fun, and freedom in its lyrics and with its stereotypical "Latin" crossover sound.[49]

The "Let's Get Loud" Zumba Wear collection singled out reggaetón with its incorporation of several Spanish phrases like "Si necesita reggaeton, dale" (a line from J Balvin's popular 2015 hit "Ginza" meaning "if he/she needs reggaetón, give it to him/her") and "Dale" printed on the clothes. Critics, both within and outside of the Latinx community, have long admonished reggaetón for promoting hypersexuality and misogyny. One common critique is that reggaetón objectifies women and only values them for their sexual availability for men, such as in Don Omar's song "Dale Don Dale," which describes seducing women on the dance floor. The term *dale*, common in Spanish and reggaetón, can mean many different things: "Go for it!," "Do it!," or "Go ahead!" *Dale* can also mean "Give it to her," as in the context of "Dale Don Dale." In that song, female artist Glory responds to Don Omar by declaring her sexual availability. The term *dale* can thus range in meaning from innocent positive reinforcement to an invitation for sex. The "Let's Get Loud" collection plays on

2.2 Screenshot from Zumba Wear website featuring the leopard-print "La Gozadera Dale Skinny Sweatpants" from the 2017 "Let's Get Loud" collection. Note the copy on the bottom that encourages consumers to "show off your wild side."

these varied interpretations. One item, the leopard-print "La Gozadera Dale Skinny Sweatpants," plastered the word *Dale* in bold white lettering on the butt. The advertisement for the pants encourages consumers to "show off your wild side," stating that "Dale means to go for it!" Still, the combination of leopard-print pants with the word *dale* on the buttocks, a body part already racialized as the quintessential symbol of Latina hypersexuality, reinforces stereotypes of Latinas as potentially dangerous yet exotic.[50]

Taken together, Zumba Wear collections like "Dance in Color," "Rhythm of the Wild," and "Let's Get Loud" reproduce key aspects of the fiesta trope: being loud, bright, colorful, and exotic. The very same traits used to declare Latinas' unsophisticated taste and inappropriate behavior transform into less threatening and more desirable qualities in the Zumba Fitness world. Zumba Wear references the Latin foreign other while distancing the brand from domestic racial and ethnic others. As a result, Zumba Wear depicts loudness, fun, and sexy fiestas as natural to Latin culture. All of these become associated with the tropics, a site of freedom and unfettered pleasure that exists outside of the norms of the Global North.

SEXY ZUMBA

If you have attended Zumba class, it's likely that you have heard the 2012 DJ Mam's song "Fiesta Buena," which translates to "Good Party." The song is a collaboration between the France-based artists DJ Mam's, Luis Guisao, and Soldat Jahman, featuring Zumba Fitness's own Beto Pérez. The lyrics shift between French Creole and Spanish to describe the ways that "la Zumba buena" grips you and makes you dance. In fact, the phrase "Zumba buena" repeats more frequently than the word "fiesta" despite the song's title. Sonically, "Fiesta Buena" mashes up synthetic accordion riffs that sound like a sped-up Colombian vallenato mixed with electronic music and a Caribbean dancehall break. Guisao's Spanish and Soldat Jahman's Martinican Creole create the perfect mash-up for Zumba Fitness— an upbeat, multilingual song that blends Latin and Caribbean sounds in a way that evokes the tropics. The accompanying music video for "Fiesta Buena" moves between scenes of the four men dancing at nightclubs, in tropical places (signified by palm trees and sun), and, in Beto's case, a massive convention-style Zumba class. Visually, then, the video links Zumba Fitness to the tropics and to parties, central aspects of the fiesta trope.[51]

The song also explicitly connects Zumba Fitness and fiestas to sexiness. The song's dancehall break slows the beat down while Soldat Jahman raps, "Dale sexy Zumba, dale sexy Zumba, dale dale." I have danced to "Fiesta Buena" in many different Zumba Fitness classes since the song is tremendously popular in the Zumba world. Each time, the dancehall break gives us a minute to catch our breath in the middle of what is otherwise a very fast routine. It also gives us a chance to do some sort of sexy move—a body roll, a belly-dance-style hip move, or a booty pop. Once again, "*dale*" encourages us to go for it and to express our inner sexy.

Sexiness plays an essential role in defining the Latin foreign other and the fiesta trope. Many scholars have documented the ubiquitous stereotypes of Latinx hypersexuality in the media. The male Latin lover stereotype most famously embodied by actors like Rudolph Valentino paints Latinos as simultaneously dangerous and desirable. Likewise, the idea that Latinas, in particular, exude sexuality in everything they do dominates representations of Latina women in film, television, advertising, popular music, and elsewhere.[52] Outside of popular culture, though, this same stereotype of the hypersexualized Latina has been mobilized by political conservatives to stoke nativist fears about Latina immigrants' allegedly uncontrollable fertility and, subsequently, so-called anchor babies who threaten the US (white) American way of life.[53] Whether considered desirable or dangerous, stereotypes of Latinx hypersexuality have their roots in modern racial hierarchies. Indeed, Frances Aparicio and Susana Chávez-Silverman note that sexuality, especially Latina hypersexuality, is a defining characteristic of hegemonic tropicalization.[54] Tropical people are sexy people. And fiestas are the perfect place for consumers to safely express their own sexualities, desires, and fantasies.

Likewise, Latin dance scenes in the United States have long been viewed as appropriate spaces for overt sexual expression. This is especially true for many white women dancers who describe the feeling of unencumbered sexual expression they do not have in everyday life or even in other dance scenes.[55] Zumba Fitness is no exception. Many instructors detailed the freedom of sexual expression that they and/or their students feel in Zumba Fitness classes. One said, "I've always thought [what makes Zumba unique is] Latin moves and sexy. And I think that there's certain times that that's what people are looking for. And it's funny. Like the people you don't expect to really enjoy it, as soon as you do a little shimmy, they're doing these sexy moves. And sometimes it's the people that you least expect, because it's like they just need to have that boundary put down." Another mentioned that she thought Zumba "objectified women," but then explained, "I always say, Zumba's like Vegas. What happens in Zumba stays in Zumba. I teach a class in the suburbs. And I think they get a kick out of the fact that they get to do things they would never do in other parts of their lives. They've learned how to swivel their hips and shimmy their shoulders. . . . I think it's a release. And nobody's watching. I think it's an essential part of the escape that Zumba provides." Yet another described the joy she felt spreading happiness to her students, which she saw expressed in their sexy movements. She said, "[You] see them smiling when we're twerking or when we're booty shaking, and they love it. You look at these people, and you're like, 'I don't think she would ever do that if it wasn't in a Zumba class.'" A Latina instructor told me, "Latin rhythms make your body move in every way that you could, and in ways that you never knew that you had. All of a sudden you start using muscles that, oh, they didn't show me this. They didn't show me to move my hips. And Latin is all hips, and that is very attractive to a lot of cultures that are not taught to do that."

Each of these instructors teach predominantly white American women. Their comments reveal several key aspects of the fiesta trope.

The idea that "Zumba is like Vegas" mirrors descriptions of Zumba Fitness as a "vacation" from regular life. Zumba Fitness becomes a space where participants not only escape the stressors of everyday life, but also move their bodies in sexy ways that they normally would not do. Significantly, Latin music makes this happen, whether because it exposes students to "new" ways of moving they never experienced before, or because it offers a "release" that students otherwise cannot have. Fiesta and sexuality become directly correlated. Just as white ballroom dancers ultimately reinforce their own whiteness through performing the Latin other, in this case, Zumba Fitness participants can engage with tropicalized Latinness and the movements of a Latin foreign other without compromising their own racial positionality. In so doing, they wind up reinforcing racial hierarchies that distinguish respectable whiteness from hypersexual tropicalized Latinness.

A plethora of internet memes that depict sexiness as a central component of Zumba Fitness reflect this contrast by juxtaposing presumably sexy Latina women's bodies with other unsexy, or even ridiculous, bodies. The popular "what we think we look like" versus "what we actually look like" comparison meme format contains two photos: the first depicts an ideal, while the second pictures someone attempting (and usually failing) to achieve that ideal. One particularly popular Zumba meme pictures this ideal as a svelte woman in a midriff-baring red top and baggy pants, facing away from the camera as she dances in the rain. Hands on her hips and chest, she separates her legs and cocks out her right hip. This is a photo of actress Briana Evigan as the character Andie, an aspiring dancer, in *Step Up 2: The Streets*. She is pictured over the text "what we think we look like." The opposite side shows a screenshot of Jim Carrey as Ace Ventura, dressed in polo shirt, shorts, and a pink tutu, and moving frantically in the grass. This comes from a scene in his 1994 film *Ace Ventura: Pet Detective*, in which Ace Ventura pretends to be a person with intellectual disabilities trying to get admittance into an assisted living facility. The juxtaposition is striking. On one side, the woman representing Zumba Fitness is young, sexy, bold, and, though a white woman, tanned and racially ambiguous. Although in the film this character is a competitive dancer, for this meme, whether or not she can actually dance is less critical than her sexy body. On the other side, we see a man dressed in a pink tutu, thus emasculating and infantilizing him, while he does erratic, uncoordinated movements. A second film character used to represent "what we actually look like" in Zumba Fitness memes is Napoleon Dynamite, the nerdy teenage boy from Idaho portrayed by actor Jon Heder in the 2004 film *Napoleon Dynamite*. The meme draws from an iconic scene in the film in which Napoleon Dynamite performs an awkward dance routine at his high school during a rally for his friend's class president campaign. Though meant to be humorous, these memes reproduce the idea that only certain bodies are sexy, while others are inherently not. In this case, the gendered nature of these memes stresses women's sexiness relative to men, who are portrayed as awkward, ridiculous, and effeminate if they participate in Zumba Fitness. This ultimately reinforces hegemonic fitness ideals wherein male bodies are meant to be muscular and strong while women are thinner and more toned.[56] Thus, for a man to perform sexiness in a way typically gendered as feminine is seen as inappropriate precisely because he does not conform to the heteronormative standards of masculinity in the fitness world and in the United States more generally.

At the same time, the whiteness of these men demonstrates the intersections of race, gender, and sexuality in the depiction of the ideal sexy body. Many people assume that Zumba Fitness primarily attracts white middle-aged women. Equating someone like Napoleon Dynamite with someone like "Sue, your regular mom who's thirty-eight," as Leah described the typical Zumba student, suggests that white middle-aged women are not sexy, or at least not *supposed* to be. It is notable that the character Andie from *Step Up 2*, though white, is also especially skilled at "urban" dance. Even in this meme, then, the reference to sexiness hinges upon Andie's involvement in a style of dance associated with hip-hop and, in the context of the film, the inner-city "streets" of Baltimore. In each of these memes, the implication is that sexiness and whiteness are an awkward and unnatural pairing, as opposed to the more intrinsic sexuality of tropicalized Latinness.

Other memes make more explicit the racial dynamics of this comparison by relying on images of famous Latina and Black women to embody sexiness. One meme contrasts "Dance Skills Before Zumba" and "Dance Skills After Zumba." The "Before Zumba" section features a photo of South Korean artist Psy doing his "horse dance" move from the music video for his 2012 crossover hit "Gangnam Style." Psy's "Gangnam Style" music video and lyrics satirized the attitudes and behaviors of wealthy South Koreans in Seoul's Gangnam District. However, as Michael K. Park observes, this satire became lost on US American audiences who did not pick up on Psy's lyrical or visual critique. Instead,

2.3 This meme follows the popular "what we think we look like" and "what we actually look like" format to compare Briana Evigan's portrayal of Andie from *Step Up 2: The Streets* with Jim Carrey's portrayal of Ace Ventura.

Park argues that Psy's meteoric rise to fame in the United States occurred because Psy conformed to stereotypes of the emasculated and asexual Asian (American) male "jester."[57] Psy's image in this Zumba meme thus connotes asexuality, undesirability, and ridiculousness.

The bottom half of the meme features a close-up shot of Colombian pop star Shakira. Taken from her music video for her 2010 song "Waka Waka (This Is Africa)," the photo features a smiling Shakira, arms raised, and paused in mid-hip shake as her black fringe miniskirt swishes around her legs. Shakira's success as a Latin crossover artist in the US mainstream involved a pronounced emphasis on her sexuality, marked by her almost always bare midriff and sexy hip-shaking moves.[58] (It is worth pointing out that Zumba Wear had a collection with the phrase "Hips Don't Lie" on the bands of sports bras and leggings—a phrase that is also the title of what is arguably Shakira's biggest English-language hit.) The meme's contrast between Psy, who conforms to the asexual Asian male stereotype, and Shakira, who embodies the hypersexual Latina foreign other, implies

DANCE SKILLS BEFORE ZUMBA

DANCE SKILLS AFTER ZUMBA

2.4 Another popular meme that compares Korean singer Psy's dance moves to those of Colombian singer Shakira, reinforcing the link between hypersexuality, tropicalized Latinness, and Zumba Fitness.

that Zumba Fitness can be a space where people who might otherwise be nonsexual, or even decidedly unsexy, can become sexy through Zumba Fitness's tropicalized Latinness.

Another meme from the popular ecard website Someecards directly compares white women with Latina and Black women. The primary image is a sketch of a slightly overweight woman with unkempt hair, a black bralette, and a sheer, flowy skirt who stands against a bright orange background with her hands on her hips and her pelvis thrust forward. She has a confident smirk on her face while she says, "I may not be sexy or a good dancer, but when I'm in my groove at Zumba class, I'm fricking J-Lo, Shakira and Beyoncé all rolled into one!" The humor of the ecard relies on the assumption that the drawn figure, with her imperfect body and eccentric outfit, cannot possibly be sexy on her own. Instead, she must turn into famous Latina and Black women in order to become a sexy dancer. That the figure's hair and clothing depart from the ideals of respectable whiteness stresses the bodily transformation that occurs when one dabbles in the sexy space of Zumba Fitness. Identifying Jennifer Lopez and Shakira, two Latina stars who exemplify both the whitened Latin look and Latina sexuality in mainstream US pop culture, reflects the broader effacement of Blackness in Zumba Fitness's constructions of tropicalized Latinness, despite references to African American popstar Beyoncé. Though widely celebrated for her voluptuous figure, Beyoncé's sexuality is often depicted as nonthreatening given her conformity to Eurocentric standards of beauty (light complexion, straight blond hair, etc.) and her embrace of respectability politics.[59] Thus, while this particular meme contrasts white women with Black and Latina women, it still limits the particular expressions of Blackness aligned with Zumba Fitness to those that conform to the nonthreatening sexuality and exoticism of tropicalized Latinness. In so doing, these Black and Latina women presumably exude sexiness in ways that white women cannot—unless they are in Zumba class.

Zumba instructors often told me that being sexy was part of what made Zumba Fitness popular and fun. Sociologists Tanya Nieri and Elizabeth Hughes found that many of the Zumba students in their study held similar attitudes; Zumba Fitness classes were fun in part because students felt sexy and free.[60] "It's all in good fun," explained Erin when I asked her about using sexy moves in class. Personally, I believe that it is important for women to have safe spaces to express their sexualities. The problem is *not* that Zumba Fitness offers opportunities to express one's sexuality. Instead, the problem is that Zumba Fitness's sexiness is intimately tied to tropicalized Latinness. The continuous linking of sexiness and Latin culture reproduces deeply entrenched stereotypes of Latina hypersexuality while simultaneously rendering whiteness as its respectable and "normal" opposite. Fiestas' tropicalized Latinness facilitates expressions of sexuality that might be considered inappropriate elsewhere. However, fiestas experienced for one hour on a random Tuesday afternoon remove the more threatening aspects of Latinx sexuality in favor of the foreign and exotic culture of the tropics, thus enabling participants in Zumba

I may not be sexy or a good dancer, but when I'm in my groove at Zumba® class, I'm fricking J-Lo, Shakira and Beyonce all rolled into one!

som**ee**cards
user card

2.5 Image from someecards.com showing an unkempt woman claiming that she becomes super sexy like Black and Latina stars when she dances in Zumba Fitness classes.

Fitness to dabble with tropicalized Latinness's sexy moves without compromising their own respectability.

- - - - - - - - - -

TO TWERK OR NOT TO TWERK

Despite the professed embrace of expressions of sexuality, there is one dance move that provokes anxiety in the Zumba Fitness world: twerking. When I asked Stephanie whether she taught sexy moves in class, she said, "Oh, they will twerk. I don't care if they want to, I don't care if they can, they're doing it." Other instructors did not embrace twerking with the same enthusiasm. Some instructors felt concerned that twerking might offend students, or pressure students into doing something too sexy that they might not want to do. What is it about twerking, specifically, that caused such anxiety, especially in an environment where sexy dancing is actively encouraged?

Twerking is a dance style that originated in the New Orleans bounce music scene. Both Kyra D. Gaunt and Elizabeth Pérez identify commonalities between twerking and other African diasporic dances from continental Africa, Latin America, and the Caribbean. Gaunt in particular lists reggaetón's perreo, Brazilian funk, and the wining found in Jamaican dancehall and Trinidadian soca as dances that involve rapid gyrations and pelvic thrusts comparable to twerking.[61] Regardless of these similarities, Gaunt and Pérez both argue that mainstream perceptions of twerking in the United States reproduce deep-seated stereotypes of African American women's hypersexuality prevalent since times of slavery.[62] By decontextualizing twerking and placing it squarely within stereotypical representations of hip-hop culture, black hypersexuality, and the jezebel trope, twerking has become a visible marker of African Americans', and especially African American women's, presumed sexual deviance.[63]

Although Zumba Fitness incorporates some hip-hop into its music and choreography, most of the Zumba instructors whom I spoke with stay true to the Zumba formula that prioritizes Latin music and dance rather than US hip-hop or pop. Zumba Fitness versions of hip-hop do not necessarily involve twerking; for example, I took Zumba International Presenters Dahrio Wonder and Gina Grant Wonder's Hip-Hop Turn-Up class on the 2019 Zumba Cruise. We did not twerk, but instead did more stylized hip-hop dance routines that one might find in something like the reality television show *So You Think You Can Dance* or in a college dance troupe. In contrast to the Wonders' hip-hop style, Zumba instructors frequently referred to twerking as an example of the limits they impose on expressions of sexuality in their classes.

A few instructors actively incorporate twerking into their classes. Erin mentioned that her students "do twerking moves" in her classes, but "we're not flipping upside down and humping the wall." Here, Erin distinguishes her Zumba choreography from seemingly more explicit and extreme "humping" styles, thus implying a more modest form of twerking in her class. Julia also integrates twerking and other "sensual moves" into her routines, but first "tests" her students by introducing more subtle gestures before using overtly sexual choreography in order to make sure that her students are receptive.

Twerking has become such a mainstream phenomenon in the United States that one can find dance-fitness classes exclusively dedicated to it. Zumba Fitness has even offered twerking workshops during its annual Zumba Convention, in part, I assume, to stay on top of this popular trend. Angela took the workshop at the Zumba Convention because of twerking's mainstream popularity and because Zumba Fitness had not previously offered twerking routines in any of the instructional materials she had received. Angela was hesitant about teaching twerking in her Zumba Fitness classes. She never felt particularly confident or familiar with hip-hop dance and generally tried to stick to Latin music and choreography anyway. But twerking added a new layer of anxiety to Angela's reluctance to incorporate hip-hop. Angela told me, "When I threw in the twerk song, I was so scared, because I thought these ladies are going to be like, 'What is she doing? Why are we doing this?'" Despite her concerns, the students in Angela's class loved the twerking routine and requested it regularly.

While some instructors like Angela and Erin limit their twerking, others reject twerking altogether. Andrea felt concerned that she would look "foolish" twerking. She noted that "we'll shake our hips," but "we don't twerk, and we're not dropping it down to the ground or whatever." Many instructors I spoke with shared Andrea's concern, which stemmed from both feeling that they had not received adequate training in twerking choreography or that twerking was simply inappropriate. Vicki frequently used body rolls in her routines. But, she said, "I never twerk in class. I just don't think it's appropriate, but that's just me." Leah "use[s] hips" in body rolls or hip circles, but she stated "I don't flat out twerk in my choreography." She framed her resistance to twerking as part of her overall style that was "not particularly like 'mm, touch yourself, sexy.'" Paula felt that sometimes instructors "abuse the twerking. As a diva, you look great if you can do all that twerking, but let's be realistic. The class is probably not even going to do 10 percent of that twerking." In a similar vein, one instructor told me she didn't "see the fitness benefit" to twerking. Vicki felt that students who could not twerk correctly were at an elevated risk for back injuries. Vicki, Leah, and other instructors I spoke with who avoided twerking often couched their decisions in relation to what they felt was appropriate for their personal style and for their students rather than a judgment of the entire practice of twerking.

Nevertheless, the fact that twerking is similar in form and style to other dances associated with popular Zumba rhythms like reggaetón or soca further reveals Zumba Fitness's commitment to tropicalized Latinness. Twerking and hip-hop do not conform to the ideas of the Latin foreign other so prevalent in Zumba Fitness. Rather than the exotic, tropical, foreign other, hip-hop brings to mind the domestic and racial other that is tied primarily to African Americans in the popular imagination.[64] The figure of the urban, working-class, young, hypermasculine African American "thug" looms large in many representations of hip-hop culture despite the complex expressions of Black masculinity in hip-hop.[65] As a stand-in for hip-hop culture and African American-ness, twerking departs from the image of the tropical, exotic Latin foreign other that embodies ideas of authenticity in Zumba Fitness. Instead, twerking reflects the allegedly more "threatening" domestic racial other.

This association between a more "threatening" domestic Blackness and twerking is also reflected in the negotiations and maneuvers that some Black Zumba instructors describe as strategies to make their classes more comfortable for themselves and for their students. Individuals' racial identities often temper their feeling of safety to express their sexuality in Zumba Fitness. Morgan, an African American Zumba instructor, incorporated twerking into her classes since she felt there was nothing "inherently dirty" about twerking. Unlike other Zumba instructors I talked with, Morgan addressed the stereotypes about twerking directly by talking with her students about why society attaches certain racial meanings to specific dance moves. This is not only educational. Morgan is also very aware of how her students might perceive her as a Black woman when doing "sexy" moves in class. She explained, "I think it's very much about the move, plus the song, plus me, because I'm always very aware that I'm usually the only Black person in the room, right? So, I have to shut down a lot of stuff when they get into, like, 'You're naturally good at dancing.' That's a whole other thing." As a Black woman, Morgan does additional labor that her white counterparts often choose not to do in order to diffuse racial stereotypes that her students may impose upon her dancing body during Zumba Fitness class.

Andrea similarly felt added pressure to navigate how she represented herself in relation to her predominantly white students. She described how in the beginning of her career as a fitness instructor, "I was nervous. It's definitely gotten better now. But I think what I was mostly worried about was being so different from everybody else, and just having a different understanding and a different attitude towards the music than everybody else." As someone who grew up listening to Caribbean and Latin music, Andrea wondered whether white students might perceive the music via more stereotypical frames than someone like her who comes from a Black community. When I asked if being a Black woman teaching Zumba for white consumers contributed to her concerns, Andrea expanded, "I felt like maybe, I hate to say too Black, but I can't think of another way to put it, like too foreign. I was worried that [the music] would be too foreign to them." Andrea does not directly speak to her students about racialization and dance in the same way that Morgan does.

However, her awareness of her positionality as a Black woman in relation to her white students added an extra dimension to her experience as a new fitness instructor. Rather than only worrying about remembering the choreography or cuing effectively, Andrea also grappled with her unease about embodying stereotypes of Caribbean music for her mostly white students. In this context, Andrea's aforementioned concern about looking "foolish" while twerking relates to the overall anxiety about being "too Black" and "too foreign" for the white students in her classes.

Of course, not all Black women I spoke with agreed with Morgan and Andrea. Stephanie thought often about the racist stereotypes of Black and Latina women in the media and in society more generally. Stephanie taught Zumba Fitness classes in very different locations—a predominantly working-class Black and Latinx urban neighborhood, and a predominantly white, wealthy suburb. She described the "culture shock" she experienced moving between the two classes, and how in the latter, her own Blackness stuck out in the class. However, she still saw Zumba Fitness as an escape from the stress of racism in her everyday life. Stephanie explained, "As much as I think we need to think about [racism] in the real world, at the end of the day, everyone needs to come and dance for sixty minutes, and I don't really care what that person thinks of me right now. But I know that we're both trying to get as low to the ground as possible, and we're both on this journey together." Stephanie is just as aware as Morgan and Andrea of the potential ways her non-Black students might view her, but she does not adjust her routines or approach to make them more comfortable. Instead, she remains simultaneously vigilant about how her dancing body might be read and committed to teaching Zumba Fitness in ways that aid her own self-care in the face of pervasive anti-Black racism.

Overall, Black women who teach Zumba Fitness must navigate the same assumptions about Black women's hypersexuality that frame popular perceptions of twerking. Regardless of their different approaches to twerking in class, Andrea, Morgan, and Stephanie all considered their own positionalities and the larger racial dynamics of their classes when deciding whether or not to incorporate certain moves into their choreography. Their Blackness added another layer to their decision-making that their white counterparts did not have to do. It is not surprising that twerking is more controversial in the Zumba Fitness world than similar dances from elsewhere in the African diaspora. Whereas reggaetón's perreo or soca's wining can be framed as part of an exotic, tropicalized Latinness, twerking's associations with hip-hop culture and, by extension, urban African American populations in the United States make it less amenable to tropicalized Latinness. Zumba Fitness may now incorporate twerking in places like Convention, but this is arguably due to market pressures and competition from other dance-fitness programs. In this context, the ambivalence around twerking in Zumba Fitness reflects the contradictions inherent in the program more broadly. It is not necessarily that twerking and hip-hop are not "Latin music," although that is part of it. Twerking represents something that is, indeed, "too Black" to be part of the trope of fiesta, thus reproducing Zumba Fitness's effacement of Blackness in favor of an exotic, foreign, and tropicalized Latinness.

BECOMING RITA MORENO

When I asked her why Zumba Fitness was so popular, one instructor told me, "It's the democratization of dance." She continued,

> It's a dispersal of something that is viewed as highly technical, as an art form. And suddenly, you can go into your gym, and you can be Rita Moreno.[66] You are dancing as if no one's watching, hopefully, and in your mind, you're whoever you want to be. . . . And it's not a technique-oriented class. There's no technique except for learning what those rhythms are. But I think that's the other thing. Suddenly people are discovering that they can dance. Especially in [the United States]. We don't dance. Latin culture, they dance. It's what you do. You start doing it when you're a baby. And you see children at birthday parties doing merengue together. And so I think it's introducing dance into a culture that I think lost the ability to dance.

On one hand, her comments underscore the ways that Zumba Fitness can introduce dance to people who might not otherwise try it, including new rhythms and styles. It is true that dance figures prominently in many Latinx celebrations and gatherings. Dancing can be a space to celebrate and affirm Latinx identity, to foster community, or to just have fun. Dance spaces can bring different groups together who might not otherwise encounter each other, such as during the famed mambo nights at the Palladium Ballroom, which attracted Latinx, African American, and Jewish patrons, among others.[67] However, drawing a stark contrast between dancing Latin culture and nondancing US American culture actually reinforces stereotypes of tropicalized Latinness, even if these comments are meant to be complimentary. This particular instructor laments the loss of dance, and of fun, in US American culture and looks to Latin music and dance as something laudable that might resurrect interest in dance. Nevertheless, this admiration for Latinxs' alleged proclivity for dancing actually reiterates racial stereotypes of the dancing Latinx body that is part and parcel of tropicalized Latinness, even if that was not her intention. Ultimately, the idea that in "Latin culture, they dance" but US (white) Americans do not implies that "Latin culture" is fundamentally different from "normal" ways of being in the United States.

The Latin foreign other is the main figure who dances, parties, and exudes sexiness at the fiesta. Fiestas happen in the tropics, not within the United States. Indeed, the desirability of the Latin foreign other does not extend to US Latinxs or African Americans who are instead depicted as too loud, too sexual, and too threatening. It is the trope of fiesta that neutralizes overt displays of sexuality often construed as so troubling when embodied by domestic racial and ethnic others. Instead, fiestas are fun and happy, foreign and exotic, and decidedly nonthreatening. Perhaps this is most notable in the marketing of something like Zumba Wear, which visualizes the trope of fiesta by transforming the same Latina aesthetics derided for being tacky, colorful, and excessive into something cool, exotic, and desirable for the wider Zumba Fitness audience. Experiencing fiestas, whether by dressing in the latest Zumba Wear or dancing sexy in a Zumba Fitness class, makes tropical Latinness accessible to consumers, while also reinforcing students' own whiteness. Indeed, the fact that Black instructors did not all feel they could move in sexy ways as freely demonstrates the racial limits and boundaries of the trope of fiesta.

In this way, the trope of fiesta aligns with authenticity in the Zumba Fitness world. Zumba Fitness might tie specific rhythms to specific places, but all of these places become linked together through homogeneous depictions of the tropics as the homes of fiesta-loving, dancing, exotic Latin foreign others. The trope of fiesta thus emerges as part and parcel of authentic tropicalized Latinness, an innate cultural attribute that marks the Global South as fundamentally distinct from the allegedly more modern United States. This can be particularly troubling because the trope of fiesta makes space for anyone to perform these stereotypes of tropicalized Latinness, and frames them as something desirable and positive while simultaneously reproducing well-worn racist ideologies. Fiesta links to one other common trope found in Zumba Fitness that obscures even further the racist underpinnings of tropicalized Latinness: fun.

SELLING FUN

IMAGINE BEING ON THE TREADMILL IN THE GYM. Everyone around you is sweaty and focused. There's a subtle vibe of competition in the air. Who is faster? Who is thinner? When is that guy going to get off that bike so you can jump on? There is some upbeat pop song you've heard a million times pumping through the speakers, and you hear it softly through your headphones no matter how high you turn up the volume on your phone. You get distracted and glance around. On the other side of the room, you see a packed class in the fishbowl-like group exercise room. People are jumping up and down, smiling, laughing, and gyrating awkwardly. They look ridiculous—and ridiculously happy. When you finish your workout, you walk slowly past and hear the syncopated rhythms of merengue, or maybe salsa. You stare in awe at all of these people who seem to have fun while they are working out. What are all these happy people doing? Zumba Fitness.

Many instructors I spoke with recalled a similar story when I asked them how they got into Zumba Fitness. Erin described, "It was at a gym. I was on a treadmill. I saw people dancing. I've danced in the past, and I was looking to lose weight. So, I just came into a class like 'What's this?' And started taking class. I fell in love right away, and started going often, and then it wasn't often enough, so I looked for a new gym that had more Zumba. The usual path. And then I was going to it five times a week." Rebecca worked out regularly at her local gym, but noticed that "this craziness was going on next door for months." Eventually, she recalled, "So one day, I'm passing by, and all this crazy merengue music is blaring out the door, and I thought, I'm going to try that, because it looks like everyone's having fun. And I went in there, and I realized that an hour went by and I didn't think about anything, nothing." Likewise, Stephanie described her experiences in Zumba class as "a party, it's like you go out to party with your friends . . . and you're all having fun, and you're smiling, and you're sweating." Leah elaborated, "Everyone's smiling. The music is bumping. It's like being in a club. It's like being at a party, but that's your cardio for the day." She continued,

> Walking past a GroupX studio with windows,[1] if you see a bunch of people being like, you know, the stereotypical GroupX instructor is someone who's fitter than you with a headpiece on, shouting over music that's really loud, and a bunch of people are doing pushups or burpees looking like they want to throw up or kill themselves or be anywhere else. That's what a lot of people think GroupX is, and some of it is like that, and some of it's not. But walking past a Zumba class, people are like, "Damn, they look like they're having fun!"

I could relate to many of these instructors' comments. I, too, was attracted to Zumba Fitness because I felt like it was more fun than other exercise programs I had tried. Although attitudes about fitness have shifted over time, US fitness culture generally centers discipline as a fundamental requirement for maintaining good health and an attractive appearance.[2] Zumba Fitness promotes weight loss and a healthy lifestyle. However, rather than the strict regimens and exclusivity that characterize most fitness programs, Zumba Fitness represents itself as remarkably open and undisciplined. The idea that anybody and any body can succeed in a Zumba Fitness class deemphasizes body modification (e.g., bigger and more toned muscles, leaner physique) and instead centers fun as the main goal of Zumba Fitness classes. It is as if exercise and weight loss are almost (though not quite) an afterthought in the Zumba Fitness brand.

Zumba Fitness's tagline "Ditch the Workout, Join the Party!" epitomizes the company's focus on fun. However, the idea that Zumba Fitness is not disciplined is a mischaracterization. Zumba Fitness instructors do a tremendous amount of labor to create and teach routines in their classes. Like other fitness programs, virtually all of the instructors I interviewed stressed the importance of working certain muscle groups, raising students' heart rates, and optimizing fitness results. Although Zumba instructors are only required to complete a one-day Zumba Basic training, many of them acquire additional fitness certifications. Other instructors arrive to Zumba Fitness with professional fitness backgrounds. Some majored in kinesiology, exercise science, or physical fitness education in college, while others already taught fitness classes like yoga or barre or worked as personal trainers. These instructors add Zumba Fitness to their repertoire in order to expand their business, and they approach the program as, above all, a *fitness* endeavor. Despite its reputation as undisciplined and carefree, Zumba Fitness actually does mandate a minimum level of certification and fitness expertise, as well as some degree of standardization.

Given that Zumba Fitness *is* actually a fitness program—one that attracts fitness professionals, that provides training for instructors, and that promotes weight loss and a healthy lifestyle—why is it represented as so different? What is it that makes Zumba fun? Instructors tell me it's the music, the sense of community, the ability to dance to cheesy songs or do sexy moves, the overall vibe. But I would venture that Zumba Fitness's promotion of tropicalized Latinness is also critical to the brand's fun. This is similar to what bell hooks called "eating the other," in which, through the process of commodification, "ethnicity becomes spice" that enables those in the mainstream to consume other cultures for fun and pleasure. hooks writes, "In the cultural marketplace the Other is coded as having the capacity to be more alive, as holding the secret that will allow those who venture and dare to break with the cultural anhedonia (defined in Sam Keen's *The Passionate Life* as 'the insensitivity to pleasure, the incapacity for experiencing happiness') and experience sensual and spiritual renewal."[3] This is not the same as cultural appropriation, or the process whereby individuals claim ownership over a culture that is not their own. I have never met non-Latinx Zumba instructors who claim to be from the communities that created the music and dance that they utilize. Instead, Zumba Fitness gives consumers temporary access to other cultures that they experience via music and dance. Like hooks argues, this temporary engagement with tropicalized Latinness actually underscores its otherness precisely because participants can revel in the exotic, tropical, sexy, and foreign without compromising their own positionalities as respectable, modern subjects of the Global North.

Of course, one's own race and gender impacts one's experience of fun. For example, much of the fun that I feel in Zumba Fitness comes from the joy of dancing and singing to my favorite songs. This is more than just musical taste. For me, many of these songs are attached to happy memories. Zumba Fitness often eased my homesickness when I lived in places far from the Caribbean Latinx communities of the Northeast. But this is not always the case. For some people, Zumba Fitness's fun comes from the ability to feel like they are transplanted to a new, exotic place. It is important to note that this does not always map neatly onto distinct racial and ethnic identities. I met instructors of all racial backgrounds, including Latinx ones, who believed Zumba Fitness could be a space where you could act differently from usual. These stories seemingly confirm Tanya Nieri and Elizabeth Hughes's assertion that abandoning one's inhibitions and feeling free is part of what people think is fun about Zumba Fitness.[4] In this context, making fun a part of the Zumba Fitness brand cannot be divorced from tropicalized Latinness since it is partially the feeling of being transported elsewhere that many people think makes Zumba Fitness more fun than other exercise programs.

The notion that Zumba Fitness is fun because it lacks discipline or structure aligns with much broader notions of the Latin foreign other as a carefree figure who prioritizes fun and fiesta over all else. Tropicalized Latinness is presumed to be devoid of stressful or difficult things that would require reason, work, and organization to overcome. So, one can have fun, let loose, and forget about the stressors of modern life through Zumba Fitness class. To be sure, exercise of all kinds is an effective mechanism for reducing stress. However, what I am trying to emphasize here is that it is Zumba's *Latinness* that makes it so fun and effective for forgetting. Tropicalized Latinness is characterized by this disregard for the dictates of "regular" modern life. The cultural elements associated with tropicalized Latinness do not necessarily require "mastery." Taking a Zumba class, then, is like going on vacation—you let your hair down, act how you might not normally act, and revel in the exotic cultures of far-off places. In the rest of this chapter, I detail how fun becomes a distinguishing factor for the Zumba Fitness brand. Zumba Fitness has cultivated a reputation for being distinctly fun and undisciplined through media coverage and their award-winning advertising campaign, "Let It Move You." However, this reputation ignores the tremendous amount of time and energy that Zumba instructors put into learning their craft. It takes a lot of work and dedication to be a good Zumba Fitness instructor, one whose fun appears effortless and natural. Ultimately, then, Zumba instructors actively cultivate a feeling of fun in their classes, but this labor becomes obscured by the idea that Zumba Fitness is inherently fun. Overall, I show that selling fun reiterates the racialized mind-body divide that equates whiteness with reason and intellect, and racial otherness with spontaneity, freedom, and fun.

I never loved exercise. The only time I ever cheated in high school was on the Presidential Fitness Test, when my friend and I added a few extra sit-ups to our count (which still remained among the lowest in the class). I was the last to be picked for the team in gym class. I attended a few aerobics classes with my college roommate, but that only lasted a few months. In graduate school, I swam because California weather allowed for outdoor pools year-round—but I stuck mostly to the slow lane, doing a not very good version of the breast stroke and typically keeping my head above water. Despite embracing a particularly competitive career in academia, I did not develop a similar interest in competitive sports.

A 2022 study published in the *International Review for the Sociology of Sport* found that a "fear of judgment" often prevents women from exercising. The authors argue that women who anticipate feeling judged or out of place in exercise environments such as gyms or fitness classes tend to avoid physical activity. Feeling like others might ridicule their appearance, ability, clothing, and the like is a strong deterrent to exercise for many women. Their fear develops "when there is a disconnect between how individuals feel they are presenting themselves and what they perceive the situation demands."[5] This is certainly the case for me. I have generally felt inadequate in gyms. It seemed that many people around me were thinner or more in shape, or just better at most physical activities. Group classes, especially ones with mirrors where other participants could consistently observe my movements, were especially daunting.

This fear of judgment impacted my ability to exercise. Even when I mustered up the courage to try something new, I often quit because of fear of judgment. But these fears melted away in Zumba Fitness classes. For some reason, Zumba Fitness became a place where I felt comfortable exercising. I began taking Zumba classes as a graduate student when trying to deal with the stress of school and feeling homesick for the Caribbean vibes of the East Coast. I loved the music. Importantly, I believed the instructor when she said no one would care if we messed up, as long as we were having fun. How many times had I gone left when the class went right? How many times had I started on the wrong foot? Flinging my arms and accidentally hitting my neighbors was not unusual, but we all just laughed it off. Sure, sometimes there were conflicts—you can only get in someone's space so much before they start to get annoyed. But overall, it seemed that this idea that I was the only person watching me was actually true. To top it all off, I thought Zumba was *fun*.

Many other Zumba Fitness enthusiasts I know similarly think of Zumba Fitness as more fun than other exercise programs. As one friend put it, Zumba Fitness is exercise that doesn't feel like exercise. This seems to be exactly what Zumba Fitness is going for. Since beginning this project (and really since I first started taking Zumba Fitness classes), the Zumba Fitness brand repeatedly incorporates words like "happy," "party," and "fun" into its various marketing campaigns (e.g., "Step into Happy," "Be an Ambassador of Health and Happiness," or "Master the Business of Fun"). This fun directly contrasts with the common assumption that exercise is hard, onerous, and decidedly *not* fun.

Shelly McKenzie argues that the 1980s saw the rise of fitness as "labor intensive," and the popularity of phrases like "No pain, no gain" or "Feel the burn" made evident that fitness was about "hard labor and accomplishment."[6] Exercisers should experience pleasure *after*, not during, their workout. Heightened feelings of morality and virtue, pride in one's dedication and self-discipline, and the external validation of one's newly fit body motivate people to become fit.[7] In this context, Jennifer Smith Maguire writes that "pleasure is to be found in and *through* discipline, and is subsequently enlisted in the service of perpetuating that discipline."[8] The social capital that ensues becomes the potential reward for continuously disciplining oneself to conform to these fitness, and moral, ideals. Beyond one's individual satisfaction, the fit body is also a visual manifestation of the discipline and self-sufficiency associated with hegemonic ideas about who is a patriotic and productive citizen.[9]

It is no accident, then, that some of the most popular fitness trends of the twenty-first century prioritize discipline and hard work. CrossFit has become one of the most lucrative fitness phenomena in the United States, and globally, since its founding in 2000 by Greg Glassman. Glassman developed the program after working as a personal trainer for law enforcement. CrossFit mushroomed in popularity, propelled by the opening of CrossFit gyms called "boxes," which are individually owned (in fact, like Zumba Fitness, CrossFit makes money based on licensing fees for trainers and gym owners). CrossFit has become so popular that there are now "CrossFit Games" in which people who train in CrossFit boxes compete by executing various CrossFit routines, also called WODS, or workouts of the day.[10] WODS consist of activities like sprints, push-ups, pull-ups, weightlifting, and other strength and cardiovascular exercises. In this vein, CrossFit prides itself on both discipline and pain. The post-workout pain and exhaustion experienced by participants serve as evidence, and rewards, for successfully completing WODs. In fact, "members often boast of 'earned' scars or other ailments and display them publicly as evidence of their dedication."[11] Pain promotes pride, and thus pleasure, in the aftermath of the CrossFit workout. Moreover, CrossFit's documented relationships with the military (e.g., military personnel actively serving in the Middle East popularized the program and many WODs are named after fallen soldiers) align the program with patriotism.[12] CrossFit exemplifies common attitudes about discipline, morality, and patriotism often found in US fitness cultures.

Barre is another fitness trend that has grown over the past two decades. Barre involves strengthening exercises using a ballet barre to sculpt participants' (usually women's) bodies into lean figures with some muscle tone. Like Zumba Fitness, barre workouts are often linked to dance—in this case, ballet. British fitness enthusiast Lotte Berk created barre in the 1960s to improve women's sexual lives with moves like pelvic tucks. Her student Lydia Bach brought the workout to the United States when she opened a studio in New York City that promoted the "Lotte Berk Method." However, in the 1980s, the popularity of aerobics combined with reduced interest in sexual liberation spurred a decline in the barre workout until the 2010s, when new studio franchises like Pure Barre and Barre Method emerged.[13] If CrossFit promotes increased musculature as evidence of its effectiveness, barre advocates for a leaner and more sculpted "dancer's body." Pirkko Markula and Marianne Clark note that the attachment to the "ballet body" as an ideal form of feminine fitness is barre's primary connection to ballet, not the workout itself.[14] In fact, barre workouts do not always involve the ballet barre from which the program derives its name. Instead of dance techniques, barre utilizes repetitive movements to strengthen the lower half of the body, especially hips, butts, thighs, and legs often identified as "problem areas" for women.[15] Repetition becomes part of the "disciplinary aspect" of barre workouts, which further links barre to ballet.[16] In the United States, ballet is frequently presented as a form of "high art" that requires complete dedication, technique, and training to perfect. Thus, it is not just the ballet dancer's body but also the larger cultural associations between ballet, technique, and discipline that inform perceptions of barre as a good workout.

Although barre classes may not celebrate pain as overtly as CrossFit, the idea that participants push through discomfort to achieve results is part of barre class culture. Like some of the instructors I talked with, my participation in Zumba Fitness emboldened me to try new exercise programs (a significant development given my aforementioned hatred of exercise). Seeking to improve my core strength, I enrolled in ten weeks of barre class at a local studio. The studio was a large, rectangular carpeted space with ballet barres and mirrors along the walls. Most participants wore spandex in dark colors like black or navy blue rather than the bright neon patterns of Zumba Wear. The instructor played loud electronic dance remixes of popular pop and country songs. Barre involves isolating one muscle group at a time in order to "exhaust" that muscle group and then allow it to "recover." As we worked our arms, abs, thighs, and glutes, the instructor encouraged us to reach our "shake zone," where our muscles would literally shake as we pushed them to the limit. She promised that reaching the shake zone would allow us to reap the maximum benefits of our class, and she encouraged us to imagine the toned physiques we would have if we could endure just a few minutes of discomfort. She praised those who had the most visible quivers or who could withstand the shake zone the longest. Barre emphasizes the importance of using proper technique in order to avoid injury, thus distinguishing it from the valorization of injury in CrossFit culture. Still, the two exercise programs buy into the "no pain, no gain" philosophy of US fitness cultures.

Both CrossFit and barre spread en masse around the same time that Zumba Fitness hit the US fitness scene. However, Zumba Fitness wholeheartedly rejects the assumption that pleasure and fitness cannot be experienced simultaneously. Instead, Zumba Fitness is *fun*. Pleasure is the point. How is it that Zumba Fitness can reject the ideology of "no pain, no gain" that has so long pervaded US fitness cultures? And, given the popularity of dance-fitness programs over the past several decades, what is it that makes Zumba Fitness especially fun?

LET GO AND HAVE FUN

Virtually every Zumba Fitness class I've attended starts with the same speech. Instructors encourage newcomers to follow along to the best of their ability. They confess to making mistakes themselves, and tell their students to just roll with it. Always keep moving. Above all, *have fun*. As

Nieri and Hughes note, "If the priority is fun, then, the priority is not having proper technique, achieving a desired heart rate, getting the steps right, or keeping up with the music. Instructors may provide guidance on these factors but communicate that they are secondary to fun."[17] Nieri and Hughes argue that many Zumba students believe Zumba Fitness gives them the "freedom to 'go crazy' and express themselves as individuals."[18] Overall, Nieri and Hughes found that people who do Zumba Fitness frequently perceive it as more fun and less "oppressive" than other fitness regimens, primarily because the party atmosphere allows for freedom of expression.[19]

Every instructor I spoke with similarly stressed fun as the primary distinction between Zumba Fitness and other exercise programs. Amanda told me that she first saw Zumba Fitness as "something fun to do," but then continued because "everyone is just moving and having fun, and laughing and smiling. And that's part of the reason I've stuck with teaching it." Angela mentioned, "It's silly. Everybody has fun. That's my favorite part. It's like, let loose, and I just smile the whole class." Part of what makes Zumba Fitness so fun is the idea that it is a place where "anything goes" and where people could move in ways that might be considered inappropriate elsewhere. One instructor jokingly told me, "I always say, where else can you do this on a Tuesday morning at 10:30? You're not going to do it in line at the supermarket! It's fun!"

In this context, Zumba Fitness is perceived as a place of freedom. Freedom from judgment, freedom from the constraints and stressors of modern life, and freedom from the norms and standards of Western modernity. Many instructors I spoke with talked about the importance of "letting go" and "forgetting" during Zumba Fitness class. Rebecca described Zumba Fitness as "an hour vacation. It's an hour away from everything that's dragging you down." Vicki explained why she began Zumba Fitness: "I needed to find something to do for sixty minutes where I could stop thinking about life." Miriam noted that her students "come and they forget about life for an hour. I mean, every person that comes to a Zumba class comes for a different reason, and they might have had a really awful day at work, at home, or just want to get away for an hour, and that's where they come." When I asked Leah who the primary audience for Zumba Fitness was, she told me

> It's like, you know, for moms, it's like the hour out of their day that they get to not be around kids. Or anyone going through any kind of massive

trauma in their life. Or it's the best part of their day. You know? I mean, that's the beauty of it, like you just go and you let loose. You shake it for a while. You forget about whatever. You don't have to worry about that email, because you're too busy singing along to lyrics that you don't know in Spanish, but they're so fun. It's a great time, and I think that's why it's so successful.

It is not my intention to dismiss the benefits that Zumba participants and instructors feel as a result of their participation in the program. Letting go of stress and having fun are not inherently problematic. In fact, I think they are laudable goals, and they were a big part of what motivated me to take Zumba Fitness classes in the first place. What's more, Zumba Fitness seems especially effective at combating mental health issues such as anxiety and depression. I met several instructors who took their first Zumba Fitness class to cope with severe hardships like deaths of loved ones, divorces, abusive relationships, health crises, or postpartum depression. Several scientific and medical studies substantiate the potential psychological benefits of Zumba Fitness such as increased self-esteem or satisfaction with quality of life; some posit that these might even outweigh Zumba's physical benefits.[20] In June 2018, *Bustle* published an article titled "The Best Workout for Anxiety Isn't What You'd Think," citing a study that established that Zumba Fitness reduced anxiety among women participants.[21] Mental health also surfaces frequently in the Zumba Home Office's profiles of ZINS in *Z-Life*, formerly the company's online publication. One especially poignant profile titled "Dancing through my Anxiety" described ZIN member Jacqueline Brummond's struggles with depression and anxiety. She wrote, "Being a Zumba Instructor with GAD [generalized anxiety disorder] and Depression is hard. I still have bad days, but with proper medication and the endorphins a good workout brings, my bad days have become fewer. In this way, the Zumba program has saved my life."[22] Taken together, all of these sources point to Zumba Fitness as a particularly effective workout for improving many people's mental health.

Of course, Zumba Fitness is not the only exercise program that has mental health benefits. Many health professionals recommend exercise for stress reduction. However, Zumba Fitness's reputation as uniquely fun is often credited for the program's effectiveness. For example, *Shape* claims that "the best way to burn more calories in [Zumba] class is to let go, have fun, and not think too much."[23] Here, the amount of weight one might lose in a Zumba Fitness class directly correlates to how well someone can "let go" and "not think." Similarly, *Z-Life* reported that ZIN member and psychotherapist Leoni Epiphaniou encouraged her clients suffering from anxiety, depression, and other mental health issues to enroll in Zumba Fitness classes that she believed would help "achieve a deeper layer of healing that is difficult to do with talk therapy alone." The article outlines three reasons that Zumba Fitness can be so effective in tackling these issues, the first being that Zumba Fitness is "easy to do." It continues, "If you let go and have fun with it, it's an opportunity to get in touch with your inner child or with your inner sexy. Dance is a great way to lift your body to an open, optimistic posture, which is the ideal gateway into brighter mental landscapes."[24] Once again, it is the fun that produces health benefits—the more fun you have, the greater relief you feel.

But this fun is not neutral. Leah's comments about singing along to "lyrics in Spanish that you don't know, but they're so fun" implies that it is, at least in part, Latinness that fosters this feeling of fun. Kimberly Lau argues that Western participants in tai chi and yoga achieve their perceived spiritual enlightenment and physical transformation through engagement with a racialized other grounded in Orientalist stereotypes of the "Far East."[25] Similarly, the ability to forget and have fun, to have a "one hour vacation" in a Zumba Fitness class, to let go, relies in part on Zumba participants' engagement with tropicalized Latinness. The capacity to be governed by reason, to make rational and strategic decisions, and to resist inappropriate, instinctual urges is central to definitions of the human within Western modernity. *Z-Life*'s assertion that Zumba Fitness enables someone to get in touch with their "inner child" and "inner sexy" directly aligns with assumptions that the freedom offered in Zumba Fitness departs from the moral and intellectual standards of Western modernity. The racialized mind-body divide is critical here. Modern constructions of racial categories characterize whiteness as exemplary of the norms, behaviors, and rationality of Western modernity. Blackness allegedly constitutes the primitive and instinctual counterpoint to this rational, modern white subject. This division is further evident in the ways that people perceive African-based dances and rhythms (including the "tropical" sounds of Latin music) as tied to a sort of instinctual and primitive way of life.[26] Jane C. Desmond argues that dance practices in the United States racialized as "Black" or "Latin" are understood to be more "rhythmic"; therefore, "this lumping together of 'race,' 'national origin,' and supposed genetic propensity for rhythmic movement rests on an implicit division between moving and thinking, mind and body."[27] This reputation of Latin music that Desmond describes surfaces in other dance scenes where Latin music circulates. For example, Joanne Bosse found that many ballroom dancers she interacted with considered "Latin dances," such as rhumba or samba, to be less technical than "modern dances" that derived from European traditions, such as fox trot or waltz.[28] The distinction between Latin and modern in ballroom dance mirrors the distinction in fitness programs wherein "Latin" Zumba Fitness is more free and instinctual than the supposedly more disciplined or skilled CrossFit or barre. The commitment (or mandate) to let go and have fun in Zumba Fitness thus exemplifies the stereotypes that Latin music and dance are spaces devoid of reason and respectability. By linking fun and forgetting with tropicalized Latinness and fiesta, Zumba Fitness's trope of fun ultimately reproduces racial hierarchies.

A key aspect of Zumba Fitness's representations of fun is that letting go allows one to lose control. This was the message of the company's 2014 advertising campaign "Let It Move You." Hailed as an unprecedented advertising campaign by a fitness company, "Let It Move You" included television, print, and online advertisements. Zumba Fitness adopted "Let It Move You" as an official tagline, which Alberto Perlman described as "a chance to make a bold statement with a campaign that promotes and elicits powerful emotion and movement."[29] Yahoo Finance claimed that "The 'Let It Move You' campaign shows the infectious and empowering influence of the Zumba lifestyle, which is fiercely linked to its addictive choreography and music."[30] Chris Mendola, chair of the advertising agency 180LA that developed the campaign, stated, "It's powerful how the Zumba classes and community all genuinely share a positive energy and way of life. It's contagious."[31] Language like "addictive," "contagious," and "infectious" connotes the idea that Zumba's fun is irresistible and uncontrollable. Such terms are eerily reminiscent of xenophobic depictions of Latin American immigrants as vectors of disease or drug smugglers allegedly "invading" the United States.[32] But in this case, these terms are meant to evoke an exciting opportunity to engage with Latinness rather than a dangerous threat to US life and culture.

The "Let It Move You" commercial visualizes the "addictive" nature of Zumba Fitness. The commercial features men and women who, out of nowhere, begin to dance. Many of them are at work: a traffic cop, a security guard, an assembly line worker, an office executive, a bouncer, an athletic coach, and a mattress salesman. Other individuals eat at a restaurant, stand in line at a food truck, or ride in a cramped elevator. They start with a small movement, like the raising of an arm or a shimmy of the shoulders. As the music, Diplo's aptly titled "Express Yourself," grows faster and louder, the dances become more involved with gyrating, jumping, booty popping, and flailing of the arms and legs, much to the shock and even discomfort of spectators.[33]

Media coverage of the campaign praised the advertisement for featuring different body types and sizes rather than the "unattainable" bodies frequently depicted in the fitness industry and advertising more generally.[34] The people included in the advertisement are white and Black, men and women, thin and overweight. The diverse cast showcased how anyone can do Zumba Fitness regardless of their background or physique. Despite their different appearances, all of their movements elicit similar reactions from bystanders, whose looks of dismay imply that these dancing bodies are behaving inappropriately. Some of the moves appear ridiculous or extreme. For example, many of the dancers break things, fall down, or make a mess, such as when the office worker shatters a pane of glass as she flings her arms around, or a restaurant customer dramatically falls over when climbing on top of his table. The mattress salesman jumps atop a mattress and swings a pillow until it explodes and feathers fall everywhere. A woman in line for a food truck spontaneously throws all of the utensils into the street in a burst of enthusiasm. And the traffic cop becomes so engrossed in her dance that she ignores two cars who collide in the intersection. These images suggest that the freedom to express oneself can actually reach a point of excess that is not only inappropriate, but potentially harmful.

The "Let It Move You" advertisement uses expressions of sexuality to further emphasize the carefree and uninhibited nature of Zumba Fitness. At least two people in the commercial do a booty pop, a common move in Zumba choreography where a person hinges forward slightly at the waist, buttocks pointed out, and rapidly jumps backward. The woman in the food truck line knocks other customers out of the way with her booty pops and the mattress salesman positions his buttocks directly in front of his male customer as he jumps up and down. In a more dramatic sexual gesture, the office executive slides on her knees across the conference table, and grabs the necktie of her male coworker as she lustily gazes into his eyes. The woman in the elevator takes down her hair and dramatically waves it around with a facial expression that suggests sexual arousal. The

3.1 Still from 2014 "Let It Move You" commercial showing a traffic cop so engrossed by her Zumba Fitness dancing that she neglects her duties and causes a car accident.

3.2 Still from 2014 "Let It Move You" commercial showing a woman "booty popping" while waiting at a food truck.

3.3 Still from 2014 "Let It Move You" commercial showing a female office worker who jumps on top of a conference table and sexily grabs her male colleague by the tie while spontaneously doing Zumba Fitness during a meeting.

3.4 Still from 2014 "Let It Move You" commercial that shows a woman with a facial expression suggestive of sexual arousal as she swings her hair around in a crowded elevator. Onlookers appear dismayed by her actions.

factory worker spontaneously throws open her uniform and thrusts out her T-shirt-clad chest. It is notable that the women in the advertisement do the most overtly sexual moves and gestures, although both the men and women appear clumsy, awkward, and over the top. In this way, "Let It Move You" implies that expressing oneself in Zumba Fitness departs from the respectability and modesty typically associated with modern subjects.

Indeed, the humor of this advertisement relies on a general understanding that these individuals dance in places where bodies are meant to be calm and controlled in order for things to go smoothly. Standing in line or in a crowded elevator, directing traffic, eating at a restaurant, or working in a factory or office all require people to adopt behavioral norms that do not involve dramatic bodily movements. The locations featured in the commercial underscore that the dancers are so entranced by the music that they literally cannot control their bodies, even if their movements might cause actual damage. The "infectious" or "addictive" nature of Zumba Fitness makes the body act out in inappropriate and unruly ways.

The assumption that Zumba Fitness can make otherwise rational people appear free (and, maybe, ridiculous or irrational) links tropicalized Latinness with instinct and primitivity. The commercial itself does not include identifiable "Latin" bodies marked by the stereotypical traits that often signal Latinx identities. Furthermore, Diplo's song "Express Yourself" is more electronic dance music than something discernibly Latin (especially given the rigid definitions of authentic Latin music that circulate in the Zumba Fitness world). Nevertheless, in the context of Zumba's widely held reputation as a "Latin dance-fitness" program, the movements of the individuals in the commercial allude to the sexuality and "spicy" Latin culture that forms the basis of tropicalized Latinness. In other words, the movements alone make tropicalized Latinness visible even without identifiably Latin bodies or a Latin soundtrack in the commercial.

Ultimately, Zumba Fitness's trope of fun naturalizes the idea that Latinness is somehow devoid of the reason, morality, and discipline associated with modern Western subjects. This becomes evident through the repeated declarations that Zumba Fitness's Latin tinge is what enables a unique type of fun that centers sexuality and lack of inhibition. On the surface, fun is an admirable quality. Everyone deserves the opportunity to freely express themselves and have fun. The problem is not fun itself, but rather that the way that Zumba Fitness utilizes the trope of fun ultimately obscures deep-seated racist ideologies that continuously depict Latinx people as primitive racial others vis-à-vis US Americanness and whiteness. Indeed, Lee Bebout asserts that this dichotomy between Latinx other and US white American keeps racial hierarchies intact and gives the illusion that whiteness is naturally superior.[35] Maintaining its reputation as uniquely fun is critical to the Zumba Fitness brand, even though, like other fitness brands, to have success in Zumba Fitness actually does require discipline.

FITNESS OR ENTERTAINMENT?

In 2016, journalist Carlye Wisel described her experiences on the Zumba Cruise in an article for *Racked* titled "Crazy Happy Zumba." Throughout, Wisel depicts the Zumba instructors attending the cruise as remarkably committed to the brand in an almost cult-like fashion. She describes the fanatical, verging on hysterical, audience reactions to classes taught by Beto Pérez. Wisel recalls her shock when someone at her dining table explained that instructors only undergo one day of training, writing, "Apparently anyone can be certified as a Zumba instructor. One teacher even joked that you 'could be on a respirator and pass.' . . . I thought she was being facetious. She's not." After considering what she sees as Zumba instructors' extreme devotion to the brand, Wisel opines,

> But then comes the hard and uncomfortable truth that for people who can't stop moving and are so dedicated to this activity that they've traveled to the Bahamas to do it, the crowd is surprisingly unfit. And remember: these people are certified fitness instructors, at least by Zumba standards. Many people take elevators between decks; those who do choose to climb the stairs do so slowly, complaining about how tiring it is. Some people are overweight, others unhealthily so. It all begs the question: how could a massive global fitness company be so successful if a notable segment of its core audience, its most dedicated fans, its *instructors*, never, ever get in shape?

Ultimately, Wisel determines that Zumba Fitness "is not exercise, this is fitnesstainment. The goal of Zumba isn't to get back into your high school jeans or wow your significant other with your toned abs, it's to spend one hour a day feeling free, gaining confidence, becoming a better you."[36] Though derisive, Wisel's review reinforces the notion that Zumba Fitness is really all about fun and therefore cannot be real exercise.

In the course of doing this project, I have met several critics of Zumba Fitness who, like Wisel, question the program's fitness benefits (this includes a woman who taught Zumba Fitness at a dance studio, and who encouraged me to pursue "real" dance instead of "just jumping around"). Despite this reputation, numerous medical studies have shown that Zumba Fitness *does* improve physical health outcomes for many participants, such as better cardiovascular function, reduced diabetes risks, and greater muscle strength, among other benefits.[37] The Zumba Home Office also frequently profiles people who have lost weight with the program. The "Zumba Stories" section of Zumba's *Z-Life* online publication profiled Zumba instructors who had achieved dramatic weight loss through Zumba Fitness. In "Smiling on the Outside, Trapped Inside," Alena Shifrin, who was rejected from life insurance because of her weight, described her experience as being a "prisoner in her own body." She lost 155 pounds with Zumba Fitness.[38] Alena's story is typical of many of the profiles of people who lost weight doing Zumba Fitness: morbidly obese, they fell in love with the music or the dancing and stuck with the program until they reached an ideal body weight. A May 2018 post on *Z-Life* featured dramatic "Before and After" photographs of Zumba enthusiasts who lost weight by regularly attending Zumba Fitness classes. The article began with the claim that Zumba Fitness "has been known to burn hundreds of calories in a single class. Woah!"[39] Other publications such as *Time* magazine and health-related websites like *LiveStrong* and *Healthline* have reported that individuals could meet weight-loss goals with Zumba Fitness (often with the caveat that the program must be accompanied by diet and strength-training exercises).[40] I met several instructors who lost significant amounts of weight with Zumba Fitness. At the time of our interview, Amanda had lost almost 75 pounds. Both Julia and Vicki reported shedding their "baby weight" with Zumba Fitness. Reflecting on her postpartum weight loss, Zumba International Presenter Gina Grant told *Smartlife Magazine*, "I found the amount of calories burned in one Zumba class was more than I would burn in an hour on the treadmill and was way more fun. Not only would I burn calories, but because Zumba is a total body workout, my body toned up as well."[41] Later in the interview, Grant states that one can burn 500 to 1,200 calories in one hour of Zumba Fitness, a statistic I've heard repeated by other instructors, as well (though I have not read any research studies that confirm this point). Zumba Fitness is, above all, a health and fitness program. Weight loss is just as important to the brand as fun, even if it does not appear to be at first blush.

The focus on weight loss, health, and fitness is also evident in the Zumba International Presenters who represent the Zumba brand on the global stage. These International Presenters have ideal fit body types. For example, Beto Pérez has a lean, muscular physique with toned abdominals and arms. He conforms to the body ideals for men in many fitness magazines that stress musculature, particularly in the upper body, and physical strength.[42] Most of the women International Presenters, such as Loretta Bates, Gina Grant, Marcie Benavides, Kass Martin, or Ecem Özam, do not have as developed upper bodies. Instead, their physiques conform to the ideal fit body for women—thin and toned, particularly in the hips, buttocks, and thighs, but never overtly muscular.[43] In addition to their slim body types, many International Presenters reflect the fitness industry's depiction of the ideal fit body as white.[44] Zumba International Presenters include people of different racial and ethnic backgrounds, but they all conform to dominant standards of beauty that prioritize whiteness, Eurocentric features, and light complexions.[45] Their racial and ethnic diversity might give the impression of inclusivity. However,

3.5 A sign advertising a Master Class with Beto Pérez on the 2019 Zumba Fitness Cruise. Pérez's physique exemplifies the ideal male fit body. Photograph by the author.

I would argue that these multicultural presenters actually embody the colorism and Eurocentric standards of beauty so ubiquitous around the world that are part and parcel of the ideal fit body.[46] By uplifting International Presenters who embody the ideal fit body, Zumba Fitness reproduces the same problematic exclusions of other bodies as the rest of the fitness industry, despite the assertion that any body can be a Zumba phenom.

On the ground, some Zumba instructors find the promotion of the ideal fit body limits their own employment opportunities. For example, Paula described herself as "kind of fitting the description of what Beto [Pérez] wanted to do, which was, he didn't want pretty and fit people in his classes. He wanted regular people with their daily problems just to get away for an hour." After taking Zumba Fitness classes, she decided to "satisfy [her] curiosity" about the choreography by getting her license. Like most of the Zumba instructors I interviewed, Paula had another job, but she wanted to "justify, especially to [her] family," the time and money that she had spent to become an instructor. She told me, "It was hard to find that regular [Zumba Basic] class [to teach], and I was like thirty-five pounds bigger than when you met me. So, I didn't really have the fit body of a Zumba instructor, and this may sound harsh, but it's the reality in many places." Paula eventually chose to get licensed in other, more low-impact styles like Zumba Gold or Aqua Zumba where she felt there was greater acceptance of instructors without "fit" bodies. She attributed this in part to the audience for these formats who she described as older people who tended to "need more exercise," thus implying that the students themselves may not be the most fit.

Paula's reasoning makes sense given that often fit bodies are the most important product of branded fitness programs like Zumba Fitness. Fit bodies show that the brand they are affiliated with actually works, and, as a result, fit bodies are important marketing tools for convincing consumers to invest in these fitness programs.[47] Indeed, the embodiment of fitness ideals is crucial for most fitness professionals. For instance, Jennifer Smith Maguire notes that personal trainers often need to rely on their "embodied capital" as proof of their effectiveness as fitness professionals.[48] She writes, "The physical bodies and private lives of personal trainers—their exercise and diet habits, especially—are central to their cultivation of professional credibility, motivation of clients, and promotion of their service and the commercial fitness industry more generally."[49] In this context, it is no wonder that Paula attributes her initial difficulty finding a job in fitness as directly correlated to her body type.

Moreover, for Paula, the teaching style differed substantially in Zumba Gold and Aqua Zumba than in Zumba Basic. She explained, "You're concerned of course about your form and the technicality of the moves, but you're not concerned about you being the diva, which is what normally happens in Zumba. And in many places, the instructors are called performers, which gives a different spin on it. A performer is not an instructor. An instructor is there for others. A performer is there for the enjoyment of others, but they are fully aware of their body position and role as the center of the universe." I met several instructors who, like Paula, felt that some of their colleagues prioritized the potential to become a fitness celebrity over fostering a sense of community, freedom, and fun that Zumba Fitness allegedly is supposed to be about. One instructor felt disillusioned at the time of our interview because of the competition and judgment she noted circulating within the Zumba instructor community. She said, "I mentioned that the zeses were like the celebrities, and everyone wants to be a celebrity. Everyone wants people to imitate them and dance like them, and they think they're the shit, and, like, some of them are. And there's a lot of longevity in a career, being a student to becoming an instructor to becoming a Jammer, to becoming a ZES. That's a lot of people's dreams, and they're passionate about it and go all the way." It is true that some instructors believed it was necessary to move up the Zumba ladder in order to have a sustainable career and a living wage. Still, many other instructors were very critical of those in their ranks who they assumed were motivated by potential fame and fortune instead of fun. In other words, despite Zumba Fitness's branding as fun above all else, it is also a space rife with the very same inequalities, norms, and competition found in other types of fitness programs.

Of course, not all instructors felt this pressure. I met instructors of various shapes and sizes throughout my time doing this project, including some who might be characterized as overweight, or, at the very least, not the most fit, and who were still very successful and talented. Some outright rejected the assumption that they had to conform to the ideal fit body to be successful instructors. Morgan considered herself a "very fat positive fitness instructor" who focused on the importance of working out rather than promoting a certain body type. She said, "I don't talk about calories burned. We're not there to work off what we ate or work on our legs. I don't do any of that talk. But I do say, 'Come. Make sure you're drinking your water . . . it's your body, your workout.'" Unlike Paula, Morgan did not seem to have strong feelings about whether or not she would make money as a Zumba instructor (like Paula, Morgan already worked full time). Morgan taught at lower-paying community centers, or sometimes offered her classes for free. Her goal was to create affordable, accessible, and fun fitness opportunities, including to those who might not otherwise feel comfortable in a group fitness class because of their body type, age, fitness level, or some other aspect of their identity. As a result, Morgan seems to actualize the emphasis on fun and the inclusion of "every body" espoused by Zumba Fitness in a way that actively distances, or even resists, the valorization of the ideal fit body.

Still, it would be a mistake to assume that instructors like Morgan do not see health benefits to Zumba Fitness. Morgan's classes often attracted older women who used Zumba Fitness as a way to improve their health, if not to become especially fit. Other instructors I spoke with, particularly those who taught Aqua Zumba or Zumba Gold formats, similarly emphasized health benefits for their students without pushing the ideal fit body as the end goal. Perhaps their impressions come from the clientele attracted to these formats. Aqua Zumba is akin to water aerobics, often attractive for those who want more gentle pressure on their joints; one instructor described Aqua Zumba as "probably the most entry level of all the Zumbas, so a lot of hip replacements are in there, people who are injured, pregnant people." Zumba Gold targets seniors and others seeking low intensity exercise. Many instructors I spoke with loved teaching these formats because of the reduced pressure they felt to be "divas" or fitness models and because they believed that participating in Zumba Fitness actively supported the health of their students. One instructor who also worked in healthcare told me,

> I think it's more important to focus the goal for them to be coming back class after class for a year or more. And this is what I tell them. I don't care if your life means that you come twenty minutes before the end of the class. You come. If they're in there moving, as a healthcare professional, I know they're getting benefits. If I can push them, you know, slowly, even better. My Gold Class is so energetic. Half of them are not gold—they are doing their moves with as much enthusiasm as regular Zumba. They're in their seventies, and they can kick twenty-year-old asses. They really can. I'm not going to be able to do a lot of strength training or flexibility. I'm really going to be able to increase their coordination, their cardiovascular fitness. It's just not a format for strength training, although I've used some squats and lunges and things like that here and there in the choreo. It is the fitness form to get out and move, and do it on a regular basis. And there are good studies to show that that increases people's fitness. I also mention safety and injury prevention a lot. Again, the hope is that they are dancing for a long time into their seventies, eighties, and beyond.

I heard similar comments from other Zumba Fitness instructors who work in healthcare, or who have higher education degrees in subjects related to physical fitness and health. For them, the point is to get students moving regularly in order to maintain, if not improve, their fitness levels. "Honestly," Amber, a Zumba instructor with twenty years of experience in the fitness industry, explained, "I tend to just do whatever my participants are going to benefit the most from and succeed [at] the most."

To that end, instructors constantly think about the health and fitness of their students—both their students' current fitness levels and their potential fitness goals—when designing their classes. For example, every instructor told me that it was critical to keep students' heart rates up throughout the class. Vicki prioritizes fitness goals, especially "hitting all the muscle groups," during her routines. She describes the popular body roll move as not just being "sexy" but also working out abs, glutes, and chest muscles. In addition to muscle toning, every instructor I spoke with also considered the cardiovascular benefits of their routines. Amanda explained, "I look for songs that I think will engage people that also get your heart rate up, and then you drop it a little just to kind of recover. So, your heart rate is always up, and then knowing when to start to decrease and get yourself to the cool down is important." Amanda constantly thinks about the overall arc of the class to ensure that her students get maximum cardiovascular benefits while giving opportunities for breaks and, eventually, a cool down and stretch. Angela also varies intensity in every class she teaches:

> I try to alternate intensity. After the warm-up, I'll have a high song, and then I'll take it down a little bit. So, like I did a fast merengue, and then I had a salsa that kind of like brings it down, and then I go back up for a soca, and then bring it down. I always try to have in the middle, right after the first half hour, a break. So, it's usually either a bachata or like a slow cumbia, so that they can catch their breath, and then go back up. And it's good to go up and down in intensity, cause it's more of an effective workout.

Other instructors agreed with Angela's comments that varying intensity throughout a single class session would guarantee greater fitness benefits. Julia explained, "If you're always at a high [intensity], you're not really exercising. You're just kind of exerting yourself. You know, there's no fitness to it, because you're exhausted. You're not working your muscles anymore, so it's just like a waste." Julia's comments reflect a common attitude among several of the instructors I interviewed who also saw the importance of working and toning particular muscle groups in addition to improving cardiovascular health. Andrea mentioned that making routines "equal" was necessary for effective muscle toning. She said, "The counts for the hooks [of the songs] have to be the same, just so we're not lopsided. . . . We can't do squats or lunges on one side more than the other." Fitness considerations thus play a critical role in Andrea's song choices. The structure, beat, and pace of a song all impact what kinds of moves an instructor can do, which in turn impacts the fitness outcomes of the class. I heard from several instructors about songs that they would not include in their classes simply because those songs would not lead to their desired fitness goals for their students.

Instructors also think about their students' physical ability, fitness levels, and potential for injury when deciding which routines to teach in their classes. Several instructors told me that they would not put similar songs back to back because that would diminish the party vibe and, more importantly, cause injuries. Leah explained, "That's how you hurt yourself, overuse, especially when your classes tend to be older. Doing too much of the same thing is how they hurt themselves." Many instructors take great care to create effective warm-ups for the beginning of classes and cooldowns at the end so that students do not overwork their bodies without proper stretches. Some instructors have even taken extra trainings specifically about warm-ups or cooldowns at the Zumba Convention, something that Amanda described as "not the most exciting class, but it's still something you need. It's still the basis of your class, how you warm people up. Because that's how you prevent your injuries." A major criticism of Zumba Fitness is that the one-day Zumba Basic training does not sufficiently address injury prevention or fitness techniques. While this may be true, most of the instructors I met were acutely aware of the physical risks of Zumba Fitness and sought additional training and resources to make sure their students could accomplish routines with minimal risk.

Taken together, the experiences of these instructors on the ground alongside the images of the ideal fit body promoted by Zumba Fitness contradict the idea that Zumba Fitness is not disciplined like other fitness programs. Despite Zumba Fitness's claims that the program is equally accessible to all bodies and all people, the promotional materials circulated by the company continue to foreground the ideal fit body understood to exemplify the morals and contributions of good, productive citizens. Moreover, the rhetorical focus on fun does not diminish the emphasis on health, fitness, and weight loss both on the part of the Zumba Home Office and by instructors on the ground. Instructors constantly think about the health benefits of their classes for their students, even if they also embrace the idea that Zumba Fitness is more fun. This emphasis on health benefits and the ideal fit body reveals how Zumba Fitness actually shares much of the same ethos as other fitness programs considered more disciplined and worthwhile despite the program's reputation as "fitnesstainment."

CURATING FUN

Presenting the trope of fun as a fundamental facet of the Zumba Fitness experience obscures one other important fact: this fun is not automatic, but rather carefully cultivated through the discipline and labor practices of instructors. Many of Zumba Fitness's critics deride the program for only requiring one day's worth of training for a license, implying that instructors are unqualified and unprepared. Wisel's depiction of instructors on the Zumba Cruise, for example, emphasizes their emotional responses and fanaticism over their physical fitness acumen. However, ZINS are indeed fitness professionals who put in a tremendous amount of time to learn and develop choreography, practice skills like cuing, and create their playlists. Most instructors I've met balance these activities with full-time employment (often in very competitive industries), caregiving, and managing their households. To be an effective Zumba instructor requires discipline and dedication.

Zumba instructors work hard to obtain the physical fitness education they need beyond the one-day Zumba Basic training. For some, this entails obtaining new fitness certifications such as a certification from the Athletics and Fitness Association of America (AFAA) that many gyms and organizations require of group fitness instructors. To earn AFAA certification, instructors must take a course and pass an exam. Additionally, many ZINS attain additional Zumba Fitness licenses in other formats, such as Zumba Gold, Zumba Toning, Zumba Kids, or Aqua Zumba. This process similarly requires investing time and money into trainings taught by Zumba Education Specialists.

Even those instructors who do not seek additional certifications to teach different formats or at more competitive gyms pursue supplementary education to keep their classes fresh and fun. Many enroll in Jam Sessions to learn new choreography during a special, ZIN-only three-hour class. Zumba Fitness's monthly dues do not include the cost of Jam Sessions, but many instructors see these classes as a worthwhile investment for improving their own skills. At Jam Sessions, instructors receive notes and "choreography breakdowns" for four to five routines that they can then integrate into their classes. For many instructors, the new choreography they learn in Jam Sessions is essential for making sure they can rotate songs on their playlists quickly and easily so that their regular student base does not get bored.

Similarly, attending the Zumba Convention in Orlando every July gives instructors the chance to learn new material and get more licenses or certifications. Instructors might spend a day becoming certified in a new Zumba format. They might take CPR classes or attend lectures about marketing their classes or, as Leah put it, about "the power of connecting and changing lives." One especially popular training among the Zumba instructors I talked with is "Pro Skills," which helps instructors improve their teaching skills, especially the silent cuing format characteristic of Zumba Fitness. Another popular Convention activity is the Personalized Feedback session. Leah described, "You're with two ZESes, and everyone does a song, and they give you feedback. You teach it to the group, and the people give you notes. They'll be like, 'This is good, but you need to improve here.'" I spoke to Amanda just before she attended Convention, where she planned to do a salsa choreography for the Personalized Feedback session. She explained that she chose salsa "because that's the rhythm I'm not comfortable with. . . . I don't want to go and pick something where I look like a shining star. I want to go and pick something where I'm actually going to get constructive feedback on things I need feedback on." Amanda's approach to Personalized Feedback is but one example of how many instructors value opportunities for improvement and professional development. They actively seek the chance to learn more skills, thus showing that teaching Zumba Fitness is not just about tapping into one's instincts or "inner sexy" but actually something one trains for, practices, and continuously improves.

Beyond pursuing additional training, Zumba instructors also put in several hours of work per week to plan their classes. They carefully organize classes that both attend to students' fitness needs and heighten the feelings of freedom and fun for their students. Zumba instructors must balance staying true to the Zumba formula, satisfying students, and keeping themselves entertained and motivated. To do so, many instructors change their playlists every six to eight weeks. A change could be incorporating one brand-new song that instructors learned at a Jam Session or from a ZIN volume, or perhaps putting in a "throwback" that is new to students, if not new to the instructor. Keeping the playlist fresh makes sure students are not bored because they hear new songs, but they still feel accomplished because they have mastered other songs, too. Instructors, then, spend quite a bit of time creating, modifying, and perfecting playlists. With each change, they must rehearse accompanying choreography with multiple modifications (e.g., low-intensity to high-intensity) as they prepare for class.

Another factor that many instructors consider when organizing classes is the "feeling" or "vibe" they wish to evoke for their students. Erin described her classes as an "emotional journey" that incorporates different "feelings" that songs can bring up. She said, "Some songs, you know, you could be romantic, and all of a sudden you move to something that gets a little bit more happy and poppy, like a merengue or something." In this context, songs communicate certain "vibes" along with physical intensity and fitness goals. Feeling something is also tied to personal preferences. At times, instructors have to incorporate songs that they do not like very much to appease their students. Miriam is not a fan of popular singers like Shakira or Enrique Iglesias, for example, but she integrates some of their songs into her playlists because students request them. On the flip side, Lauren loved Destra Garcia's song "Lucy" so much that she kept it on her playlist too long and had to remove it after students approached her and said, "It is time to retire 'Lucy.'"

Still, as the arbiters of Zumba's "fun," instructors must balance their musical tastes with their students' interests in order to ensure that they can convey their own enthusiasm during class. Although Miriam sometimes used songs that she did not especially like, she rejected songs that she just could not "connect" with. She told me, "I cannot teach a class [when] I'm not connected to the music. That would make me very robotic, and I can't do that." Similarly, Vicki explained that she had to "feel" a song in order to teach it. Vicki recalled the advice she gives to newly minted Zumba instructors: "When you go to practice [a song], if your body says no, something in you says that doesn't fit there, then it doesn't fit for you. Don't do it. I've taken ZIN volume songs that I absolutely love, but when I go to do it, I don't like it. I won't use it. The class is going to know that it's not a favorite of yours. And then you won't smile. Who wants to take a class from an instructor who's miserable?" For both Vicki and Miriam, their own feelings of connection or joy about a given song strongly impact their teaching style. They have to emit fun vibes themselves so that students can feel the party, too. Weighing all of these competing factors indicates that instructors put in substantial effort to cultivate fun in their classes.

In fact, it is imperative that ZINs must always communicate they are having fun. Although ZINs actively foreground fitness and health when determining what to teach in their classes, they rarely talk about fitness during class. Of course, the silent cuing method of Zumba Fitness minimizes speaking already. Still, when choosing to speak, most instructors must limit their comments to having fun, expressing yourself, and being free. They marry these comments with exaggerated gestures, facial expressions, and moves. Overall, this performance style conveys that instructors, too, are "lost in the fun."[50] As Nieri and Hughes write, "The Zumba Instructor models how to party."[51] Instructors' expressions of joy and fun must be effortless in order to be convincing. Nieri and Hughes show that students' perceptions of the amount of fun and enthusiasm an instructor has is a key motivating factor that keeps them going during classes.[52] The stakes of communicating fun, then, are high since dissatisfied students may not return to an instructor's class. It is certainly true that many instructors do have fun in Zumba Fitness classes. However, they also work hard to create this fun atmosphere for their students. As Amanda told me, "You have to give 150 percent so your students will do 100 percent."

Being a Zumba instructor is hard work. It takes time, energy, money, and dedication to learn choreography, create playlists, and complete new training and professional development to make a safe and fun Zumba Fitness class. Successful Zumba instructors must be disciplined and dedicated in order to keep their classes fresh and popular, especially since many of them have other full-time careers. My experience talking with other people who take Zumba classes is that many students are unaware of the significant amount of time and money that their instructors have invested in their classes. This, too, is part of the labor of constructing fun. Instructors must be so well-versed in their choreography that it appears natural, unrehearsed, effortless, and ecstatically fun. This reality flies in the face of the notion that fun is a guaranteed, organic outcome of Zumba Fitness's tropicalized Latinness.

. . . .

"GET HAPPY"

It is the end of February 2021. My favorite local instructors are doing a throwback class where we request some of our favorite hits. I intended to sleep in, but my children's arguing woke me up early. I slogged out of bed, made coffee, and decided to cook French toast. But it burned, and we ran out of eggs, and it was overall a big fail. And it is only 9:00 a.m. I decide to log into a 9:30 virtual Zumba Fitness class. I go to the playroom and frantically move Legos and Hotwheels out of my way so I can start class on time. I'm tired. I almost give up. Then I remember that I requested Pablo Vittar's "Pose" and they haven't done that one in a while. And I love it. So I sign on.

The class immediately lifts my spirits. The instructors have included all of my requests! "Pose," Destra Garcia's "Lucy" and "Permission Slip," the salsa remake of "La Tusa," Grupo Treo's "Pégate," and J Balvin and Farruko's "6 a.m." all get played. I sweat my way through class. I stomp hard on the floor. I sing loudly, not worried that my neighbors can hear me through the open window (open because I am so hot although it is snowing). This is the perfect antidote to my sour mood. I got happy.

Almost one year into the COVID-19 pandemic, Zumba Fitness adopted a new slogan, "Step into Happy." As the pandemic surged and gyms closed, fitness instructors tried to move their businesses online. Zumba Fitness's business model relying primarily on instructor licensing fees meant that it did not face the same types of challenges as gyms or studios that were forced to close during the pandemic. Still, Zumba Fitness had to encourage people to stick with their Zumba classes so that it would be worthwhile for instructors to continue paying fees to the company. In the context of increased fear and anxiety brought on by the pandemic, Zumba Fitness's new marketing campaign "Step into Happy" focused on the program's mental health benefits. A new website featured three brief "trial workouts" that could "lift your mood—and your booty."[53] In many ways, the "Step into Happy" campaign aligned perfectly with increased attention to mental health during the COVID-19 pandemic, and the role of exercise in easing stress, anxiety, loneliness, and depression.

"Step into Happy" was also the latest in Zumba Fitness's long-standing effort to represent the program as fun. Of course, fun is important. We need spaces for people to express themselves, have fun, and improve their physical and mental health. But "Step into Happy" fell into the same traps that associate the trope of fun with tropicalized Latinness in Zumba Fitness. In typical Zumba fashion, the videos of the three trial workouts featured Zumba International Presenters dancing in front of bright, colorful backdrops, often with florescent colors and busy patterns on their Zumba Wear clothing. The colors, upbeat Latin music, and happy smiles on the presenters' faces epitomized the assumption that fun is only accessible via engagement with tropicalized Latinness. Those people who can access fun temporarily through Zumba Fitness's tropicalized Latinness can achieve the benefits of this fun, like weight loss, happiness, and sexiness, without compromising their own positionalities as modern subjects. "Step into Happy" is thus the latest in a long line of Zumba Fitness marketing campaigns that reproduce racial hierarchies rooted in the mind-body divide intrinsic to Western modernity.

The hyperfocus on fun also obscures the reality that Zumba Fitness takes work, dedication, and discipline. Zumba instructors and many participants remain as dedicated to their exercise regimens as practitioners of allegedly more disciplined exercise programs. Moreover, the continuous elevation of Zumba Presenters with the ideal fit body as the face of the brand further aligns Zumba Fitness with the same hegemonic expectations around discipline and health that pervade the fitness industry. Likewise, the focus on fun also renders invisible the time and labor instructors put into creating a fun, party atmosphere in their classes. This is critical. The whole point of Zumba Fitness's fun is to give the impression that no one is being judged, stigmatized, or held back by the norms of behavior and expectations in other, more "disciplined" exercise programs like barre. Instead, fun is supposed to be natural, embodied by an instructor who has tapped into her "inner child" and "inner sexy" and can model the types of freedom available to participants. Not only does tropicalized Latinness's supposed natural inclination toward fun make instructors appear authentic but it also reproduces stereotypes of racialized others as instinctual, pleasure-loving, and uncontrollable. On the flip side, detailing how instructors learn to manifest and represent fun in their classes shows that fun is not organic, but rather is manufactured by the people on the ground.

Fun is not always bad. Rather than dismiss the importance of fun, my goal here is to show how the trope of fun can be carefully constructed in ways that preserve racial stereotypes, which, in turn, become hidden through the idea that fun is natural and desirable. One especially insidious aspect of the trope of fun is its positive connotations. Who doesn't want to have fun or spread joy? However, closely interrogating how the trope of fun operates alongside tropicalized Latinness shows that we cannot take seemingly positive representations at face value. Instead, we must consider how even these admirable and positive ideals can sometimes bolster racist ideologies and hierarchies.

SELLING DREAMS

‹‹‹‹›

THE COVID-19 PANDEMIC TRANSFORMED THE FITNESS WORLD. The shared equipment and close proximity of exercisers breathing heavily on each other made gyms a particularly undesirable place to be during the pandemic. Mask mandates and intensive health protocols added burdens to the fitness industry, too. Moreover, the ever-evolving nature of the pandemic with the emergence of new variants and shifting hotspots made planning for gym owners and fitness professionals particularly difficult.[1] On top of the health risks, job losses and an uncertain economy made people cut back on spending, meaning fewer customers had the means to go to the gym at all.

Group fitness seemed especially problematic. By the time the United States shut down in March 2020, South Korea had already become a major hotspot for COVID-19 infections. In February 2020, news outlets reported that the Shincheonji Church of Jesus in Daegu accounted for a major outbreak in the area.[2] However, in the summer of 2020, new research emerged that a second large gathering contributed to the outbreak in Daegu: an in-person Zumba instructor training that took place in the nearby city of Cheonan on February 15, 2020.[3] The *New York Times* reported the story in an article titled "What's the Future of Group Exercise Classes?" The article began, "During 24 days in February and March, 112 people were infected with the Covid-19 virus in South Korea after participating in or associating with participants in Zumba classes." It continued with damning evidence of the Zumba Fitness instructor training as a petri dish for the virus, reporting that "researchers discovered that the common thread connecting infections was Zumba," and that "of the 27 newly minted Zumba teachers attending, eight later tested positive. But in the meantime, they taught classes, without wearing masks, and in a few instances while coughing." Within a week, as the *New York Times* reported in a summary of the study, the Zumba outbreak had an "attack rate" of 25 percent, meaning that one-quarter of the people who interacted with infected Zumba instructors became infected themselves.[4] Zumba Fitness found itself listed as one of the primary super-spreaders of South Korea's early and virulent outbreak.

The Zumba outbreak reflected many experts' warnings about group fitness more generally. The study of South Korea's Zumba outbreak noted that "characteristics that might have led to transmission from the instructors in Cheonan include large class sizes, small spaces, and intensity of the workouts. The moist, warm atmosphere in a sports facility coupled with turbulent air flow generated by intense physical exercise can cause more dense transmission of isolated droplets."[5] As more information about COVID-19 circulated, it seemed that nothing could be worse than an enclosed space full of sweating fitness participants packed in together, breathing heavily.

But there was some good news: virtual fitness took off during the pandemic.[6] The global popularity of Zumba Fitness gave the company a head start at developing their own online platform since the Home Office heard from Chinese instructors about the need for support during the pandemic in January and February, two months before the US shutdown.[7] Prior to the pandemic, Zumba instructors could only teach Zumba Fitness classes in person. Within a matter of weeks, the company launched a new online platform called ZIN Studio. Instructors could now livestream and prerecord classes, accept payment directly through the app, and chat online with their students. Many instructors had already begun teaching on Zoom, but with ZIN Studio they could use Zumba Fitness's music license and thus avoid paying any potential fees for streaming songs.[8] Access to ZIN Studio was now one of the offerings included in instructors' monthly dues.[9] Alberto Perlman told NPR that instructors kept all of the revenue from their virtual classes, which, he argued, allowed them to earn substantially more per class; whereas in person Perlman noted instructors often earned $25 to $30 per class, he claimed some earned up to $150 per class virtually.[10] In addition, the company offered financial assistance to Zumba instructors, especially those who were also nurses and frontline workers, or were affected by COVID-19 due to hospitalization, death of a family member, or lack of childcare.[11] Perlman declared that the Zumba Home Office did not garner any revenue from online classes.[12] He explained that the company's primary motivation

4.1 Author's at-home Zumba Fitness setup during the COVID-19 pandemic. Photograph by the author.

for shifting online was so that instructors could continue to earn income while gyms were closed.[13]

While it is technically true that the Zumba Fitness company does not earn direct revenue from individual students or classes, this is not the whole story. Zumba Fitness's main customers are instructors. Anxious students and shuttered gyms meant that for many instructors, paying monthly dues for a program they could not teach, with no timeline for reopening, would be a financial loss. Perlman does not mention this in any of his interviews about creating ZIN Studio. Instead, Perlman depicts Zumba Fitness's approach to the pandemic as altruistically motivated to help struggling instructors; however, the reality was that if ZINs stopped paying their monthly fees, Zumba Fitness's profits would suffer. Perlman's comments are similar to Zumba Fitness's frequent pronouncement that the company gives potential instructors all the tools they need to be successful. If instructors consistently pay dues to maintain their license, Zumba Fitness promises to provide them with music, choreography, an official website, a supportive community, and "everything that they need."[14] However, the Home Office does not help ZINs find jobs or get their foot in the door in their local fitness scene.

According to the Zumba Home Office, instructors can have very lucrative incomes if they dedicate themselves to the program. I have never found information about the average income for a Zumba instructor in the United States. This could partially be because salaries depend on a variety of factors such as whether instructors teach at a private gym or a community center, what format they teach, how often they teach classes, and the going rate for Zumba Fitness classes in their local area. Sometimes instructors open their own studios, which has more overhead cost but can potentially increase profits since they keep all of their revenue. Although the Zumba Home Office does not guarantee a specific salary, the company often paints a rosy picture of the potential financial success that an instructor can have. For example, in a 2016 interview with the *Cut*, Perlman answered the question "Out of curiosity, how lucrative is a career as a Zumba instructor?" by touting the success of an instructor in California who earned $24,000 per month. He explained, "She has seven classes a week. She pays us $30 a month. . . . She started teaching Zumba classes with five people. Now she has 200 to 300 people per class. She rents a basketball court. So she pays, like, $100 to rent that basketball court and charges, like, $10 per person. We give her all of the support for marketing; we give her a website, music, choreography, everything she needs to teach that class."[15] By all accounts, a monthly income of $24,000 seems extreme; however, that Perlman chose to answer the question with this exceptional story indicates how the Zumba Fitness brand promotes the program as a path toward wealth and financial success. The implication is that other people with the same persistence and dedication as this particular California instructor could also earn over $100,000 annually if they worked hard enough.

The stories about super financially successful Zumba Fitness instructors often center these individuals' drive and perseverance over obstacles as key to their success. In essence, instructors like the one Perlman praised on NPR achieve the American dream through Zumba Fitness. In so doing, Zumba Fitness brings together tropicalized Latinness with neoliberal ideologies of the American dream. This further renders tropicalized Latinness nonthreatening to the status quo. For example, one stereotype of Latinx hypersexuality cautions that Latin American immigrants, especially women, come to the United States, bear children, and reap the benefits of social welfare without contributing to the economy. Attaching tropicalized Latinness to the American dream erases these concerns by transforming Latinx sexuality into a commodity that can produce wealthy contributors to the US economy. Moreover, this provides fodder to those who argue that institutionalized racism and xenophobia are no longer significant barriers to Latinx immigrants in the United States by stressing that anyone can make it if they just work hard enough. This is especially salient in the frequent retelling of Beto Pérez's journey from impoverished Colombian youth to successful US-based multimillionaire that distinguishes him from the "Latino Threat" often associated with Latin American immigrants. A Latinx immigrant like Beto Pérez is not a drain on US resources; instead, he embodies the American dream.

This chapter analyzes how Zumba Fitness sells the American dream. The figures of Beto Pérez and other Zumba International Presenters who immigrated to the United States play a critical role in showcasing the possibility of financial uplift through Zumba Fitness. Importantly, these narratives are also racial ones that foreground these International Presenters' ethnic and racial otherness while simultaneously depicting them as exemplars of the American dream and, by extension, ideal potential citizens. However, for many Zumba instructors, immigrant or not, the American dream never bears out. The numerous fees and certification costs combined with what one instructor described as a "saturated" New England market mean that many of the instructors I spoke with aim merely to break even each month. This inconsistency reveals that the American dream becomes a marketing tool, one that idealizes certain Latinx bodies as assimilable, desirable, and even patriotic, while rejecting those who do not conform to normative expectations of capitalist success. In turn, selling the dream contributes to the construction of tropicalized Latinness as something consumable, nonthreatening, and assimilable into US culture.

FROM "LATINO THREAT" TO "MODEL MINORITY"

The COVID-19 pandemic laid bare many inequities in the United States. Discrepant access to healthcare, childcare, food, transportation, employment, and housing (among other things) all came into stark relief. Many jobs that had hitherto been disregarded as unimportant, unskilled, or undesirable became labeled "essential." Grocery store workers, delivery drivers, and agricultural laborers were viewed as equally important as the doctors and nurses who treated sick patients. Just like medical professionals, these workers risked their lives so the rest of us could avoid COVID-19. Importantly, immigrants and people of color made up the bulk of this labor force. Indeed, this is why so many of them had been invisible before the pandemic. For the first time, many Americans started thinking about how their food got from the farm to their tables, and all the human beings whose labor made that happen. "Thank you, Grocery Workers" signs popped up alongside ones that said "Thank you, Doctors" in neighborhoods around the country.

But unlike medical doctors or nurses, many of these essential workers' jobs offer very low wages. Many low-income essential workers had no choice but to work. COVID-19 had tremendous consequences for these communities, whether because of disproportionately high infection and death rates or high rates of evictions, food insecurity, and other problems. Congress responded to the pandemic with stimulus bills, eviction moratoriums, and child tax credits that kept many low-income families afloat. But critics of these measures claimed that these "free handouts" would make poor people too reliant on state benefits. They recycled old arguments that have historically represented Black and Latina women, in particular, as people who prefer to take advantage of public benefits than to work.[16] And so, the very same communities that comprised most of the newly lauded essential workers became derided as people who did not contribute to US society, but instead actually threatened the economic stability of other, more industrious citizens.

COVID-19 stimulus programs also excluded undocumented immigrants and their families (including those of mixed status). The rationale for excluding them reiterated the "Latino Threat Narrative" outlined by Leo Chavez. He writes, "In this narrative, Latinos, especially Mexican immigrants and their children, are seldom represented as signs of positive change, because their unwillingness to integrate denies them the opportunity to influence the larger society in any appreciable way, except in the negative—as threats to existing institutions (e.g., education, social services, medical)."[17] One especially acute anxiety stoked by the Latino Threat Narrative is that undocumented immigrants arrive to the United States eager to take public benefits like welfare programs away from taxpaying citizens (notwithstanding the fact that undocumented immigrants do pay taxes). This was, in fact, the reasoning behind excluding even undocumented immigrants' immediate family members who were US citizens from COVID-19 stimulus benefits. The very same essential workers praised for feeding us during the pandemic were left out of the government programs that aimed to help low-income families despite many immigrants bearing the brunt of the economic and public health impacts of COVID-19. For example, in Massachusetts, where I live, a high "proportion of foreign-born noncitizens was the strongest predictor of the burden of COVID-19 cases within a community" precisely because many members of these communities worked in critical industries that required in-person, face-to-face labor.[18]

Such discourses around the role of undocumented immigrants in the pandemic revealed a fundamental contradiction in the depictions of Latin American immigrants and US Latinx communities more broadly. On one hand, the US economy could not function without their labor; on the other, they were assumed to be lazy cheats. These conflicting representations are not new. Instead, as Arlene Dávila argues, they work in concert to support the logics of neoliberalism and postracial ideologies in the United States. Dávila shows that the praise of Latinx communities as potentially upwardly mobile, middle-class consumers who harbor conservative family values furthers postracialism because it de-emphasizes ongoing systemic racism in favor of highlighting those who have "made it" based on their own hard work and values. Dávila points out that the uplifting of US Latinxs who have achieved educational and economic mobility contrasts them with Latin American immigrants assumed to be poor, unskilled, and unassimilable. And yet, despite these uplifting narratives, Dávila underscores that Latinx people have not achieved full civic rights in the United States. It is just a small few who actually have the types of upward mobility touted by pundits and market researchers.[19]

The success of these small few serves a crucial function in upholding neoliberalism and postracialism in the United States. They become exemplars of the American dream whose exceptional life stories serve as evidence that those who do *not* succeed presumably fail due to their own poor choices, lack of will, or troubling behavior. As Lázaro Lima shows, someone like Supreme Court Justice Sonia Sotomayor, the child of working-class Puerto Rican migrants in the Bronx, becomes a symbol of all that is possible for everyone in the United States if they choose to take advantage of the opportunities afforded to them.[20]

Lima notes that Sotomayor's ascendancy "also functions as both a performance of and an attachment to a particular American patriotic identity premised on assimilation."[21] Assimilation has long been assumed to be a unidirectional and holistic process in which an immigrant becomes completely integrated into US society. This includes changes like adopting the English language, cultural norms, and the American dream ethos. However, as Catherine Ramírez argues, assimilation has not been available to everyone. Instead, race is a critical factor in determining whether someone can be fully assimilated. Americanness and citizenship have long been tied to whiteness, thus barring even nonimmigrant people of color from accessing their full citizenship rights.[22] Racist ideologies have painted groups like domestic Latinxs and African Americans as unassimilable because of their perceived primitivity and distance from whiteness.[23] These are the so-called failed citizens, those who do not live up to the neoliberal ideals that undergird Americanness.[24] In this vein, Ramírez argues that assimilation is best approached not as an automatic, unidirectional integration into society, but instead as a "paradox" wherein only a few people of color are actually recognized as assimilable, while most remain excluded from mainstream US society.[25] In this context, only those domestic racial and ethnic others like Justice Sotomayor and other so-called model minorities who have overcome obstacles to achieve financial success and to acculturate into the values associated with (white) Americanness can be assimilated into mainstream life.[26] Diversity becomes visible through the bodies of these exceptional individuals of color whose mere presence serves as "ocular evidence" of the end of racism and the viability of the American dream.[27] The success of a few model minorities, then, actually bolsters the racist policies that stymie progress for other members of even the same marginalized groups.

And yet, there are instances in which embodying stereotypes enables certain figures to achieve this American dream. Leah Perry notes that the success of 1990s Latinx stars like Jennifer Lopez or Selena Quintanilla relied in part on capitalizing on their ethnic and racial difference as "heterosexual, exotic, sexy, bilingual embodiments of otherness."[28] Media depictions of Quintanilla and Lopez routinely represented them as embodiments of the American dream whose presumably immigrant families sacrificed for them to be successful. However, not only were Quintanilla and Lopez each born and raised in the United States, but Quintanilla's parents were both born in the United States, and Lopez's parents are, like all Puerto Ricans, US citizens even though they were both born in Puerto Rico. Leah Perry argues that the emphasis on Quintanilla and Lopez as connected (however distantly) to immigration purposefully followed the passing of the Immigration Reform and Control Act of 1986, which, among other things, provided amnesty to undocumented immigrants who had arrived in the United States prior to 1982. Showcasing the success of Latinas like Lopez and Quintanilla reinforced the power and possibility of the American dream for those who worked hard enough. At the same time, their marked ethnic and racial difference indicated that racism no longer posed a serious obstacle for success.[29]

Capitalizing on tropicalized Latinness to achieve financial success is a clear example of the mutual construction of postracialism and neoliberalism in the contemporary United States. The fun, fiesta-loving, dancing Latin foreign other has long been central to representations of Latinx populations in popular culture. Latin foreign others are assumed to endorse the values of neoliberalism, thus removing any possibility of their reliance on the state typically associated with undocumented immigrants and domestic Latinx groups. Their achievement of the American dream occurs in part because they personify stereotypes of tropicalized Latinness that bolster racial hierarchies, but, ironically, this same achievement is mobilized as evidence of the absence of racism. To embody tropicalized Latinness, then, is not only to be sexy, fun, authentic, and foreign. It is also to be an independent economic contributor to the United States who embraces and lives out the American dream's entrepreneurial spirit.

BETO PÉREZ DREAMS BIG

Perhaps no one embodies the marriage between the American dream and tropicalized Latinness better than Beto Pérez. He is more than the cofounder of Zumba Fitness, he is also the face of the brand. Alongside his frequent declarations about reaching "your dreams" and fulfilling "your destiny," Beto models how to marshal tropicalized Latinness into a marketable commodity. Beto Pérez stands out as *the* figure whose innovation, hard work, tenacity, and persistence exemplify the possibilities of a career as a Zumba instructor.

To be sure, Pérez's accomplishments are impressive, and I do not mean to diminish them. Instead, I want to call attention to the ways that his biography depicts him as a "good immigrant"—someone who does not conform to the so-called Latino Threat, but has instead become an active contributor to US economic, cultural, and civic life. Beto's life story has been told and retold in various magazines, interviews, and even a 2018 Colombian novela aptly titled *Nadie me quita lo bailao* (No one can stop me from dancing). These biographical sketches repeat the trials and tribulations Pérez experienced on his transformation from a poor child in Colombia to a multimillionaire and entrepreneur in the United States. In fact, in 2017, CNBC declared him one of the top five "self-made Hispanic immigrant millionaires," alongside a banker, real estate developer, tech entrepreneur, and supermarket chain CEO.[30] Situating Zumba Fitness alongside other industries like finance or robotics legitimizes the fitness program as a viable and valuable career option. These sorts of profiles reinforce the ubiquitous narrative that perseverance and hard work can make anyone a millionaire.

Pérez offers his own version of his biography in his 2009 book *Zumba: Ditch the Workout, Join the Party! The Zumba Weight Loss Program*. In the chapter dedicated to his life story, Pérez stresses his humble beginnings and the hardships that he endured before becoming a successful entrepreneur. Pérez begins the chapter with an epigraph: "My dream was always to entertain people. You will find that when you have a dream, you may not always see the way to make it come true; you just have the dream. Maybe you know where you want to go but you do not know how to get there. Do not even worry about it. Just hold on to the dream, keep it alive, and let destiny take its course. This is what happened to me."[31] Here, Pérez attributes much of his success to dreaming—dream big, keep dreaming, and eventually dreams will come true. He begins with the story of his birth in Cali, Colombia, which he describes as a "cosmopolitan city" whose "landscape is mountainous and jungle-like—semi-tropical but not too muggy."[32] Pérez discusses how his mother became pregnant after meeting a married doctor who took advantage of her innocence. She met him, as fate would have it, on the dance floor. Pérez describes, "Because Colombia is a country of warmth, people tended to exude a little more sensuality when they dance, and this man was no different."[33] Pérez inherited his dancing from his father and nurtured it in a society that, according to him, was infused with dance, music, and sensuality. The focus on sensuality, fecundity, and tropical climates references some of the basic tenets of tropicalized Latinness. Consequently, Pérez becomes the embodiment of both authentic Latin American culture since he was born and raised in Colombia, and the exotic and sexy tropicalized Latinness so fundamental to the Zumba Fitness brand.

After Pérez was born in 1971, he and his mother endured several hardships including poverty, domestic violence, and housing insecurity. They lived in a barrio where he "played in the dirt streets."[34] His mother worked tirelessly in a local restaurant to "[provide] food on the table and love in our home."[35] After she overcame several obstacles, including leaving her abusive drug-dealing boyfriend, Pérez encouraged his mother to move to the United States where she worked as a housekeeper in Miami for ten years.[36] Characteristics like poverty, violence, and association with drug trafficking are common stereotypes associated with Colombia and the Latino Threat Narrative as a whole. However, Pérez repeatedly stresses the love, happiness, and *decency* of his family. In this way, these stereotypes seem like especially onerous challenges rather than inherent cultural or familial traits. Moreover, readers know that at the time of this writing, Pérez has already achieved the American dream, thus distinguishing himself from the Latino Threat Narrative and from domestic racial and ethnic others.

By the time his mother emigrated from Colombia, Pérez was a teenager who had achieved some modicum of success dancing in local competitions and nightclubs. Still, his mother's departure made life difficult. "At times it was a struggle to survive," he wrote. "I often subsisted on a glass of milk and one banana a day."[37] Rather than wallow in despair, Pérez chose "to grow up and take responsibility for myself and muster up more confidence, all on my own. In the face of this hopelessness, I did the only thing I could: ignore it. I kept my head up, worked slowly and steadily, and did what I believed in."[38] Pérez kept on dancing.

Dance opened up new opportunities for him. Pérez started teaching aerobics and dance classes in Bogotá.[39] He won some high-profile dance competitions and even started working as a choreographer for local stage productions and celebrities, most notably Shakira.[40] Perhaps most importantly, he created his new aerobics format based on Latin music, which had become very popular in Bogotá. Eventually, Pérez had the opportunity to travel to Miami for the first time in 1996. He took several trips to Miami in order to find opportunities to teach his new aerobics format until he found a gym willing to give him a chance.[41] After settling in Miami with a fellow Colombian immigrant, Pérez eventually met Alberto Perlman and Alberto Aghion, and the rest is history.

Popular media profiles of Beto Pérez similarly recount his perseverance and ability to overcome even the most difficult obstacles. Like in *Zumba*, the key to success is to keep dreaming and have hope. Profiles mention Pérez's lifelong passion for dance, his willingness to take advantage of any opportunity no matter how small, and his unwavering faith in the American dream.[42] Often, these articles include advice for would-be fitness entrepreneurs. For example, a 2015 profile of Pérez in *Women's Health* offers five steps to help these entrepreneurs achieve their goals. Some are very practical, like "Do Your Homework" (i.e., research material and hone your craft), or "Marketing Your Idea Is Half the Battle" (i.e., have a pitch that could get your foot in the door). But several other suggestions are less tangible, like "Believe in Yourself" or "Don't Let Setbacks Stop You from Following Your Dreams."[43] This advice ignores any structural inequities or barriers that might impact someone trying to establish themselves in the United States, whether in fitness or any other industry. Instead, it implies that all anyone needs is hard work, tenacity, optimism, and faith. Depicting Pérez as a prime example of the American dream fulfilled thus separates him from other Latin American immigrants assumed to be economic drains on US society as depicted in the Latino Threat Narrative.

This distinction is particularly important because at one point, Beto Pérez lived as an undocumented immigrant in the United States. There are not many details about his daily life as an undocumented immigrant or his path to legalizing his status in the United States. Of the many, many profiles of Pérez that I have read, the vast majority do not mention his legal status at all. A 2019 article from the BBC briefly states that "in 1999 he moved—illegally—to Miami." It continues with an incredibly short discussion about how his initial experiences in the United States were difficult "because he didn't speak enough English and didn't bring enough money with him."[44] Similarly, Pérez addressed his undocumented status directly in a 2017 Hispanic Heritage Month essay for the popular women's lifestyle website PopSugar. The essay, titled "The Moment I Realized That I—and Zumba—Had Achieved the American Dream," once again tells the story of Pérez's achievements. But, this time, his advice specifically targets Latinx readers. He describes the difficulty of establishing himself in Miami: "I tried to move to the United States four times before I made it in 2000. I didn't speak English. I didn't have papers. Again, I had nothing."[45] The image of the impoverished, Spanish-speaking, undocumented immigrant dominates the Latino Threat Narrative. However, Pérez notes how he overcame these challenges in order to counter xenophobic arguments that Latinxs are not active contributors to US life. He writes, "It's very important for me to change the idea that Latinos aren't an important part of the economy and culture of the country. I want people to say: 'Hey, the creator of Zumba is Colombian.' I want people's perspectives about Latinos to change."[46] Pérez foregrounds Latinxs' economic contributions multiple times to highlight that Latinxs do not steal jobs, they create them. On one hand, this is a very important critique of xenophobia and the Latino Threat Narrative. On the other, this reinforces neoliberal ideologies that individuals' contributions to the market determine their value to society. Pérez distinguishes himself as someone who achieved economic success despite his background as a poor, Latinx immigrant. Beto Pérez thus joins Sonia Sotomayor, Jennifer Lopez, and other model minority figures whose success supposedly makes evident that the United States is a meritocratic society where anyone can achieve the American dream.

Pérez reinforces this point with his advice to Latinx readers: "To young Latino entrepreneurs everywhere, I say don't stop dreaming and never forget where you came from. Remember, your parents, grandparents, and family worked hard to get here so you could have opportunities. Appreciate your hard work to get where you are today. But know that dreams only come true with perseverance, passion, and hard work. You must wait for the right moment. I waited 25 years! I promise your moment will come."[47] In addition to keeping hope alive, Pérez strongly recommends patience. If one works hard enough and waits for their "moment," they will certainly be rewarded. The emphasis on patience discounts the role of luck in the American dream. Mark Rank contends that the focus on individualism and agency in the American dream narrative dismisses the important roles that chance and luck play in creating the conditions of possibility for any single person to achieve the American dream.[48] Luck is certainly central to Zumba Fitness's origin story. If Pérez had not forgotten his aerobics tape, he never would have created the new dance-fitness format. If Alberto Perlman's mother had not attended Beto Pérez's class in Miami, the two men never would have met. These kinds of coincidences are often critically important for people who are able to achieve the American dream. Luck helps a lot, whether that takes the form of being lucky enough to be born into a wealthy family or the luck of simply being in the right place at the right time. To acknowledge the importance of luck, though, is to take away from the rugged individualism so central to the American dream. Likewise, Pérez's emphasis on patience ultimately discounts any role that racism or xenophobia might have played in his own story. Here, the key to overcoming racism is not enacting systemic changes that would benefit Latinxs and other people of color. Instead, racism is merely something that an individual must endure until the right moment comes around and they finally get their due.

Throughout his essay, Pérez stresses that one should not "forget where you came from" or the role of family members in paving the way for younger generations. If the Latino Threat Narrative reproduces stereotypes of Latinxs' (and especially Latinas') alleged sexual pathology, a conflicting representation of Latinx communities depicts them as having traditional family values.[49] Dávila notes that the assumption that Latinxs adhere to conservative family values reiterates stereotypes of Latinx communities as steeped in tradition, separated from the more modern and sophisticated lifestyles of the "average" American.[50] Pérez's comments emphasize the importance of maintaining Latinx cultural traditions, while simultaneously recalling a common origin story of Americans' ancestors arriving to the United States to seek better opportunities for future generations. Consequently, he inserts Latinx immigrants into hegemonic narratives of assimilation and success. In so doing, Pérez ignores the systemic racism that, as Catherine Ramírez documents, precludes the ability of immigrants and other people of color to be considered assimilated and American.[51]

Beto Pérez has certainly achieved something remarkable—he created one of the biggest global fitness programs in history. This obviously takes perseverance and hard work. My point here is not to discount what are

clearly important sacrifices and hardships that Pérez has made in his lifetime. Nevertheless, his story is also part and parcel of the Zumba Fitness
brand. Zumba Fitness needs tropicalized Latinness to distance the brand
from the negative stereotypes associated with the Latino Threat Narrative. Pérez not only embodies the sexy and exotic qualities of tropicalized
Latinness, but effectively capitalizes on these qualities to achieve financial success. Pérez's story of achieving the American dream represents
him as an exceptional Latin American immigrant who can easily be assimilated into mainstream US society even as he maintains his foreign
and ethnic difference. In so doing, Pérez's status as the face of the Zumba
Fitness brand both uplifts tropicalized Latinness and models all that is
possible for those who wish to become Zumba instructors and achieve
their dreams.

AMERICAN (CITIZENSHIP) DREAMS

Beto Pérez is not the only person celebrated for achieving the American
dream in Zumba Fitness. The Zumba Stories YouTube series showcases the
lives of successful Zumba instructors. Zumba Stories often focuses on the
myriad challenges people face on their way to becoming successful ZINS.
Not all of these obstacles are the same, however. Zumba Stories almost always feature migration in the profiles of Latinx instructors. On the other
hand, they generally depict American women—often white, but sometimes not—as facing issues related to physical and mental health. There
is also a striking gender dimension to these profiles. Many of the Latinx
immigrant instructors are men. While this may be a coincidence, centering male immigrants does a lot of ideological work to neutralize the
Latino Threat Narrative, which often conjures up images of dangerous
men clandestinely crossing the border. They are contrasted with white
women, in particular, who become representative of authentic Americanness given their locations in small-town, rural America. To be sure,
there are some exceptions: for example, Nour Jabri briefly describes her
immigration from Saudi Arabia to the United States before addressing
her battle with breast cancer.[52] Still, reading the Zumba Stories of white
American women and Latinx men together underscores how Zumba Fitness uses the trope of dreams to distinguish tropicalized Latinness from
the Latino Threat Narrative.

Former Zumba Jammer Jhon Gonzalez's Zumba Story tells a similar story as that of Beto Pérez about immigrating to the United States to achieve the American dream. He describes coming from Colombia to the United States at the age of ten, and feeling just as American as Colombian while he was growing up. As the video shows scenes of Gonzalez roaming along the Santa Monica pier and jogging through the Hollywood Hills, he says, "When you move to the United States, you move with the idea of the American dream, and the American dream for me was to be able to give back to my family what they did for me."[53] Gazing at the Los Angeles skyline, Gonzalez continues, "It was always in the back of my mind, 'Will I ever be able to have a regular job? Will I ever have enough money to support my family?'"[54] In this particular clip, it is unclear exactly what keeps Gonzalez from achieving his goals. A second Zumba Stories video titled "Meet 5 Zumba Choreographers" profiles Gonzalez alongside four other Zumba Jammers. There, the same interview goes into more detail about his immigration status when Gonzalez states he did not know "if I ever was going to become legal—which I am" before talking about his goal of supporting his family.[55] There are no details about Gonzalez's immigration journey or legalization process. What is clear, though, is that despite the brevity of this statement, Gonzalez is differentiated from undocumented immigrants who make up the Latino Threat. Instead, Jhon Gonzalez is an ideal immigrant who achieved financial success, became culturally integrated into the United States, and is "living [his] dream right now."[56]

Another Zumba Jammer featured in Zumba Stories is Puerto Rican choreographer Rony Gratereaut.[57] Gratereaut describes his childhood in Residencial Las Margaritas in San Juan, Puerto Rico. These residenciales, also known as caseríos, have been historically depicted as sites of crime, poverty, and urban blight in Puerto Rico.[58] Gratereaut states that growing up, "I saw things I don't regret, but I don't wish anyone to ever see. But that helped me make decisions in my life that I don't want that type of life for me. I deserve more."[59] While he speaks, we see images of Gratereaut walking his pit bull past some yellowish buildings. The video appears to be filmed in his current city, Orlando, Florida, yet these buildings look similar to the typical residenciales of San Juan. The image of a pit bull—a dog that signals aggression—and the urbanesque space where this takes place signals race and class positionalities that mark Gratereaut as some kind of Latin other. The music shifts from somber to upbeat as we learn about Gratereaut's interest in dance and performance. He

Pero no le desearía a nadie pasar por lo mismo.

4.2 Still from YouTube video "Zumba Stories: Rony Gratereaut." The still of him walking a pit bull surrounded by buildings similar to public housing developments in San Juan, Puerto Rico, frames Gratereaut as a racialized and foreign Latinx other.

describes following his siblings to Orlando and seeking opportunities to dance professionally. Although he did not get bites as a professional dancer, Gratereaut met Jhon Gonzalez who encouraged and mentored him as he became a Zumba Fitness instructor.

At the beginning of the video, Gratereaut identifies performing at the Fitness Concert at the Zumba Convention as the pinnacle of success—"the dream"—for Zumba instructors.[60] After describing his journey, we see Gratereaut break down into tears when the producer tells him "Rony, you are going to be performing at the Fitness Concert this year at Convention."[61] Triumphant music plays while we watch Gratereaut perform alongside Beto Pérez on the big stage. He says, "Coming from Puerto Rico and [the] struggle with the way that I grew up, with society and the environment, to get the chance to achieve such a big dream, a big goal, with Zumba Fitness, it's a life chang[ing] experience. It was a dream come true."[62]

Rony Gratereaut's Puerto Ricanness functions in two important ways here. First, his story of migrating to the United States to escape poverty conforms to the narrative of the ideal immigrant who seeks new opportunities in the United States. However, like all Puerto Ricans, Rony Gratereaut is a US citizen. Consequently, his story of uplift from poverty is especially important to distinguish him from domestic racial and ethnic others. Poverty has often been construed as the antithesis of being a "good" American citizen who is self-reliant and independent. Catherine Ramírez argues that the connection between poverty and alleged "failed citizenship" pertains primarily to domestic African American and Latinx populations, who are assumed to be culturally deficient and therefore incapable of achieving the American dream and normative standards of US citizenship.[63] In this context, Rony Gratereaut's narrative of escaping poverty, violence, and trauma to live out his American dream both reinforces an idealized (im)migration story and differentiates him from other domestic US Latinx and African American communities, all while diminishing the impact of structural racism on Black and Latinx lives.

Even when Latinx Zumba Jammers do not focus on hardships related to immigration, immigration remains a central trope of their Zumba Stories profiles. For example, Henry Cedeño describes immigrating to the United States from Venezuela as a child, and the many challenges he faced learning a new language and navigating a new culture. However, he stresses the pain of being bullied because he was overweight and "different." His mother took him to Zumba Fitness classes, where he started to develop more self-confidence and committed to a healthy lifestyle. Although Cedeño mentions the extra income he earned as a teenager, much of his story focuses on less tangible benefits of Zumba Fitness like happiness. Cedeño's comments are more focused on the impact that bullying and being overweight had on him than his immigration story. Still, the framing of his Zumba Story as one that begins with racial and ethnic difference prioritizes his immigrant experience despite Cedeño himself talking primarily about his struggles with weight loss.[64]

Gonzalez, Gratereaut, and Cedeño are all featured in the Zumba video "Meet 5 Zumba Choreographers" alongside two white American women, Marisa Stani and Kaitlyn Murphy. The three Latinx men's stories underscore the financial security and success associated with the American dream as their motivating factor for joining Zumba Fitness. However, Stani's and Murphy's comments focus primarily on their love of dance. Stani mentions that she has danced since she was a toddler, and Murphy describes her dream as being "Britney Spears's back-up dancer."[65] While all the choreographers in the video talk about helping people achieve greater wellness and happiness, this particular video only mentions Gonzalez's and Gratereaut's entrance into Zumba Fitness as part of their American dream story. Besides knowing that Murphy and Stani have danced since childhood, the video offers no information about how they got into Zumba Fitness in the first place. This juxtaposition of three Latinx immigrant men who achieved the American dream alongside two white women who inspire others further emphasizes the importance of achieving the American dream for Latinx people, in particular, who seek inclusion into US society.

Like with Stani and Murphy, more in-depth profiles of women instructors from the United States differ from the profiles of men like Gratereaut and Gonzalez. Women ZINS also face adversity, but this almost always involves managing a mental and physical health crisis, be it depression and anxiety, cancer, or autoimmune disorders. For example, Josette Tkacik of Santa Barbara, California, joined Zumba Fitness in order to stay physically active in the wake of her rheumatoid arthritis diagnosis. In her Zumba Stories profile, she recalls the myriad emotions she felt when she was "first being told, 'you're gonna end up in a wheelchair.'"[66] Tkacik also mentions the importance of proving to her son that she could take care of herself and that she would not let her illness stop her. Tkacik differentiates herself from stereotypes of the physically disabled who cannot work or care for themselves, thus ascribing to the neoliberal philosophy of individual perseverance as the key to success in all realms of life including curing disease. At the same time, the visuals accompanying the video locate Tkacik in prototypical "rural America." We first see her while she rides a horse through a farm. Later, she ambles through a field of wildflowers with her family and dog in tow. These images evoke the idea that the "real America" is rural, simple, and unsullied by urban blight.

The association between Americanness and rural landscapes is even more striking in the Zumba Stories video about Maggie Engels's Zumba Fitness journey. It begins with shots of farmland, including barns and silos with American flags plastered on them, while Engels narrates, "Life in Nicholville, New York, is very simple."[67] In fact, when she says the word "simple," an Amish family riding a horse and buggy passes by. These images make clear that Engels is from a very rural place characterized by hard work and American values. Engels suffered from low self-esteem as an overweight teenager, but she eventually moved on and did what was expected of her by her community: "You go to school, you get a job, you get married, you have kids."[68] But she still wasn't happy. She decided to quit her job, telling her boss, "I'm going to follow my dreams, I'm going to do my passion, and I'm going to teach Zumba."[69] We ultimately learn that Engels has been successful at building her business and supporting her family not just financially but also, as her husband

4.3 Opening shot of YouTube video "Josette Tkacik's Zumba Story," featuring Tkacik riding on a horse to suggest a more rural, "authentic" American landscape.

4.4 Still from YouTube video "Josette Tkacik's Zumba Story." This image of Tkacik and her family roaming through wildflowers in the California hillside locates her in a rural place.

4.5 Still from opening sequence of YouTube video "Zumba Stories: Maggie Engels." Using this shot of a barn and silos (including one with an American flag) while Engels narrates that Nicholville, New York, is "simple" reinforces the associations between Americanness and rural landscapes.

describes, in "raising [their children] the way [they] wish to."[70] Images of Engels and her family, including several close-up shots of her kissing her toddler, reinforce this point. The video profile of Engels thus stresses family values and women's roles as caregivers even if Engels also works as a Zumba instructor. Therefore, just as the videos of Latinx men depict them as ideal immigrants, Engels is represented as the ideal American mother who does not require public assistance, but instead successfully balances a lucrative career with involved childrearing. That this takes place in rural America reinforces the notion that authentic Americanness is both rural and white.

Maggie Engels and Josette Tkacik de-emphasize monetary success. Although Engels supports her family, this was not what motivated her to pursue a career in Zumba Fitness. Instead, she freely chooses to leave her formal employment and make her way in Zumba Fitness, implying that she had enough economic support to take this risk. Tkacik explicitly minimizes the importance of money in her Zumba Fitness journey. She recalls, "When I started teaching in Santa Barbara, I had never planned on making tons of money. I just planned on maybe being able to move a little bit."[71] Tkacik describes the persistence it took to get her business off the ground, at one point facing potential cancellation because of poor attendance in her classes. But she mobilized her social media, offered free classes, and continued to develop relationships with students that substantially increased her audience and, subsequently, her revenue. Tkacik declares, "I am not the anomaly. Anyone can do this. For me I always say, 'I never planned this. I was just trying to walk.' . . . I never thought in a million years I would make six figures doing what I absolutely love to do."[72] Regardless of their original goals, the profiles of Engels and Tkacik both highlight the commitment and perseverance through adversity typical of the neoliberal philosophy of the American dream while upholding financial success and independence as the pinnacle of success.

Comparing the Zumba Stories of Latinx (im)migrant men like Henry Cedeño, Jhon Gonzalez, and Rony Gratereaut with those of American women like Maggie Engels and Josette Tkacik uncovers several key tropes in Zumba Fitness's selling of the American dream. On one hand, race and national origin distinguish these two groups in significant ways. Although all of them face obstacles, the women's obstacles primarily deal with health challenges. Cedeño, Gonzalez, and Gratereaut grapple instead with migration stories and adapting to life in a new country. Moreover, Gratereaut and Gonzalez in particular must overcome structural barriers like poverty to achieve their dreams. The stakes of their success differ substantially. Whereas Gratereaut and Gonzalez seek the safety, security, and financial means to support their families, Engels and Tkacik prioritize passion, joy, and family values. This difference marks Gratereaut, Cedeño, and Gonzalez as racial others vis-à-vis their American women counterparts who instead embody authentic, "simple," rural America. These differences make Gratereaut, Gonzalez, and Cedeño marketable for the Zumba Fitness brand. Like Beto Pérez, they embody "authentic" Latin American cultures through their immigration stories, which, in turn, imply their natural affinity for Latin dance. At the same time, their achievement of the American dream distances them from the negative stereotypes associated with the Latino Threat Narrative.

These narratives enable Zumba Fitness to capitalize on tropicalized Latinness as a culturally distinct phenomenon that is compatible with dominant US ideals of self-sufficiency, economic independence, and meritocracy. In this way, Zumba Fitness promotes the notion that the American dream is available to everyone, from rural white Americans to recently arrived Latin American immigrants, thus erasing institutional racism, xenophobia, and other forms of structural inequality. Beyond affiliating Zumba Fitness with the hegemonic ideology of the American dream, though, these stories are also marketing tools to attract new dues-paying Zumba instructors. The message is clear. Zumba Fitness gives their instructors everything they need to make it. If Beto Pérez can do it, anyone can. But whether the typical Zumba instructor, Latinx or not, can achieve similar financial success is another story.

DOES SHAKING YOUR MONEYMAKER MAKE YOU MONEY?

As the pandemic wore on, advertisements about becoming a Zumba instructor continuously popped up on my social media feeds. Amid extended shutdowns and rising unemployment, one ad started to appear more frequently. The question "Pandemic got you worried about your future?" flashed across my screen. According to this advertisement, becoming a Zumba instructor promised financial security in an uncertain world, all while having fun and receiving virtual support from experts and trainers in the Zumba Home Office.

This particular advertisement's reference to the pandemic struck me because of how blatantly it preyed upon people's fears about employment, financial security, and health during this tumultuous time. It also spoke to another jobs trend during the pandemic, what news pundits termed the "Great Resignation." Apparently, the pandemic had really shifted many people's priorities in life. News media frequently featured stories about people who quit jobs that seemed unfulfilling or that required too much time away from their true passions. Zumba instructors, however, made money doing something they loved, and even helped people along the way. Potential Zumba instructors could enjoy flexible work hours, be their own bosses, and prioritize what made them happy. Now they could even work from home, thus avoiding the possibility of contracting COVID-19 at work. What's more, Zumba Fitness would provide all the tools needed to jumpstart a brand-new career in fitness, even for those with no previous experience.

When Zumba Fitness touts that the company gives instructors "everything they need to be successful," the implication is that the company offers more than training to be a fitness instructor—it helps instructors start a small business. Zumba Fitness creates entrepreneurs, not just fitness instructors. This is the moral of Maggie Engels's Zumba Story. She quit her regular job to be her own boss, create her own schedule (giving her more family time), and follow her passions. But what exactly did Zumba Fitness offer Engels, and other instructors, so that they could be successful? Is what the company offers enough?

The Zumba Home Office grants individuals who complete their Zumba Basic 1 training a license that permits them to teach the Zumba Fitness format. At the time of this writing, the license from the Basic 1 training lasts six months.[73] However, the license will not expire as long as newly minted instructors join the Zumba Instructor Network (zin), which requires additional monthly dues payments that instructors reported to me cost about forty dollars per month. Of course, it is possible to take a Zumba Basic training without becoming an instructor. I have met several people who have taken Zumba Basic training simply because they are curious about the four core rhythms or want to learn how to do them "right." However, if anyone (trained or not) claims to teach Zumba Fitness without paying for a license, they can be subject to legal action. In fact, Zumba Fitness maintains a website called "Stop Party Crashers" where individuals can report anyone who they feel is an "illegal instructor."[74] Although joining the Zumba Instructor Network might at first appear optional, it is absolutely required for those who aim to have a career as a Zumba Fitness instructor.

In exchange for their monthly dues, zins receive access to new music and choreography, and an app that helps them organize their playlists and classes. The license gives instructors the legal permission to use Zumba Fitness's official branding materials like logos. The company provides zins with a personalized website to advertise their classes, and links their classes to the official Zumba Fitness website so potential students can find them when searching the company's website for a local class. zins receive discounts on things like Zumba Wear and the Zumba Cruise, and they have exclusive access to the Zumba Convention and Jam Sessions. Despite their exclusivity for dues-paying members, zins still pay extra fees to attend these special events. As I noted previously, many zins consider these extra training opportunities essential for their own professional development. The Zumba Convention is especially expensive, requiring travel to Orlando, Florida, in addition to the hefty registration fee. I met several instructors who never attended Convention because of the expense, and others for whom Convention was their primary vacation each year. Although Zumba Wear might also be considered optional, many instructors see it as crucial to their own self-branding. Virtually every ZIN whom I have met invests in these additional costs because they view things like Jam Sessions or Zumba Wear as absolutely necessary in order to have a successful career in Zumba Fitness.

There are other costs to having a successful Zumba Fitness career beyond what an instructor pays to the Zumba Home Office. One example is additional certifications. Many gyms require that instructors have a group fitness certification administered by the Athletics and Fitness Association of America (AFAA). Though ZIN members can receive a discount for this certification, Zumba Fitness does not cover the cost of enrolling in AFAA classes, taking exams, or maintaining certification. Similarly, ZINs are responsible for their own insurance and liability coverage, or they must negotiate this coverage with the gyms or organizations where they teach. Full-time fitness instructors often must purchase their own health insurance. Several instructors identified the need for health insurance as a particularly onerous barrier to teaching Zumba Fitness full-time. Many mentioned that one could only teach so many classes in a week without potentially harming themselves. Moreover, since their bodies are their livelihoods, a more substantial injury could seriously derail their careers and impact their income-earning potential. In this context, health insurance is even more important since their careers may put them in greater need of healthcare coverage. Many Zumba instructors I spoke with saw these things not as electives but rather as essential tools they needed to actually have a viable fitness career.

There is one more perhaps surprising thing that the Zumba Home Office does not help instructors find: a job. Once instructors have their license and join ZIN, they can access choreography and mentoring programs to help get their foot in the door. But, as many instructors told me, they are responsible for finding their own jobs. Local networking is absolutely essential for finding a Zumba class to teach. Some instructors begin by "subbing," or filling in for regular, established ZINs who need a substitute once in a while. As the new instructor increases her following, she might have the opportunity to have her own class at that gym.

Others look out for open auditions at local gyms and fitness centers. Auditioning usually involves teaching anywhere from one song to an entire class to a handful of people, or sometimes no one at all. Leah described the process of auditioning for major sports clubs like Lifetime, Boston Sports Club, or LA Fitness:

They have auditions like every few weeks, every month or something, and you have to book an audition, where you go in, and you usually have like five or six songs prepared. You do them, and the GroupX directors or the managers watch you teach, or they might have a group of their own staff there that you teach to. You might just be dancing by yourself or you might be teaching to a group. You never know. And they might stop you after, you know, a minute and a half into your first song and make their decision there, or they might have you do the entire thing. And sometimes they'll offer the job to you on the spot, and other times they'll get back to you later, or you'll never hear from them again, and then you'll have to reaudition, because they had forgotten about you, 'cause that's sometimes how fitness works.

Auditions can be intimidating, grueling, and time-consuming for instructors. Miriam described auditions she had attended where she acted as a student for other auditioning instructors who taught a variety of fitness formats such as Tabata or kickboxing. She said it was a "few hours of auditioning, and then once it gets to your time to audition, you're exhausted because you've been doing all this cardio, and then you have to give it your 100 percent." Being high energy and overly enthusiastic is critical for a successful audition, especially given Leah's arguments that sometimes zins do not even have the chance to perform an entire routine for potential employers. Given this imperative, Miriam's experience shows just how exhausting auditions can be. However, if successful, teaching in an established gym can substantially increase an instructor's profile, student base, and earnings.

Other instructors cold-call facilities to see if they are looking for Zumba Fitness instructors, especially if they are not tapped into local fitness networks already. Julia describes herself as an "aggressive" jobseeker. She regularly calls gyms and rec centers in her area to see if they have openings for Zumba instructors. Some instructors whom I met considered obtaining their first job as pure luck. One instructor posted on Facebook that she had obtained her license and was looking for a class. By chance, an acquaintance who owned a fitness center needed a Zumba instructor and immediately hired her. Another instructor got her first regular class when a parent from her child's school just happened to staff the front desk of her local rec center on the day that she went in to inquire about openings for a Zumba instructor. Being in the right place at the right time is critical for many of these instructors to get their first jobs.

Another common strategy that instructors use to obtain a regular Zumba Fitness class is to take on unpaid classes in order to establish themselves and become competitive for future jobs. One instructor worked as a journalist. When on assignment at a local gym, she asked if they needed an instructor. The gym could not pay her, but she jumped at the opportunity because, as she said, "I needed a class." From there, this instructor became more integrated into the local Zumba Fitness community, eventually meeting someone at an exclusive ZIN event who hired her for her first paid job. While taking on unpaid positions might make Zumba instructors more competitive applicants in the future, it also means that they are paying Zumba Fitness dues and certification fees without earning any income. The time and energy they spend teaching without compensation can be interpreted as yet another type of investment in their business since it requires that they operate in the red for a while.

Other instructors distinguish themselves from the competition by pursuing certifications in additional formats. When Paula had little success getting a regular Zumba class, she decided to teach Zumba Gold and Aqua Zumba. She believed adding these formats expanded her reach and limited her competition; indeed, Paula reported that her swift procurement of a regular Aqua Zumba class confirmed her suspicions that teaching Zumba Basic was simply too competitive. On the other hand, some instructors believed adding new Zumba formats was, essentially, a waste of time. Erin obtained certifications in four Zumba formats, but she only teaches Zumba Basic because there is "not really a market" for formats like Zumba Kids or Zumba Toning. Julia felt that "invest[ing] in any other format" would not be financially beneficial. She said, "I don't think it'll fly in the area we're in. We're suburban. We have gyms in every corner. They offer so many classes that it doesn't make sense for me to do anything else at this moment." Paying for additional certifications may or may not lead to a higher income as a fitness instructor depending on many factors outside of ZINS' control.

Despite the fact that Zumba instructors pay money to the Zumba Fitness company in order to teach classes, Zumba Fitness is not a multilevel marketing company like Herbalife or Avon. Instructors are not compensated for recruiting other Zumba instructors. In fact, recruiting new instructors might actually harm ZINS' bottom line given the "saturation" of the Zumba Fitness market in the Boston area that so many of them described. Instead, Zumba Fitness's financial model is similar to other fitness programs such as CrossFit, where the owners of CrossFit boxes (or studios) pay the CrossFit corporate office for a license to teach CrossFit and to use the brand's logo and materials. Other dance-fitness programs like Nia or BollyX similarly require potential instructors to pay for a training and, subsequently, monthly fees to maintain a license to teach.[75] Still, such business models do not necessarily benefit fitness instructors. I learned that many instructors pay so many fees to Zumba Fitness in order to teach that they often just break even. One instructor told me, "I think Zumba instructors should actually make money. That's what I think. And some don't. Some are operating in the negative, which is not sustainable for them and their families. Still others get so much benefit out of teaching that they don't mind." Although she conceded that some instructors do make most of their income from Zumba Fitness, this particular instructor, who combined teaching three classes per week with a high-paying full-time job, expressed concern that for many instructors, Zumba Fitness was actually costly.

Julia agreed. When I asked her whether one could make a living wage from teaching Zumba Fitness alone, Julia said, "Probably not." Julia worked full-time at a local small business. She noted that even if she were a full-time Zumba Fitness instructor, "I would probably get licensed in other things, because there's just not enough money." This was the case for Amber, who had worked in fitness for twenty years prior to teaching Zumba Fitness. Amber mentioned, "I have seen so many fitness trends come and go, and I kind of thought that Zumba was going to be one of those, so I just put it off to the side. I didn't really pay much attention to it. But, then I heard it come up, and then I was seeing it grow, and thought, I'm going to go ahead and get my license." Amber incorporated Zumba Fitness into an already-established fitness career. Miriam similarly combines teaching five different Zumba classes a week in three different formats with teaching yoga and other types of aerobics classes. Both Miriam and Amber exemplify Julia's comments that one must be fully immersed in the fitness industry to really make a living with Zumba Fitness.

The vast majority of ZINS whom I met over the course of my research had other full-time jobs in industries such as finance, healthcare, and education. The few exceptions included stay-at-home moms, who often had wealthy partners, and those who moved up the Zumba Fitness ladder to become Zumba Jammers, Zumba Education Specialists, and International Presenters. ZINS with other full-time jobs often commented that they had reached a point where they were taking so many Zumba Fitness classes, they figured they might as well get paid for it. Many of these women saw teaching Zumba Fitness as more of a hobby than an actual career option.

Still, I met several instructors who saw Zumba Fitness as a viable career option, even if they also held other full-time jobs. When I asked Erin if it were possible to have Zumba Fitness as one's main source of income, she responded, "Anything's possible! I don't view it as a hobby. I view it as I have two careers. I have a career in the corporate sector, and I have a career in fitness. What you do with that career is up to you. Whether you treat it as a career or a hobby, that's up to you. It's possible. It's just finding a way to make it happen." Erin is profoundly dedicated to Zumba Fitness, including activities outside of her regular classes. She has certifications in several formats, and she regularly volunteers to organize local Zumba Fitness fundraisers and events. Her approach to Zumba Fitness as a career just as worthy or significant as her career in the corporate world implies that Zumba Fitness could be financially viable if people were dedicated to it. Paula, who also worked in the corporate sector, agreed: "As an instructor, your business is to teach. If you want to do it 24/7, or if you want to teach for a couple of hours a day, or a full-time job. So, you have to choose to do whatever you want with it." Rebecca noted that sports clubs "vet their instructors pretty carefully. . . . The cream will float to the top. So you do have a lot of people who get their licenses, but stay sort of relegated to sub lists or struggle to secure classes because they just don't have the teaching skills." All of these comments reiterate the Zumba Home Office's assertion that someone who works hard enough and takes advantage of all of the support that the company offers can make it as a full-time instructor.

Despite Zumba Fitness's claims that anyone can become a successful entrepreneur with the program, the reality on the ground is that many instructors encounter significant challenges to their ability to earn a viable income with Zumba Fitness alone. These limitations do not stem from a lack of will, perseverance, commitment, or innate skill. Instead, they reflect much broader structural issues facing entrepreneurs more generally, like access to start-up funds, professional networks, and other resources. Though Zumba Fitness provides ZINs with some essential tools like choreography, these tools are ultimately useless if instructors cannot find adequate employment. In this context, the advertisement I saw claiming that becoming a Zumba instructor could offer financial security in precarious times made me especially uncomfortable. On the surface, the promise of a job one can do on their own terms with only a one-day training to earn the appropriate credentials seems a lifesaver in the context of a raging pandemic where people lost jobs or could not leave their homes. But for many would-be instructors, this is simply a dream.

DREAMS VERSUS REALITY

About one year prior to the start of the pandemic, I visited Vicki's regular weekend Zumba Fitness class at a sports club in a rural Massachusetts town. I had arrived ten minutes early, but I could barely find a spot in the back of the room. There must have been fifty people there. Vicki has worked hard to cultivate a following of Zumba students. She invests tremendous time and energy into developing choreography for her classes, attending Jam Sessions and Convention, mentoring new instructors, and organizing Zumba-related events. She told me that becoming an instructor "makes business sense. It's a part-time job. I teach four times a week. I get paid decent money to spend an hour working out. You do have to pay Zumba dues. Once a month, we pay Zumba a fee. One class once a week pays for my Zumba fee for the entire month. So, in the grand scheme of things, I'm still making money from this."

Vicki fits the typical profile of a successful Zumba instructor more than people like Beto Pérez, Rony Gratereaut, or Josette Tkacik. She is a model instructor who has, indeed, taken advantage of all of the tools Zumba Fitness offers her for success. Vicki's dedication has paid off, but she still does not rely on Zumba Fitness for her sole income. Instead, Zumba Fitness provides her with supplementary income to pay for things like her kids' extracurricular activities or her family vacations. In this way, Zumba Fitness enhances Vicki's quality of life, but it does not earn her enough to cover her basic needs. By all accounts, Vicki has a very successful Zumba Fitness career, but it is still nowhere near the six-figure salary that Alberto Perlman claimed was possible in Zumba Fitness.

Zumba instructors might be entrepreneurs, but they are also the primary consumers of the Zumba Fitness brand. They buy clothes, go to events, and, most importantly, pay dues. All of these things add up. Regardless of whether or not Zumba instructors saw Zumba Fitness as a lucrative career option, almost none of the women I interviewed for this project used Zumba Fitness as their primary source of income, even if they wanted to. This reveals a fundamental limitation of how the Zumba Fitness corporation sells dreams to instructors. The dream may be achievable, but only for a select few. These few already have time and money to invest in their business. They already have networks that can help them secure their first jobs. Many instructors I spoke with, especially those who come from white, upper-middle-class suburbs, describe these challenges as more of a nuisance than anything else. They share more with Maggie Engels, who had the financial means and familial support to follow her dreams, than with Beto Pérez, who struggled with undocumented immigration status, homelessness, and other structural barriers.

If the average instructor does not have the same type of experience as Pérez, then why are his and other comparable immigration stories so central to selling dreams in Zumba Fitness? Selling dreams is not only a marketing ploy to attract potential dues-paying ZINs. Selling dreams also helps cement Zumba Fitness's connections to tropicalized Latinness. The stories of people like Rony Gratereaut, Jhon Gonzalez, and, especially, Beto Pérez portray them as ideal immigrants who arrived to the United States, sometimes without papers, knowledge of English, or money to support themselves. These characteristics make someone like Beto Pérez the embodiment of the Latino Threat—a potentially unassimilable and financially needy Latin American immigrant. However, framed through Zumba Fitness's trope of dreams, Pérez and others overcome these obstacles to become successful and, even more importantly, financially independent of the state. Through achieving the American dream, figures like Beto Pérez maintain their cultural distinction while still conforming to the neoliberal ideals of US life. Their success renders them ideal immigrants who are job creators, business innovators, and economic contributors to US society.

The COVID-19 pandemic did not kill Zumba Fitness. Instead, the company adapted its business strategy to incorporate digital platforms for instructor training and teaching, while marketing itself as an easy, fun, and lucrative career option for those who may have lost their jobs or were unable to leave their homes for regular employment. Although Alberto Perlman presents the company's approach to COVID as almost altruistic, the reality is that the company needed ZINs to keep paying dues, buying merchandise, and attending special events in order to maintain its business model. The problem here is not necessarily the business model itself. Instead, the problem happens when Zumba Fitness promotes its company as a way for downtrodden individuals to easily and quickly achieve financial success. The reality reported by many instructors is that actually earning a living with Zumba Fitness is not that different from other small businesses; one must have time, energy, and capital to invest in their business. While Zumba Fitness might guide people through the program's cultural elements, it does little to help ZINS obtain steady employment that enables them to earn a profit. This is what one instructor told me was the "underbelly" of Zumba Fitness.

Of course, this contradiction between experiences on the ground and the promises peddled by Zumba Fitness is not actually unique to the brand. Other business models and programs, such as buying into franchises or multilevel marketing programs, also promise participants the opportunity to run their own business with relatively little help or preparation. What makes Zumba Fitness unique, however, is how the brand incorporates this financial success into tropicalized Latinness. This reproduces hierarchies of value wherein only those immigrants who achieve the American dream can actively participate in and contribute to US life and culture. At the same time, this financial success requires an embrace of the racial stereotypes associated with tropicalized Latinness. Consequently, the problem with Zumba Fitness's selling dreams extends beyond the company's reliance on instructors as its main consumer base. Selling dreams eliminates any acknowledgment of systemic racism while commodifying racial stereotypes that continuously render Latinx people as foreign, exotic counterpoints to the allegedly more modern white US American. In this way, Zumba Fitness exemplifies the complex and often contradictory intersections of race, citizenship, and neoliberalism that are part and parcel of the American dream.

SELLING LOVE

HURRICANE MARÍA DEVASTATED PUERTO RICO in September 2017. The Category 4 storm, one of the worst in the island's history, left behind massive destruction that resulted in an estimated 4,645 deaths. Some of these occurred long after the storm due to lack of healthcare services, life-saving medications, and electricity (in some areas, for an entire year) to power essential things like oxygen tanks and refrigeration. The storm and its aftermath laid bare the inadequacies of the US government's readiness to respond to such natural disasters and confirmed the inequalities and racial biases inherent to the colonial relationship between Puerto Rico and the United States. Individuals and charitable organizations sought to fill in the gaps left by FEMA's lackluster response.[1]

Zumba Fitness was among the numerous organizations that contributed to Puerto Rico's disaster relief. The company "partnered with [reggaetón singer] Daddy Yankee and Feed America, an organization dedicated to fighting hunger in the US, to provide food and relief items to those in immediate need on the island."[2] The Zumba Home Office also worked with ZINS and ZESES to distribute aid to ZINS living in Puerto Rico.[3] Across the United States, individual instructors hosted Zumbathons to raise funds for Hurricane María relief. Zumba Fitness defines Zumbathons as a "Zumba dance-fitness party for a cause! These events are open to the public and raise funds and awareness for a selected charity, organization, individual or community in need."[4] Zumba instructors organize Zumbathons in their own communities for causes that they select.

In November 2017, I attended a Zumbathon organized by Zumba instructors in the Boston area to raise funds for hurricane relief. I entered a public school gym, which was adorned with Puerto Rican flags. Many attendees also wore clothes with the flag or the words "Puerto Rico" emblazoned across the front. Some even had Puerto Rican flag shirts with the official Zumba Fitness logo (I don't know if the Zumba Home Office created this shirt to raise funds, or if instructors acquired it some other way). Another popular clothing item was the "Spread Love" baseball cap. Joshua Saadi of the Polo Spreads Love organization produces these hats, which are typically black with the words "Spread Love" on the front in different colors, in order to raise money for health-related causes.[5] In this case, several participants wore Spread Love hats with the Puerto Rican flag embroidered on the side. Organizers offered free snacks and water. Participants could buy raffle tickets for donated goods and other services from local vendors. I had a lot of fun at the two-hour Zumbathon. I appreciated that my twenty-dollar entry fee would go to support Puerto Ricans on the island, a cause that directly impacted my own friends and family, and that I could get a good workout in the process.

This was an exemplary Zumba charity event—an event organized by local instructors for a cause that already had widespread public support, especially in Massachusetts, a state with a substantial Puerto Rican population. Zumbathons such as this one epitomize the final trope used to sell tropicalized Latinness in Zumba Fitness—love. Selling love in Zumba Fitness involves working on or modifying the self in service of others. The discourses of multiculturalism infused into the Zumba Fitness brand and marketing strategy promote love of the other—those culturally unlike the average (presumably white American) Zumba participant often due to their Latin American heritage. Thus, the individual who takes Zumba Fitness classes works both mind and body, increasing cultural tolerance and appreciation alongside their own physical fitness and happiness. In this instance, the Zumbathon gathered together local instructors and Zumba enthusiasts seeking to raise funds for a place with significance on both the local level (given the large Puerto Rican population in the area) and in Zumba Fitness more broadly (since Puerto Rico is critical to the development of core rhythms like salsa and reggaetón).

Like most aspects of Zumba Fitness, selling love does not appear to be problematic, at least on the surface. Increasing one's self-confidence and health, fostering intercultural appreciation, and helping those less fortunate are all laudable goals. However, such goals center individual, profit-driven mechanisms to address deep-seated social problems. These neoliberal projects bolster discourses of postracialism and postfeminism that declare systemic racism and patriarchy, respectively, relics of the

5.1 Selling "Spread Love" gear from the Polo Spreads Love organization at a Zumbathon in the Boston area in 2017. Photograph by the author.

past.[6] Instead, work on the self—improving one's physical fitness and mental outlook and providing service to others—is promoted as the way to help make a more just and equal society.[7]

Furthermore, selling love reinforces many of the dictates of health-related charity events wherein individuals pay money to exercise and support a charitable cause. In turn, these events, like other health-related charity "-thons," reproduce neoliberal ideals that equate health with good citizenship while also relying on private funds rather than the state to provide social safety nets.[8] Zumbathons promote the trope of love by offering spaces for Zumba Fitness enthusiasts to financially support causes they care about without addressing, let alone committing to, any type of structural change. In this context, spreading love becomes a commodity accessed through one's dedication to the Zumba Fitness brand. The discourse of love that permeates the Zumba Fitness brand is deeply rooted in the assumption that one can make the world a better place if she just loved hard enough, accepting herself and others no matter how different they might be.

But there are limits to this type of love. In addition to reproducing neoliberal ideologies of self-help, selling love also adopts a postracial approach to race relations. Postracialism acknowledges racial difference while simultaneously dismissing the significance of systemic racism. In this case, the trope of love entails the acknowledgment of tropicalized Latinness as a defining feature of the Zumba Fitness program while ignoring systemic racism, xenophobia, and stereotypes embedded within Zumba Fitness (and society at large).

Selling love thus differs from some of the other tropes that form part of Zumba Fitness's brand culture. On one hand, selling love involves Zumba Fitness's general commitment to multicultural tolerance. On the other, this love renders the cultural difference of tropicalized Latinness inconsequential, much like how selling dreams obscures the structural barriers and racial inequality facing Latinx immigrants. Selling love's simultaneous recognition and disavowal of tropicalized Latinness reflects a fundamental contradiction in the Zumba Fitness brand that enables Zumba Fitness to capitalize on difference in times of racial strife without having to take any explicit position on controversial issues like immigration (unless it becomes expedient to do so). This chapter details how this contradiction manifests through the trope of love in Zumba Fitness, which ultimately serves to tamp down attempts at structural changes that might upend the racial status quo. For instance, Zumbathons reproduce the link between citizenship and health while distancing the brand from contro-versial topics like anti-Black racism or immigration policy. Zumba's "love songs" further this distancing from controversial topics by instead fore-grounding inspirational messages that promote diversity and multicul-turalism typical of postracial rhetoric. But what is the effect of this love? Does selling love actually impact people's thinking about cultural differ-ence? While some instructors try to use Zumba Fitness to address issues like racism, most of the time they perceive Zumba Fitness as a program that exposes people to new cultures more than one that changes people's hearts and minds. The trope of love thus plays a critical role in neutral-izing tropicalized Latinness and distinguishing it from the Latino Threat Narrative by promoting postracial discourses that declare racism a thing of the past. Consequently, experiencing tropicalized Latinness becomes one way that Zumba enthusiasts can demonstrate their love of self, love of others, and commitment to social change.

LOVE IN POSTRACIAL PARADISE

Roopali Mukherjee, Sarah Banet-Weiser, and Herman Gray call post-racialism *"the* racial project of our time" (emphasis in original).[9] In the post–civil rights era, terms like colorblindness or multiculturalism sur-faced to call attention to the presumably more racially egalitarian society that followed the end of Jim Crow segregation. For example, colorblind-ness posits that racial difference is meaningless. However, as Eduardo Bonilla-Silva has so clearly demonstrated, colorblindness only further entrenches systemic racism in US social institutions.[10] Jodi Melamed argues that multiculturalism enables the incorporation of certain non-white figures into elite society as evidence that neoliberal policies work for everyone, thus ignoring ongoing systemic racism.[11] In this context, antiracism becomes part of the official stance on race relations in the United States.[12]

Neoliberal multiculturalism enables postracialism to thrive. Roopali Mukherjee notes that "post-race [*sic*] necessitates the recognition and, indeed, explicit avowal of some racial differences deployed as evidence of the declining significance of race in the life chances and experiences of whites as well as non-whites."[13] In this context, racism is understood as a thing of the past, and racial and ethnic difference are seen as desirable and commodifiable within the multicultural marketplace. Perhaps this is best exemplified by the election of President Barack Obama in 2008, which led to many people declaring the end of racism precisely because they recognized Obama as Black. In this way, postracialism furthers neoliberal multiculturalism's dismissal of systemic racism as no longer a concern. If racism has been overcome, postrace claims that ongoing racism is simply the work of a few individuals, and that contemporary US society embraces difference and rejects structural hierarchies or exclusions.

Popular culture is one site where postracial ideologies come to the fore. Racial difference becomes rendered a marketable commodity that does not disrupt racist or white supremacist logics. Instead, despite appearing to be inclusive, these postracial forms of representation actually maintain exclusionary systems grounded in racist logics.[14] If tropes like fiesta, fun, and authenticity work to naturalize tropicalized Latinness then the trope of love neutralizes tropicalized Latinness's racist underpinnings. The perception of tropicalized Latinness as fundamentally distinct from US Americanness both reproduces racial stereotypes *and* makes the Zumba Fitness brand unique within the postracial marketplace. In true postracial fashion, selling love in Zumba Fitness entails highlighting and even celebrating tropicalized Latinness while insidiously obscuring systemic racism. And so, as Herman Gray notes of the idea of postrace more generally, the trope of love actually "provides cover for cultural styles of racism where quotidian ideas of racial tolerance and inclusion thrive, where racism does not need racists and is communicated in the form of codes."[15] In the case of Zumba Fitness, the tropes of authenticity, fiesta, and fun serve as codes that communicate the ongoing stereotypes of hypersexuality, foreignness, and otherness of Latinness, but they are couched within the seemingly positive rhetoric of cultural tolerance and appreciation. As a result, the trope of love renders tropicalized Latinness an acceptable representation of Latin(x) American culture without disrupting and, in fact, strengthening the status quo.

Since the trope of love reproduces postracial assertions that racism is now the work of a "few bad apples," one's participation in Zumba Fitness can reflect one's commitment to antiracism. Just as a membership to a gym or sports club conveys one's dedication to health and wellness, consuming products from companies that support various social causes can display a consumer's values as well. This "commodity activism" leads to "rituals of consumption increasingly stand[ing] in for other modes of democratic engagement."[16] Consumers are encouraged to support companies that profess to make the world a better place, and companies aim to "align themselves with social causes that bolster their reputations as good citizens."[17] In the case of Zumba Fitness, selling love gives the company an image of a culturally sensitive and racially inclusive organization, even as it peddles racist stereotypes.

Sarah Banet-Weiser's concept of "brand cultures" is especially useful here. Banet-Weiser argues that branding has shifted from merely marketing to brand cultures that involve "cultural contexts for everyday living, individual identities, and affective relationships."[18] Brand cultures foster communities of individuals who imagine themselves as dedicated not exclusively to a product, but rather to a set of values, morals, and ideas.[19] Fitness programs can be especially fruitful sites for the development and promotion of brand cultures. Devon Powers and DM Greenwell argue that fitness programs such as Bikram Yoga or CrossFit (and, I'd add, Zumba Fitness) are forms of "branded fitness" wherein participants "frequently enjoy strong community," and sometimes become "proselytes engaged in a 'way of life' that warrants substantial time, social, and financial investment."[20] In turn, they write, "Fitness can act as a marker of status, a form of social capital, and a way to invest (and communicate investment) in one's well-being. It is, in short, an element of one's personal brand, and also a brand itself."[21] Powers and Greenwell detail how the modification of the body becomes both the product and the brand in branded fitness. Moreover, many kinds of branded fitness involve not only fitness but also social and political ideals. So, for example, one could showcase their body and their patriotism in CrossFit, or, their body and their cultural appreciation and open-mindedness through Zumba Fitness.

Commodity activism thus becomes one way that participants in Zumba Fitness can demonstrate their commitment to antiracism, civic engagement, and multicultural appreciation. Zumba Fitness's messages of love, acceptance, and corporate social responsibility give the impression of contributing to efforts to combat inequality, but do little, if anything, to actually encourage structural changes. Selling love is critical to this process. First, selling love reproduces the idea that consumer activism and individuals' charitable actions are the most effective strategies for sparking social change. Second, selling love entails embracing and celebrating cultural differences. As perhaps the most fundamental characteristic of Zumba Fitness's brand culture, selling love ostensibly brings people together who are interested in engaging with different cultures, people, and worldviews. Selling love, then, commodifies a set of values like joy, acceptance, fun, and care as central aspects of Zumba's brand culture. In so doing, selling love obscures the racial and imperial underpinnings of tropicalized Latinness both in its emphasis on individual action as the key to social change and in its reiteration of racial stereotypes. Instead, consuming tropicalized Latinness via Zumba Fitness serves as evidence of one's cosmopolitanism and cultural appreciation.

DANCE FOR A CAUSE

Fittingly, Zumba Fitness calls the charitable arm of the company "Zumba Love," which raises funds for a variety of charitable causes. More often than not, these causes are health-related, with funds donated to various organizations tackling complex and common diseases like heart disease or cancer. Zumba Fitness often implies that their charity efforts are part of a broader communal effort. For example, in 2012, Zumba Fitness touted the power of a "global network of instructors" who could "encourage 12 million Zumba enthusiasts worldwide to 'join the party' in support of great causes."[22] Despite the community-oriented language, most Zumba Fitness charitable efforts, especially Zumbathons, ultimately rely upon *individual* efforts to raise money for charity.

The Zumba Home Office regularly praises the "global network of instructors" for contributing to its charitable causes. And rightly so. It is a tremendous amount of labor to put together a Zumbathon. Organizers must recruit a set of instructors to teach the class, secure a space (especially if they do not own their own studio, which was the case for most of the instructors whom I spoke with), find cosponsors, advertise to the local community, and enlist people to man doors, hand out snacks, and do other more menial tasks the day of the event. According to the company's website, Zumba Fitness does not actively promote anyone's event. However, zins can use the company's online platform to list their Zumbathon so that when people search for activities in their local area, it will appear. Zumba Fitness's legal team reviews and approves Zumbathon announcements (along with other events) prior to posting them on the company's website.[23] But putting one's event on the Zumba Fitness official website is only one very small part of organizing Zumbathons, and it is not necessarily the most effective publicity. I rarely find out about Zumbathons by looking them up on the company's website. Instead, I receive advertisements in email newsletters, or see flyers circulating on social media platforms. Sometimes I hear about Zumbathons from instructors who invite their classes to attend. Zumbathons attract local Zumba enthusiasts, and so advertising through the networks already established in that area via social media or word of mouth seems to be as useful an advertising strategy, if not more so, than being included in a vast online database of international Zumba Fitness–related events.

Much like how the Zumba Home Office does not help local instructors find jobs, the company also does not seem to offer much logistical support for managing Zumbathons. No instructors relayed to me anything about the Zumba Home Office contributing to their organizing efforts. Instead, they all mentioned how much extra time and hard work it took to pull off a successful Zumbathon. I met Julia at a Zumbathon. During the event, she not only taught a portion of the class, but she also appeared to me to be an organizer—replacing snacks when they ran out, taking tickets at the door, and checking in with local vendors. From my perspective as an attendee, Julia appeared actively involved in every aspect of the Zumbathon. But she seemed surprised when I mentioned that to her. Julia explained that, actually, she had not taken the lead on the event, but was invited to participate by another Zumba instructor she knows. "Oh my God, it was so much work," she explained. "I kind of got thrown into it. It was extremely overwhelming. So it got me very nervous. I would never do that on my own." Another instructor described the "pressure" she feels to contribute to charity events. She helped organize an annual Zumbathon for a health-related cause. Her role involved advertising and recruiting participants. "I get a lot of pressure to get ZINS to come to things," she explained. Zumbathons need to attract enough participants to cover costs with more to spare in order to be effective fundraisers. In addition to recruiting attendees, instructors who teach at Zumbathons must coordinate with each other to create playlists, plan routines, and make sure everything goes smoothly. Zumba instructors like Julia put in a tremendous amount of uncompensated time and labor to host successful Zumbathons with little, if any, support from the Zumba Home Office.

And yet, the Zumba Fitness corporation receives a lot of praise from instructors and the media alike for its charitable giving. For example, in a promotional video for its "Zumba Love, philanthropic platform," Zumba Fitness claims that in "11 years, 1000's [sic] of Zumbathon Charity Events, you raised more than $7,500,000."[24] The "you" here is presumably ZINS.

Still, reporting the cumulative amount of money raised by ZINs implies that the Zumba Home Office has taken on a more comprehensive role in these fundraising efforts.

Moreover, the types of charities that Zumba Love highlights have historically prioritized noncontroversial, health-related causes. Zumba Fitness has raised funds for heart disease, ALS, and childhood obesity. Zumba Fitness focuses most intently on raising money for breast cancer. The company has long partnered with the Susan G. Komen for the Cure to raise money for the Zumba Global Research Grant for Breast Cancer Prevention. In fact, Zumba Fitness launched the "Party in Pink" movement in 2010 in order to directly link their fundraising efforts to breast cancer. In 2011, Zumba Fitness reported that 30 percent of Party in Pink Zumba Wear profits would be donated to Susan G. Komen for the Cure along with 75 percent of ticket sales for Zumbathon events.[25] Over the years, successful Party in Pink campaigns have raised several million dollars for breast cancer research.

To accompany its 2015 Party in Pink campaign, Zumba Fitness created a music video to the song "Dance 'Til You Feel Better!" that featured Beto Pérez alongside "Zumba instructors and breast cancer warriors Paula, Jocelyn, Carla, and Helen."[26] One of these women, Jocelyn, was also profiled in a Zumba Story video called "Jocelyn's Persistence Saved Her Life." ZIN Jocelyn recalls how her doctor found an abnormality during a routine breast exam. She had a biopsy and subsequently traveled to Los Angeles to attend a Zumba instructor conference. While she was "literally putting on [her] Zumba clothes," her doctor called to inform her that she had a positive cancer diagnosis. Rather than wallow alone in her room, Jocelyn picked herself up and attended a three-day Zumba Fitness event, where she met another instructor, Diane, who had "danced her way" through cancer treatments. The video ends with Jocelyn saying that she hoped her story would encourage women to seek adequate medical treatment.[27] Jocelyn's profile is fairly typical of most of the breast cancer survivors featured in Zumba Fitness's breast cancer awareness materials. In each case, the overall message is that Zumba Fitness restored their happiness, gave them meaning, and fostered community that supported them through their treatment. Indeed, Leah told me that she saw Zumba Fitness's promotion of happiness as "another reason why Zumba's so involved with fundraising for breast cancer research, because so many people come to [Zumba Fitness] when they're at the most difficult times.

A lot of these women have come to it once they've been diagnosed, or even when they're in treatment, or when they're recovering, and it gives people a place to go and be happy."

My purpose here is not to ridicule those individuals who find meaning and support in Zumba Fitness to get them through a health crisis like breast cancer. Rather, I aim to call attention to the ways that Zumba Fitness presents its program as a key element of patients' recovery through promoting happiness, individual drive, and a positive outlook. The emphasis on one's attitude as a part of cancer recovery puts the onus on the afflicted individual, as if one's level of happiness directly correlates to their ability to be cured. Once again, the myriad structural barriers to healthcare are obscured in favor of a more individualistic attitude toward overcoming adversity.

Several instructors told me that they believed Zumba Fitness encouraged them to do charity events. Julia recalled that breast cancer awareness is "something they talk about at Convention. They have somebody from Dana Farber [Cancer Institute] come in. They talk about all the money that we raise through Zumbathons throughout the world, not just the US. They're everywhere. It's a huge platform." It is laudable that Zumba Home Office uses its platform to raise awareness about breast cancer, which undoubtedly impacts many Zumba enthusiasts. At the same time, though, the type of presentation that Julia describes once again places the responsibility for fundraising on individual instructors while simultaneously representing their work as part of a bigger, communal fundraising goal.

The trope of love brings together individuals in a community but also enables them to express their care for others through their own charitable giving. This move helps integrate the trope of love within Zumba Fitness's brand culture. On the individual level, someone who organizes or contributes to a Zumbathon can brand themselves as a person who cares about breast cancer research, and who strives to help others. The larger Zumba Fitness brand also embraces these qualities as key to its ethos. In other words, expressing care for others through such neoliberal charitable initiatives exemplifies the type of corporate social responsibility that Banet-Weiser notes "is not the logic of social justice, or what a corporation might do beyond the confines of its own bottom line to create a more equitable market. Rather, the logic of CSR [corporate social responsibility] is about the various ways in which a corporation's support of social issues—be they sweat-free labor, the environment, or fundraising for AIDS or breast cancer research—can build the corporation's brand and thus bring in more revenue and profit."[28] Zumbathons for breast cancer also avoid political risks. Breast cancer is a relatively innocuous cause. Few would quibble with the importance of finding a cure for such a common and devastating disease. As Banet-Weiser posits, "CSR campaigns tend to attach to politics that are legible in brand vocabulary, are palatable to an audience of consumer citizens, and are uncontested as socially important issues."[29] Breast cancer research fits squarely within the Zumba Fitness brand, from the convenient alliteration of its "Party in Pink" slogan to the fact that breast cancer disproportionately affects women, especially those who are middle-aged or older, who make up a significant proportion of Zumba Fitness's audience. The emphasis on breast cancer avoids any overt political stakes that might play a role in healthcare or any other social inequities. Instead, Party in Pink and other Zumbathon-style fundraising efforts center individualistic efforts to tackling problems that already have widespread support as *the* most effective way to spread the Zumba love.

Although tropicalized Latinness forms the crux of the Zumba Fitness brand, it remains conspicuously absent in the trope of love. Instead, the trope of love assumes that everyone has equal resources and opportunities to make healthy choices and, therefore, become a productive citizen. Health-related charities of all kinds align with the dominant, yet often unspoken, assumption that health is an individual choice. As Samantha King writes, "As self-responsibility for health has come to figure prominently in measures of proper citizenship, and as consumer-oriented philanthropy has become the preferred mode through which to demonstrate responsibility to others, physical activity-based fundraisers represent a potent site for the celebration and recirculation of dominant norms and values."[30] Party in Pink thus helps integrate dominant notions of healthism and neoliberal charity into the Zumba Fitness brand while, in true postracial fashion, avoiding any acknowledgment of systemic inequality or discrimination.

Although the trope of love more broadly neglects discussions of racial inequality, some instructors actively sought opportunities to address these issues in their fundraising efforts. Morgan told me that she wanted to raise money for causes pertinent to the Black and Latinx communities who created many of Zumba Fitness's rhythms. She explained, "The president [Donald Trump] is talking about building this wall. So what is our responsibility as instructors in this moment?" Rather than health-related causes like breast cancer, Morgan wanted to address systemic racism and inequality. At one point, Morgan proposed to raise funds for activists who were jailed after protesting Confederate statues in the US South. In 2015, Bree Newsome Bass climbed a flagpole in front of the South Carolina state capitol and tore down a Confederate flag to protest a white supremacist's murder of nine African American worshippers at an AME church in Charleston. Inspired by that action, Morgan said, "I thought, well, wouldn't it be great to use our bodies the way that Bree Newsome used her body to go and pull down that flag? We could use our bodies to do this stuff. And they were like, well, that's a little political, but you can raise money for love in general." Morgan did not clarify who "they" were; it could be the gym where she worked, or the Zumba Home Office itself, which, as I mentioned earlier, must approve requests to host a Zumbathon. Regardless, the message that Morgan received is that no official Zumba Fitness events could raise funds for something so overtly "political"; instead she could only organize around the significantly more vague and innocuous idea of "love in general."

It is no accident that Zumba Fitness as a larger brand did not explicitly address anti-Black racism, xenophobia, and homophobia until 2021.[31] In the wake of the Black Lives Matter protests against the killing of George Floyd, companies from Amazon to L'Oreal suddenly made explicit statements about their support for racial and social justice. Zumba Fitness joined the fray. The Zumba Home Office launched a new version of the Zumba Love online platform. The new Zumba Love website includes resources and, especially, recommendations for those who would like to donate to charitable causes related to social justice initiatives such as Black Lives Matter, Stop Asian Hate, or Juneteenth that all emerged in the wake of hypervisible violent attacks against Black and Asian Americans during the Trump administration and the COVID-19 pandemic. The statement begins, "Every Zumba class is not only a place of celebration, but also inclusivity. Where happiness is not only a priority, but a right."[32] This statement diminishes the systemic nature of racism faced by Asian Americans and African Americans by promoting the idea that happiness and the right to party are the keys to dismantling inequality. In a similar vein, an August 2022 promotional video for Zumba Love features people across the world dancing and "moving for change every single day." The video continues by listing the types of causes that Zumba Fitness instructors have supported. These include the typical health-related issues such as breast cancer, autism, Alzheimer's, and childhood obesity. But they also list an array of heritage months and days such as "Black History Month," "AAPI [Asian American and Pacific Islander] Heritage Month," and "Pride Month."[33] To be fair, some of the health-related causes are also listed as special days; for example, the video mentions "World Autism Awareness Day" and "World Alzheimer's Day." Still, I assume that many of the funds raised for these causes go toward research and advocacy organizations, much like the Party in Pink initiative. On the other hand, it is difficult to ascertain what, exactly, is funded for "Black History Month" or "Pride Month." Is it a particular advocacy organization? An awareness campaign? Given Zumba Fitness's reluctance to address potentially controversial political topics, it is not surprising that these non-health-related causes are vague. Supporting Black History Month or Pride Month is much more innocuous than fundraising for organizations like Black Lives Matter that call for an end to systemic racism, or taking a stand on hot button issues like trans rights. Overall, this very safe approach to acknowledging racial and ethnic difference fits easily with the postracial trope of love. Zumba Love exemplifies the perfect form of commodity activism, in which consumers purchase goods (in this case exercise classes) and donate to charities in ways that render them good individual citizens doing their part to create change, all while maintaining the very same structures of inequality that make these charities necessary in the first place.

Together, the emphasis on fitness and philanthropy ultimately reinforces the notion that individual behavior, whether it is one's own attitude or charitable giving practices, is the most effective remedy to systemic problems. But these efforts do little, if anything, to actually address the structural issues that impact the communities that Zumba Fitness claims to support, be they breast cancer patients or Asian Americans or LGBTQ youth. Much like the ways that selling dreams ignores the racist and xenophobic policies that restrict Latinx immigrants' lives, selling love in Zumba Fitness contributes to our postracial moment's neglect of ongoing systemic inequalities. King notes, "In requiring participants to take responsibility for their fitness and to demonstrate compassion for those who will be recipients of their private fundraising efforts, the thon supplies an 'ethical rationale' for privatization and the shift away from general taxation toward corporatized individual philanthropy."[34] Selling love in Zumba Fitness blends fitness and philanthropy together to reward those with the resources to stay fit and give money, all while suppressing any discussion of systemic racism and other forms of inequality. In this context, tropicalized Latinness can be easily consumed via Zumbathons as a way to express multicultural tolerance and cultural appreciation despite the fact that tropicalized Latinness promotes racist stereotypes. This is the fundamental contradiction of the trope of love—and postracial ideology more generally—that both acknowledges and flattens racial and ethnic differences in order to maintain racial hierarchies that privilege whiteness.

ZUMBA LOVE SONGS

The cooldown at the end of a Zumba Fitness class is a chance to do some mild stretching and get your heart rate down. Many Zumba instructors I've met do not understand the Spanish lyrics of the songs they use in class. Discerning messages in lyrics is not necessary to perform tropicalized Latinness; indeed, this unintelligibility is partly what makes tropicalized Latinness foreign and exotic. However, cooldowns are meant to be understood. They offer students' bodies a moment to rest and their minds a moment to reflect. For this reason, many instructors select English-language cooldown songs that have inspirational messages. Vicki explained, "I always use an inspirational cooldown. It's something that motivated me from when I first started taking Zumba, so I always look for the songs that have the words. Some of them will make you cry. Some of them will talk to you on a level that I will never understand. But that's okay. It's for you to take with you."

Vicki's cooldowns demonstrate how self-care and self-love are part of Zumba Fitness's trope of love. Popular discourses of self-care often claim that you must love yourself before you can love others. However, as Shani Orgad and Rosalind Gill argue, the growth of self-care and self-love discourses happens alongside increasing levels of social inequality and precarity.[35] In other words, self-care and self-love discourses reproduce the individualized approach to social change and wellness: the way to overcome problems is to make sure you have the proper rest and confidence to tackle them. This emphasis on self-care and self-love follows neoliberal logics that center individual attitudes and perseverance as the keys to success. Orgad and Gill refer to this as part of a larger "cult(ure) of confidence" that emerges with "the media's growing emphasis on self-transformation, and neoliberalism's construction of enterprising and 'responsibilized' subjects called on to take full responsibility for their lives no matter what constraints they may face."[36] This type of self-love and self-care discourse thus aligns with healthism's links between fitness, health, and citizenship.[37] In fact, self-care discourses have become part and parcel of health and fitness marketing where, as Orgad and Gill describe, "You 'train' your body, but you also make over your mind as well."[38] In so doing, self-care gives you the confidence to be your best self both physically and mentally, thus enabling you to love yourself and others, too. On the flip side, those who do not adequately care for themselves lack the capacity to care for and accept others for who they are.

In this vein, the cult(ure) of confidence involves specific ideas about the body. Orgad and Gill identify "love your body" discourses as exhortations to accept yourself as you are, no matter how different. They argue that love your body messages rely in part on visible representations of diversity. For example, advertisements for body products can sometimes feature people with different races, gender identities, religious markers, or abilities to emphasize that all bodies are worthwhile. Orgad and Gill place such love your body discourses in relation to postracial critique, writing that in these instances "visibility becomes an end in itself—a marker of progress and inclusion, which signifies that nothing has to change, since the politics *is* the visibility."[39] Consequently, the diversity represented by love your body discourses does not upset the racial status quo. Rather, it hides the ongoing effects of racism through visual images of racially diverse subjects coming together in love and happiness.

Zumba Fitness similarly blends the discourse of self-love with post-racial celebrations of multicultural diversity, both in visuals included in their marketing materials (e.g., utilizing images of models with different racial backgrounds although they all conform to hegemonic perceptions of the fit body) and, often, in English-language lyrics used in songs. Many English-language songs in Zumba Fitness are already popular hits (sometimes contemporary, sometimes not), or from "global rhythms" like dancehall or soca. Still, inspirational songs play an important role in spreading the trope of love. Like Vicki's cooldowns, some songs focus on individual acceptance and self-care. But others implore everyone to love each other across racial and ethnic difference. These Zumba love songs generally identify love as the antidote to hate and, by extension, racism. Zumba love songs thus reproduce neoliberal and postracial assumptions that systemic racism is no more, and what remains can be overcome with shifts in individuals' behavior and attitudes.

One popular Zumba love song that exemplifies this trend is "LOVE," by Italian DJ Gianluca Vacchi with vocals by Colombian singer Sebastián Yatra. "LOVE" was originally considered the unofficial anthem of the 2018 World Cup Colombian soccer team. The music video featured giant images of Yatra, Vacchi, and Colombian soccer stars Radamel Falcao, Yerry Mina, and James Rodríguez kicking around soccer balls and dancing in various locations around the globe.[40] Zumba Fitness recommended "LOVE" as a "New HOT Track" in June 2018.[41] The *Z-Life* article announcing "LOVE" included a video clip of Zumba International Presenters Prince Paltu-ob and Loretta Bates performing the choreography on a stage in front of the Egyptian pyramids of Giza. After a few bars, the video shifts to Rony Gratereaut and Ana Georgescu dancing in a space suggestive of an ancient Egyptian tomb with dark, candle-lit lighting and brown stone walls with hieroglyphics. That such popular Zumba International Presenters performed in the promotional materials reflects the extent to which Zumba Fitness embraced and promoted the song, which was included on ZIN Volume 75.

Since its release, "LOVE" has made its way into many of the Zumba Fitness classes that I frequent—and, I admit, I really like dancing to it. It is a catchy tune that combines upbeat Spanish verses with a slower English chorus that is easy to sing along to. The music itself is typical dance music. Loud syncopated beats punctuate the chorus that dramatically proclaims, "We all need / A little bit of love." This is the exciting part to dance to in class. We open our arms wide, lift them over our heads, come back down and open them again as if inviting a big embrace, our movements following the thumping, dramatic beats. Next, we shift to a few, slowed-down body rolls before going into our quick step-touch. This slower chorus enables us to catch our breath, and the simple choreography ensures that the class can get back in sync. Our synchronization creates a feeling of belonging and community. There is a sense of connection and joy in those moments when we are all belting out the same lyrics and flinging out our arms, even if I don't necessarily know the women around me. But I know we are all enjoying this moment together and that feels good.

"LOVE" is, in fact, a song about unity. The bilingual Spanish-English lyrics of the song celebrate love and tolerance for people around the globe. The song proclaims that everyone is the same, regardless of color, and that love unites all—for example, "Nos unió el amor / Ahora soy mejor / Esta es la bandera que yo siempre seguiré (Love united us / Now I'm better

/ This is the flag that I will always follow). In this way, "LOVE" certainly makes sense as a hype song for a major sporting event where everyone comes together to support their team and express their patriotism. But in the context of Zumba Fitness, the "flag" becomes much more ambiguous. The repetition of the chorus "We all need / A little bit of love" shifts the song's message from a patriotic sporting anthem to a broader proclamation of love as the quality that heals and joins together everyone around the world. It is no wonder, then, that the song has become so popular in Zumba Fitness circles. The message of love uniting across difference aligns perfectly with Zumba Fitness's promotion of love as a method for social change. In my Zumba Fitness classes, the choreography to "LOVE" links us together while the lyrics encourage us to embrace one another across racial and ethnic difference.

Another popular Zumba love song comes from the Zumba Kids program. Zumba Fitness describes Zumba Kids as a class that features "kid-friendly routines" along with "games, activities, and cultural exploration" for kids ages 7–11 (Zumba Kids Jr. classes are similar but for ages 4–6).[42] I met several instructors who were licensed to teach Zumba Kids, although few actually taught it. For some instructors, the limited market combined with the extra preparation required to learn new, age-appropriate songs and routines did not make the investment worthwhile. Still, several commented that Zumba Kids was valuable because it encouraged kids to exercise and it included an interesting cultural education component. Stephanie explained, "With Zumba Kids training, they have a section of the class called the 'Culture Corner.' And so in an authentic Zumba Kids class, ideally you stop and teach them one rhythm or dance move from a merengue, and you explain to them where merengue comes from." Morgan was the only ZIN I met who taught Zumba Kids regularly at the time of our interview. She described how she would integrate this cultural background information into her class structure: "In the Kids class, we'll say, 'Well this is merengue,' or 'This is salsa.' First, we'll say, 'What do you know about salsa?' And then we'll go, like when we did cumbia, say, 'This is Colombian.' That's what we learn in the Zumba Kids training, that you come and you show them a flag of the country. Here are some famous people from there. So, they get a little bit of what they call 'cultural enrichment' as a part of the class." This is a marked difference from many Zumba instructors' approaches to teaching Zumba Fitness formats that cater to adults. Although some instructors would occasionally bring up background information about their songs to their adult students, they could not substantially pause class to impart information to their students since most adults came to Zumba Fitness for a high-energy aerobic workout. Zumba Kids distinguishes itself from other Zumba Fitness formats with its mandate to incorporate cultural enrichment into the class.

Zumba Fitness provides Zumba Kids instructors with specific music to use for their class. Morgan described some of these songs as "Kidz Bop in Spanish," where a child sings an age-appropriate version of a popular song. In addition, Zumba Kids songs often meld their lyrics with movement commands. One such song is the 2016 Zumba Kids hit, "Spread Love." Zumba Fitness produced a video for the song that demonstrated "official choreography for Childhood Obesity Awareness Month, dedicated to teaching our kids about a healthier and happier future."[43] The music video starred Rony Gratereaut and the Zumba Kids, a group of children who serve as back-up dancers in the video.[44] It begins with Gratereaut walking through an alleyway with brightly colored murals on the walls. He passes by different kids lounging about in their Zumba Wear who begin to follow him as the song starts. "Spread Love" is a soca song whose lyrics primarily relay directions for dancers—step to the right, thunderclap, jump, and the like. There are two brief verses where the choreography changes slightly. The first verse describes a kid who "just want[s] to dance" and "turn[s] off the TV" to get moving. The reference to television is significant here, since much of the discussion about childhood obesity identifies watching television as a major driver of the problem. In addition, this verse places the responsibility for health and fitness directly on the child who is motivated and disciplined enough to avoid the lure of television. The second verse begins, "Can we just spread love?," and proceeds to instruct kids to "make this a nice place to live amongst each other." Unlike "LOVE," this Zumba Kids song does not explicitly address hate or mention characteristics like skin color. Instead, "Spread Love" uses more vague terms to declare love something that makes the world a better place. In one of the final shots of the video, Rony Gratereaut poses with his fingers shaped like a heart and outstretched to the sky.

Although "Spread Love" does not mention race explicitly, it is interesting to note that the Zumba Kids themselves appear relatively diverse. Gratereaut, a Black Puerto Rican man, is the only adult featured in the video. The Zumba Kids, however, are mostly girls who range in age and racial background, including one who is overweight. This is precisely the type of visible diversity that Orgad and Gill describe as central to love

5.2 Still from music video for "Spread Love" featuring Rony Gratereaut and the Zumba Kids. The diverse body sizes and racial identities of the Zumba Kids reflect the postracial ethos of the trope of love.

your body discourses. First, the inclusion of one noticeably overweight child in a group that is otherwise quite thin implies that thinness is the standard. Importantly, she is also the child with the darkest skin complexion in the video. This is notable given that Black and Latinx youth are often stereotyped as the children most at risk of childhood obesity, presumably because of cultural attitudes rather than systemic inequalities that limit their access to healthy lifestyles. In contrast, this particular overweight child has made the choice to join her thinner peers in a dance to a song that exhorts everyone to get up and move. This reiterates the assumption that health is an individual choice, even for children, with no acknowledgment of structural and social barriers to adequate medical care, exercise space, or nutritious foods. Second, the diverse group of kids in a song about love visually stresses racial tolerance and multiculturalism, even if the lyrics do not explicitly address racial difference. In this context, "Spread Love" reflects the fundamental tenets of our postracial and neoliberal moment wherein individuals' attitudes about others along with their lifestyle choices presumably ameliorate societal problems more effectively than collective efforts to enact structural change.

Zumba love songs stress joy, happiness, togetherness, and acceptance. Any mention of racial, ethnic, or national difference happens only at the very superficial level of visible diversity. In so doing, Zumba love songs ignore any structural inequality that might have severe consequences for those communities from which it draws inspiration. Incorporating these postracial Zumba love songs into its repertoire further distances Zumba Fitness from any public stance on potentially controversial topics unless it is politically expedient to do so. Still, even then, these political statements do not make their way into Zumba Fitness songs. Instead, Zumba Love promotes the perfect postracial vision of a multicultural community of individuals whose capacity to love is so strong that it can even cure racism. But whether ZINS experience this on the ground is another story.

BREAKING DOWN BARRIERS?

Of all Zumba enthusiasts, instructors, and celebrities that I met, Kathy was perhaps the most optimistic about Zumba Fitness's potential to contest racism and xenophobia. Kathy believed that Zumba Fitness could offer much more than health benefits; she also thought that Zumba Fitness could help people to learn about and appreciate other cultures, something that she hoped would have a larger political impact. Kathy explained,

> I don't know. It's all very complicated. We are all about getting people together to dance, get fit, and be accountable to each other. In the end, I think what makes Zumba different is the social connections and the huge amount of charitable efforts. And for me, it's also an opportunity to promote cultural competence, in a very organic way. So if someone who believes in deporting the Dreamers,[45] wants to close down immigration, and doesn't want anyone speaking Spanish in the schools, gets into a Zumba class and really enjoys dancing to "Despacito," that's a win. Maybe they'll go home and influence their family away from the xenophobic politics that are really frightening these days. That's my hope.

Like most Zumba instructors I spoke with, Kathy was incensed at the anti-immigrant and racist policies of the Trump administration. She considered herself politically liberal and dedicated to promoting equality and human rights both domestically and around the world. Kathy saw Zumba Fitness as an antidote to the white supremacist and nativist policies promoted by the federal government.

But to what extent is this actually true? In some ways, Zumba Fitness differs from other types of commodity activism in that one does not buy an actual product like an electric vehicle, green cleaning supplies, or fair-trade coffee to demonstrate their commitment to a cause. However, Zumba Fitness's brand culture conforms to the emphasis on individual behavior, attitudes, and habits consistent with commodity activism. Part of what Zumba Fitness consumers receive is the ethos attached to the brand culture—the focus on fun, wellness, and expanding one's cultural horizons. Additionally, brand cultures enable people to see themselves as part of a larger community with shared values and ideals. One important marker of these shared values is the charitable causes that a company embraces as part of its corporate social responsibility efforts.[46] Participating in a particular brand culture like Zumba Fitness, which is ostensibly committed to dealing with racial inequality, affiliates the consumer with the same ideals. This is what enables Kathy and others to see their work in Zumba Fitness as extending beyond fitness and health to part of a bigger movement to teach about cultural diversity in ways that might lead to political change.

Still, Kathy expressed some reservations about Zumba Fitness's potential to spark social change when she said it was "complicated." Her example of the potential students whose anti-immigrant sentiments might change as a result of participating in Zumba Fitness shows some of the limitations of this impact. In this hypothetical, the hope for change rests on one person changing their views and then speaking to others. It is certainly true that these types of personal interactions can make a difference in people's points of view. Still, since these actions are solely up to the individual, it is also difficult to measure the extent to which these changes actually happen, or if they have any influence on efforts to create more systemic change. Indeed, Kathy notes this limitation when she says, "That's the hope."

Similar to Kathy, Miriam viewed Zumba Fitness as a program that could potentially influence individuals' attitudes. She said, "Maybe someone that has never been to a Zumba class before would have never thought of going to a salsa lesson, or going to Latin America, traveling to Latin America. It has opened that horizon for them. People that always thought that traveling was Disney World, or maybe Canada. I mean, all of a sudden they are thinking, 'Oh, maybe we should go to Costa Rica, and take some Spanish and salsa lessons.'" For Miriam, Zumba Fitness offers students exposure to foreign cultures and practices, specifically from Latin

America, that might open their horizons and show them something new. However, this does not extend to political action. Miriam's observations thus address the limits of the trope of love's focus on cultural appreciation on actual political and social issues.

Miriam's perception is similar to many other instructors who see their classes as primarily impacting students' musical tastes. Several instructors related stories of students asking for the names of specific songs on their playlist to enjoy outside of class. But, as Julia said, "I don't know necessarily if they go and search out the history [of the music] or do any more research." In other words, students' tastes may change to incorporate new sounds and genres, but whether or not this actually lends itself to a broader interest or increased education about other cultures is uncertain. While Zumba Fitness's brand culture might promote the program as an effective avenue for cultivating love and understanding, I found it striking how many instructors—white and nonwhite—felt this was extremely limited in practice.

Indeed, I met several instructors who were very skeptical of the potential for Zumba Fitness to do anything more than expose students to new music and dance styles. Morgan questioned whether or not the trope of love that permeates Zumba Fitness's brand culture actually did anything for people. She said,

> OK, you say you love Zumba, but what do you love about it, and how does this love make you do something different than you would have done otherwise? How does it make you connect? Or do you change your mind about stuff? Or does it fall under the same kind of consumption as Taco Tuesday and you have no critical engagement? I do think it's really mixed, because I have talked to some people who I think are really, genuinely interested in learning about things and having conversations and stuff, and it's like they are just sort of starting. And then I talk to other people who say they're doing it, but then they'll say lots of other things that make you wonder what they're getting out of it.

Although Morgan left open the possibility of Zumba Fitness being a space for exposing students to something new, she also implied that that alone is not enough. Morgan believed strongly that Zumba Fitness across all levels, from individual instructors to the company itself, should have a more overt political commitment to communities of color. To do something in the name of love is not enough for Morgan, who feels she has a responsibility to use her platform as a Zumba instructor to speak to issues affecting the Black and brown communities from which Zumba Fitness draws its music and choreography.

Other instructors simply discounted any possibility that Zumba Fitness could expand worldviews or shift one's racial politics. Amanda told me she doubted Zumba Fitness would actually transform anyone's political views since most people attend Zumba Fitness classes exclusively for exercise. Andrea agreed. Andrea believed that Zumba Fitness introduced her students to music and dance that they might not otherwise hear. But for Andrea, that's where it ends. She explained, "I don't think it promotes cultural tolerance. I think it might for a short amount of time, but folks just go back to being who they are. I know that sounds cynical, but I think that's how it works . . . because, in terms of politics, folks are who they are. They're going to think what they think. I don't really see Zumba making vast changes in that area, and I don't expect them to either. I think at the end of the day, folks are going to just see it as fitness."

Andrea's experiences as a Black Zumba instructor informed her opinion. She said, "I think I get seen as one of the cool Black people and not one of the angry ones, you know what I mean? Not the 'other' kind." My interviews took place during heightened tensions around the Black Lives Matter movement and increased attention to police murders of Black men in particular. Andrea's comments that her mostly white students see her as "cool" rather than "angry" address the contradictions inherent to Zumba Fitness and our postracial moment more generally. Since an important aspect of Zumba Fitness's brand culture is the emphasis on respecting and accepting cultural difference, a member of the Zumba community can demonstrate their cultural tolerance and antiracist bona fides through their participation in the program. Nevertheless, Andrea's interpretation of her students' perception of her as a "cool" Black woman reflects Zumba Fitness's ambivalence toward a more critical politics dedicated to systemic change. Seeing someone as a "cool" Black person rather than an "angry" one implies that the normative image of a Black person is, in fact, angry, or perhaps aggressive or even violent—all stereotypes associated with Blackness in the United States. One can both appreciate Andrea as a "cool" Black woman *and* ascribe to racist stereotypes or ignore the systemic racism that impacts Andrea's daily life.

This is, in fact, how the trope of love works to limit racial critique. On one hand, as made evident in Zumba love songs, the trope of love acknowledges racial and cultural difference in order to then declare it irrelevant through a discourse of sameness and acceptance. However, Andrea's comments demonstrate that only *certain* types of difference are acceptable within the postracial Zumba Fitness community. In her case, the "cool" Black woman is integrated into the community while the "angry" Black woman is not. Andrea does not expand on what she means by "cool" aside from being nonthreatening. However, mainstream US popular culture has long drawn from African diasporic cultural practices and repackaged them as markers of a "cool" aesthetic that is cutting edge, fresh, and modern. In this context, Andrea's comments show how she represents all that is desirable about Blackness without any of the stereotypically threatening characteristics normally imposed upon Black communities. Tropicalized Latinness functions similarly in Zumba Fitness. Tropicalized Latinness as marked by fun and fiesta is acceptable and desirable, while the more threatening images of Latinx hypersexuality, cultural unassimibility, and racial difference are not. In this context, only those embodiments of cultural or racial difference that are nonthreatening to the status quo can really be loveable. To express love, then, is not to work in a decolonial way that might challenge hegemonic racial hierarchies.[47] Instead, the trope of love does the opposite, upholding many stereotypes of Blackness and Latinidad while dismissing structural racism as a thing of the past.

Still, some instructors like Kathy or Morgan saw an opening to at least *try* to influence others' attitudes in an attempt to spark change. Although Kathy generally avoided songs with explicit political lyrics, she integrated songs that related to current events into her class playlists. For example, in the aftermath of the 2017 mass shooting at a Las Vegas country music festival, Kathy used country music as her cooldown. In other instances, she incorporates what she's learned about a place or a particular situation into her routines. For example, Kathy described how she used a Venezuelan song to address the economic crisis in Venezuela with her class: "I said 'Let's go to Venezuela!,' and then we do 'Pa' Venezuela.' And I say, 'This sounds like a fun song, but this is actually a really thoughtful song.'... When they did it in [the Zumba Convention], after it was over, people were emotional. They said, 'We don't know what we're going home to. People are starving. Babies are in the hospital because they're starving to death.' And so, I make it as dramatic as I can make it. I make it so it's insanely dramatic, because it is a love song for Venezuela." Kathy used what she learned at Convention about the dance to inform her choreography for "Pa' Venezuela" as well. She explained, "It's tambores, two dancers in the middle of the circle, they're eye to eye, and then one dancer leaves the circle and another takes her place. It can be dramatic." In her class, she teaches the song in a similar fashion. Her students make a circle, and individuals "battle" in the middle. Many Zumba instructors incorporate these kinds of interactive moments (e.g., dance battles, dancing together in a circle) into their classes as a strategy to create a feeling of community, though not always with this kind of political slant. For Kathy, the tambores routine addresses several of her primary goals in her Zumba classes. She is particularly concerned about having authentic routines in the class and making sure her students know the cultural origins of their Zumba choreography. In this instance, her choreography draws from aspects of tambores in Venezuela. But Kathy sees potential for this to have an even deeper meaning in her class. She learned about the plight of Venezuelans from Venezuelan instructors at the Zumba Convention, and she tries to bring that emotion into her routine. Kathy did not report to me whether or not her students grasped these politics around her choreography and musical choices. Nevertheless, she sees such moves as part of her overall obligation as a Zumba instructor dedicated to promoting love and tolerance, in addition to fitness.

Morgan similarly thought about the specific messages she promoted in her classes. She approached teaching Zumba Fitness as a "feminist thing, this like pro-Black, pro-brown, pro-fat, pro-everything cool thing." This was partially due to her own politics and beliefs and partially to address how her white students might react to her as a Black woman fitness instructor; as Morgan stated, "I was bringing this into a space where everybody was trying *not* to look like me." Morgan intentionally selects T-shirts with slogans that make clear to her students her "pro-everything" stance. She said,

> I have a shirt that says "Black Girls Rock." Or I have a shirt that says, "We All Belong Here," and "Riots Not Diets" in addition to shirts saying like, "My Favorite Dance Club is the Gym." I love Beyoncé, so I have "Beyoncé Wasn't Built in a Day." I have a shirt that says, "I want to dance with somebody." So, I try to use my clothes, to use my body as a way to do this messaging because I thought that was all a part of creating a different type of gym experience for people, so that you knew how I felt about a particular issue. So, you're not going to come up to me talking out the way, because I have this shirt that says "Body Positive" on it, right? And I knew that it probably wouldn't—I mean, I didn't know how it was going to go over, but I said, if I'm consistent, if I'm always the same, then it'll work out.

On one hand, shirts like the ones that Morgan selects conform to aspects of the "love your body" discourses that Shani Orgad and Rosalind Gill see as consistent with neoliberalism and postracialism.[48] Given the ubiquity of love your body messages in our current moment, it is possible that Morgan's students interpret her T-shirts not as a political statement, but rather as a more innocuous embrace of body positivity. On the other hand, Morgan works hard to make sure that her positionality as a Black woman fitness instructor in a predominantly white space is understood. She wants her students to realize the ideas about Black women's bodies that they bring to the class, whether it is stereotypes of Black people as inherently rhythmic or their implicit bias about the fitness acumen of a Black woman instructor. In this context, her shirts serve as a type of messaging meant to attract and encourage those students committed to an inclusive, feminist approach to fitness.

Morgan openly recognizes that her strategy of conveying messages with her outfits has a limited impact, and that these messages alone will not erase systemic racism even if they influence students' thinking. In this context, Morgan combines these messages with other efforts to raise awareness about current events that impact the countries from where Zumba Fitness's music originates. After Hurricane María devastated Puerto Rico and the US Virgin Islands, Morgan used her Zumba Fitness platform to encourage her students to donate to hurricane relief. She recalled,

> I told all my classes that if you donate to whatever organization you want around hurricane relief in the Virgin Islands and Puerto Rico, I will match it. And so I did it for like six weeks, and it wasn't anything connected to my gym or anything that anybody was reimbursing me for. But I said, "It is irresponsible of us to come into this class week after week and listen to this music and feed off of this. I feel like we should also be giving back because if it wasn't for these countries, you wouldn't have this class. You wouldn't have this music. So, we need to honor that." And so, I do things like that and it goes over really well, because they know it's me.

Morgan's charitable efforts may appear on the surface to conform to Zumba Love, but they differ in several significant ways. First, in this example, she did not organize a large, one-time Zumbathon event, but rather incorporated charitable giving into her regular class. Morgan did not explain whether or not her previous attempt to fundraise for Bree

Newsome informed her decision to avoid a major Zumbathon for hurricane relief in the Caribbean. Regardless, though, her choice to organize the fundraiser over a longer period of time allowed her to talk with her students about the impact of Hurricane María repeatedly over a few weeks. Second, Morgan intentionally utilized this fundraising effort to make a commentary about where Zumba Fitness's music comes from. Morgan taught other dance-fitness formats that used US pop and hip-hop in addition to Zumba Fitness. She believed her students considered Zumba Fitness "something that feels tropical" when compared to other programs. Connecting this vague notion of something "tropical" to a very specific location makes visible the places where Zumba Fitness's music comes from through foregrounding the realities of contemporary life there. Morgan's approach distances itself from the rigid tropes of authenticity normally utilized in Zumba Fitness when talking about Latin America. This also attempts to decenter tropicalized Latinness by paying attention to cultural specificity in a way that tropicalized Latinness typically ignores.

Aspects of Morgan's attempts to give back to the places where Zumba Fitness's music comes from conform to commodity activism projects where the Global North "helps" those from the Global South in ways that confirm the former's modernity vis-à-vis a primitive other.[49] But in the context of Zumba Fitness, where authenticity is frequently decontextualized, Morgan's efforts are significant. She departs from the trope of authenticity by presenting Puerto Rico and the Virgin Islands as contemporary places that are negatively impacted by their colonial relationship with the United States. This involves a discussion of structural inequality often left out of the tropes of love and authenticity in selling tropicalized Latinness.

Instructors like Morgan and Kathy try to infuse an explicit politics into their classes. They not only offer their students exposure to diverse cultures, but also attempt to situate these in relation to a larger politics that calls attention to issues pertaining to the Latin American and Caribbean countries from which Zumba Fitness culls its music. This is similar to Lynn Comella's discussion of sex-positive retail. She argues that feminist and sex-positive sex toy retailers not only sell products but also offer important spaces where people of all gender identities can access safe and reliable sex education. Consequently, Comella writes, "elements of neoliberalism . . . can be rearticulated and marshaled towards socially progressive ends."[50] In the case of Zumba Fitness, students may come to

Zumba Fitness because it "feels tropical," but perhaps they can leave with a greater understanding of larger social issues.

Overall, it is hard for even the most committed instructors like Kathy or Morgan to determine how much of an impact their efforts actually have. This problem is amplified by the reality that most students come for exercise, so there is little time to forge intimate bonds with them during class that would enable instructors to assess how their students interpret their actions or words. While some instructors do make strong friendships with some students, many described their relationships with students as more cordial. They talk to students before and after class or check in with students who might be dealing with something difficult. Stephanie described, "I love my students. We talk a lot, and I do things for them, and I ask them about their mom. You know, 'How's your mom? How's the dog?' . . . I have some students I feel like I'm close with, but generally, I think it's more just wanting to be there for them." Most instructors I spoke with see themselves as offering a form of emotional support to their classes, whether it is through the stress relief that comes from one hour of intense cardio or through checking in to see that everything is OK. But, most instructors, including Kathy and Morgan, did not know the extent to which their efforts to educate students about different social and political issues were actually effective. In this way, the trope of love severely curtails Zumba Fitness's overall political work. While individuals may spend time, energy, and even their own funds on these projects, the brand culture itself instead centers the trope of love that leaves virtually no room for substantive critique. Instead, the trope of love enables the contradictions inherent to Zumba Fitness to flourish, thus substantiating the brand culture's commitment to postracial ideologies.

BUILDING MULTICULTURAL
COMMUNITIES?

I met Angela at a Zumba Master Class that she attended with her close friends who were also Zumba instructors. Angela moved to the Boston area without any established connections. As she described, "I met most of my friends through Zumba." At this point in her life, all of her closest friends are somehow connected to the Zumba Fitness world. Additionally, Angela, who is white, notes that her community is much more diverse than it was before. "I got to know them outside of Zumba," she told me, "so I really opened my mind culturally. A lot of my friends are Haitians or Latinos. So I would learn about their culture, not just their music." She noted that before participating in Zumba Fitness, she interacted with a very homogeneous, predominantly white group of friends. Angela credits Zumba Fitness with giving her the opportunity to forge lifelong friendships with people from different backgrounds. The types of communities created by people like Angela and her friends show the potential for Zumba Fitness to foster deep social bonds across difference.

This type of community building is one reason many people keep coming back to Zumba Fitness. Amanda hesitated to join an exercise program but became attracted to Zumba Fitness in part because of the "community-based nature of it. Developing a community with a group of people who are not judgmental, it's not threatening." Like Angela, many of Amanda's closest friends come from Zumba Fitness classes, including both other instructors and a few students. Miriam called Zumba Fitness a "community-based kind of workout" where you can "get really friendly with the teachers and the people in the class." Julia thought that the communal nature of Zumba Fitness classes motivated more people to return who would otherwise give up on exercising. For me, personally, the experience of participating in a Zumba Fitness class does motivate me to keep exercising. I like the feeling of togetherness I have in class with the other women. The women in my classes are friendly and nonjudgmental (or at least it seems that way). Their regular presence makes the class more enjoyable and makes me more excited to go. This feeling of togetherness in Zumba class is different from other group exercise programs I've done like barre or yoga that prioritize individual body posture and technique. Barre and yoga are quiet spaces of individual concentration. Zumba Fitness is loud, full of music but also laughter, jokes, and yelps. That's what I like about it.

But rarely, if ever, have I personally made very close friends with other people in my class. Perhaps it is because of my shyness, or because I have to juggle my exercise schedule with the demands of working full time and parenting young kids. Some people do become friends, but a lot of the time, class ends, we grab our coats, wave good bye and head out the door. If we are feeling especially chatty, we might ask about each other's families or jobs, or swap names of realtors, cleaning people, tailors, hairdressers, and babysitters while we grab our waters or tie our shoes. Instructors like Angela spend a lot of time together at master classes, Jam Sessions, and other events. These instructors are often tapped into larger networks of other Zumba Fitness enthusiasts, usually ZINS. However, the structure of a class where students want to do aerobic exercise with minimal talking makes these bonds more difficult to make during the class itself.

Even when people become friends or have a tight-knit community in their Zumba classes, it can still be difficult to overtly address political and social issues, especially in this polarized political moment. Zumba instructors may be invested in community or politics, but they are also, essentially, running a small business. To that end, they must prioritize maintaining their student base, which means offering a sense of community but not necessarily addressing controversial politics that could turn some students off. It is worth mentioning that Morgan, the instructor whom I interviewed who was most willing to take these risks, approached her Zumba Fitness career not as a money-making enterprise but more as a way to make fun and rigorous exercise accessible to all, regardless of how much she earned in the process. In contrast, most of the instructors I talked with avoided these sensitive topics, instead checking with students about their parents, kids, pets, or jobs. Few actually integrate political commentary about racism or other social injustices into their classes, regardless of their own personal beliefs. They know that students are there to have fun and exercise, not necessarily to learn about other cultures or social issues.

As a whole, Zumba Fitness avoids potentially controversial issues. The company has instead aligned itself with public health campaigns like breast cancer awareness that affect people, regardless of race, class, nationality, or political affiliation. While supporting these causes is noble, Zumba Fitness's prioritization of innocuous causes with established broad-based support shields the company from criticism from either side of the political spectrum. This also removes tropicalized Latinness from any political efforts to fight for civil rights for Black and Latinx communities. Because Zumba Fitness does not address racial conflict, the trope of love is decidedly race-neutral. Whereas tropicalized Latinness is front and center in many of the other tropes that Zumba Fitness sells, it remains conspicuously absent in Zumba Fitness's trope of love. Instead, love in this case is a postracial, neoliberal one that prioritizes individual attitudes, beliefs, and choices. Expressing this love comes as a form of charitable giving to acceptable causes that do not address systemic inequality or at most do so on a very superficial level. And, like most commodity activism, this investment centers the values of the individual giver rather than a commitment to collectivity or challenging the status quo.

Perhaps the most nefarious aspect of selling love is how the trope of love depicts Zumba Fitness as a racially progressive space. However, the heart of the Zumba Fitness brand is tropicalized Latinness and the circulation of deeply rooted stereotypes of Latin(x) cultures and people as foreign, hypersexual, and exotic. These are the very same racist discourses used to justify limiting Latinx citizenship rights. Softening these stereotypes through discourses of love reproduces the fundamental basis of postracial ideology where racism is propagated through the actions and beliefs of a few bad apples. Systemic racism becomes obscured in favor of narratives of meritocracy and the American dream. In the final analysis, selling love shows what is at stake in contemporary forms of commodity activism and reveals how even the most benign or even positive ideas on the surface can actually reinforce systemic racism.

COOLDOWN

∧∧∨∧∧∨

I GOT IN LINE EARLY FOR RONY GRATEREAUT'S "Puerto Rican Flow" master class. The long line snaked around the court that served as the dance floor, shaded by the waterslides overhead. We were on the 2019 Zumba Cruise floating somewhere between Labadee, Haiti, and Miami, Florida. As we sailed the seas, we shimmied and booty popped our way through classes with some of Zumba Fitness's most sought after International Presenters. Students who gathered in line around me wore a mix of typical Zumba Wear. Many people had Puerto Rican flags somewhere on their outfits, and one man wore a T-shirt with Puerto Rican salsa legend Hector Lavoe on it. A group of women stood in a line with balloons that spelled out "Rony" as they waited for him to arrive. It was obvious to me that not only the instructors I talked to back in Boston loved Rony Gratereaut, so did everyone else. Good thing I had arrived early, then, because Gratereaut only offered one chance to take the "Puerto Rican Flow" workshop on the cruise (he normally taught it during the Zumba Convention). I was super excited to take the class that so many instructors had recommended to me. I had heard that Gratereaut often included information about Puerto Rican music in his class and that his music and routines were, simply put, awesome.

Instructors had told me that Gratereaut often began with information about Puerto Rican music, especially bomba and plena, when he taught Puerto Rican Flow at the convention. Sometimes he even had an introductory video about Puerto Rico.[1] Gratereaut didn't do any of the educational programming from Convention that instructors had described to me. Still, Puerto Rican symbolism abounded in the class. He wore Puerto Rico athletic gear, including a baseball jersey from the Puerto Rican national team that competed in the World Baseball Classic. He hung a Puerto Rican flag on the back of the stage. Although Gratereaut used recordings from Puerto Rican artists almost exclusively, his choreography was fairly typical of most Zumba Fitness classes—merengue marches, salsa back steps, reggaetón stomps. But then, toward the end of our class, Gratereaut jumped into the crowd and instructed us to kneel down in a circle. He tied his Puerto Rico jersey around his waist and began using it as a skirt to perform bomba-style moves to the plena song "Mañana por la Mañana" while we clapped and cheered him on. Once he was finished, three audience members—all women wearing Zumba gear—danced one by one. I don't know how Gratereaut selected the three women to dance in the circle—if it were spontaneous or planned, if they were people he knew already or not, if they were Puerto Rican or not. Comparing their dancing to Gratereaut's was striking. Whereas I recognized Gratereaut's moves as derivative of classic bomba and plena, these women's dancing style felt more directly tied to Zumba Fitness moves. Their salsa steps tended to be more like the salsa two-step of Zumba Fitness classes than the complex footwork I grew up with at my parents' parties. All three of them, at one point, spun in a circle while vigorously shaking their hips, one even getting low in a "twerking" style move. The three women's dances were very brief. Gratereaut stopped them during a spoken part of the song, where he lip-synched with the recording. He then gathered us around to finish the routine before our final stretch.

At the end of the class, we all waited in line to meet and take photos with Rony Gratereaut. When it was my turn, I told Gratereaut that I had never seen bomba in a Zumba Fitness class before. He seemed excited that I knew what bomba was and that I appreciated the integration of this routine into the grand finale of the class. However, since I did not have the opportunity to talk with other participants after the class, I had no idea how they interpreted the "Mañana por la Mañana" routine. Did they believe they had just witnessed an authentic Puerto Rican dance performance? Did they see this as an exotic and tropicalized form of Latin music? Did they see it as a source of Puerto Rican pride?

After taking Puerto Rican Flow on the Zumba Cruise, I wrote in my fieldwork journal:

> The bomba part of Rony's class got me thinking a lot about authenticity. Zumba's marketing doesn't always fit how people experience it. A lot of Puerto Ricans in his class were obviously very proud to be there. The bomba was meaningful to me, but I wonder about other people who don't know what it is. You can't say that Zumba only does stereotypes. It presents that way in its marketing, but it's obviously not always like that.

I noted a similar experience in a "Colombian Fuego" class taught by popular Colombian Zumba presenters Wally Díaz and Mauricio

C.1 Rony Gratereaut leads a version of his "Puerto Rican Flow" Zumba Fitness class on the 2019 Zumba Cruise. He wears a Puerto Rico baseball jersey and directs the class from on stage in front of a Puerto Rican flag. Photograph by the author.

Camargo. In that class, Colombians waved flags and shouted along to popular songs by artists like Carlos Vives and Joe Arroyo. For the Colombian participants of Colombian Fuego or the Puerto Ricans in Puerto Rican Flow, it could be that the excitement they expressed was because they related the songs and movements in these classes to their own personal experiences. That was certainly the case for me. It was exciting to see so many people bouncing along to songs that I listened to during my formative years like Hector Lavoe's "Mi Gente" or DLG's "Quimbara." The fiesta feeling was much more palpable to me in a class where I recognized all of the songs from my own personal life experience than one where I was unsure about the instructor's understanding of the music they used in class. It wasn't just that I thought these were "authentic" routines. It was also the joy I felt belting out songs from my own life on top of a cruise ship with a bunch of other people who also loved these songs.

My experience at Puerto Rican Flow reflects the contradictions I have experienced ever since I began taking Zumba Fitness classes as a graduate student. The truth is, even though (as readers have learned by now) I am exceedingly critical of Zumba Fitness, I also love it. It *has* taken me through tough times. I *do* have fun in Zumba Class. It really is the only exercise I can stand precisely because, for me, it doesn't feel like exercise—just like the Zumba Home Office promises. So how can I love something that I also think can be so problematic?

This is a question that my students bring up in virtually every class I teach. Whether its reggaetón or *The Bachelor* or Zumba Fitness, we all consume products that may not square exactly with our own beliefs. Like Amanda, Leah, Miriam, or Andrea, I accept the reality that what Zumba Fitness offers me is not always going to be what I think is "accurate." Sometimes, I am like Stephanie when she twerks—knowing intellectually that Zumba Fitness might not always jibe with my own definitions of Latinidad but still taking the time to enjoy myself for myself. For whatever reason, it works for me.

I'm also aware that not all Zumba Fitness spaces conform to hegemonic notions of tropicalized Latinness. When I first moved to Massachusetts, I began attending a class once a week that took place in the basement of a Christian church with a predominantly Brazilian parish. Virtually everyone in the class was Brazilian and spoke Portuguese with each other. The instructor, herself a young Brazilian immigrant, led us in routines to very popular Latin songs. Her steps were not always the most faithful to the Zumba Fitness formula, nor did she take us on a "trip around the world." Instead, we danced almost exclusively to reggaetón, pop, and Brazilian funk. At the end of every class, we cooled down to a slower, inspirational Portuguese-language song. This was a class that in some ways followed the typical Zumba Fitness format but in other ways catered to a very specific population and community. Tropicalized Latinness did not feel like a big part of this class, although, like in all of Zumba Fitness, it is always lurking. Latinx people are not immune from tropicalizing others or even themselves.[2] Perhaps it was the other students' familiarity with the songs, or the continuous integration of Brazilian songs and references in the class, but there was something about this class that hit me differently, just like Puerto Rican Flow or Colombian Fuego.

Throughout this book, I have highlighted how people have different interpretations of Zumba Fitness's promotion of tropicalized Latinness. I see Zumba instructors as critical agents in this story. Their interpretations of the Zumba Fitness brand are especially crucial given the almost nonexistent oversight of their individual classes on the part of the Zumba Home Office. Zumba instructors are the face of the brand for their students, and how they represent Zumba Fitness on the ground communicates to others what Latin music is. And yet, even when they might disagree with what Zumba Fitness promotes, the structure of the fitness industry and the logistics of planning a one-hour class impose some limits on what they can convey to their students. By highlighting their different opinions about what happens in Zumba Fitness, I aimed to underscore that consumers of Zumba Fitness are not uncritical "dupes" who buy into everything they learn. Like all of us, they grapple with the contradictions inherent in the brand that they love, and they make do with what they have available to them.

At the same time, focusing on how the Zumba Fitness brand thoroughly integrates stereotypical tropicalized Latinness is absolutely critical in our current moment. Over the course of conducting this research, two old, yet significant, representations of Latinx people and culture came to the fore. First, Donald Trump won the 2016 election on a platform that focused intently on racist and xenophobic rhetoric targeting Latinx communities. His campaign and subsequent presidency routinely demonized Latinx people and immigrants, reproducing the Latino Threat Narrative's focus on Latinx people as dangerous for the health, safety, and culture of "real" Americans.

Then, just one week before Trump's inauguration, Puerto Rican artists Luis Fonsi and Daddy Yankee released their hit song "Despacito."

After dominating Latin music charts for a few months, they recorded a new remix with pop star Justin Bieber. This bilingual hit stayed at the top of the US pop charts for sixteen weeks, and it became only the third Spanish-language song in history to reach number one.

How could it be that a predominantly Spanish-language hit could be such a massive cultural phenomenon at a time when extreme xenophobic and anti-Latinx rhetoric circulated so widely in US political and civic life? Considering how tropicalized Latinness circulates in Zumba Fitness sheds light on this seeming contradiction. Zumba Fitness's embrace of postracial politics makes it a particularly effective site for thinking about how racist ideas continue to flourish in spaces that claim to be progressive and antiracist. The tropes of authenticity, fiesta, and fun that shape tropicalized Latinness reproduce deep-seated stereotypes of Latin America as an exotic, primitive, titillating but also potentially dangerous place. These same stereotypes have grounded imperial enterprises in the region since the times of the conquest of the Americas. Spaces like Zumba Fitness promote these stereotypes as desirable cultural qualities that can be experienced by others through neutralizing their more threatening and negative connotations.

Ironically, though, the very things that make tropicalized Latinness desirable—its exoticism, hypersexuality, and foreignness—is also what undergirds the Latino Threat Narrative. Although they are seemingly opposed, both tropicalized Latinness and the Latino Threat Narrative make stereotypes appear natural and authentic in their own right. Following this logic, Latinx people dance and party because it is part of their culture and very essence, but without the proper precautions, these same Latinx people can actually upend US ways of life. In turn, the naturalization of these stereotypes then provides alleged justification for the continued exclusion of Latinx people from full national belonging. Latinx people continue to experience systemic racism that blocks them from equal access to key resources like healthcare, housing, educational and employment opportunities, voting rights, and the like. The tropes of fiesta, fun, and authenticity may appear to celebrate Latinx cultures, but in actuality they simply reframe existing stereotypes in more positive and innocuous ways that ultimately reinforce rather than challenge them.

The tropes of dreams and love further naturalize the stereotypes embedded within tropicalized Latinness by discounting the continued impact of systemic racism on Latinx communities. The trope of dreams emphasizes hard work and perseverance as the keys to success. Success then becomes a marker of the self-sufficiency that has been constructed as paramount to hegemonic definitions of citizenship. In this context, those Latinx people who can capitalize on their tropicalized Latinness are represented as exceptional figures who differ from other Latinx people assumed to embody the Latino Threat Narrative. Despite their exceptional status, these same Latinx figures exemplify the possibilities for all Latinx people. In other words, if someone like Beto Pérez made it, then everyone else can, too. Those who do not achieve the same embody the Latino Threat Narrative, which supposedly justifies their exclusion, and in some cases removal, from US civic life.

The trope of love furthers this distinction by focusing primarily on individuals' capacities to accept others as the key to dismantling systemic oppression. Love renders everyone the same, regardless of their different race, gender, or class positionalities (among other things). In fact, these are considered insignificant precisely because the trope of love dismisses systemic racism and inequality. Following this logic, racism happens as the result of a few problematic individuals rather than a historically rooted, deeply entrenched system that impacts all facets of US life. Thus, love and dreams work together to depict the United States as a fundamentally equal and meritocratic society such that anyone can succeed. Those who cannot, then, fail presumably because of their own faults.

Overall, the Zumba Fitness brand's combination of transforming stereotypes into marketable, nonthreatening commodities alongside thoroughly embracing neoliberal and postracial ideologies plainly shows how it is possible for Latinx popular culture to be trendy at the same time that Latinx immigrants are demonized and scapegoated. In this book, I mapped out this contradiction within the Zumba Fitness brand as one example of how popular culture, politics, and national identity coalesce in ways that strengthen systemic racism even if love and antiracist ideas are central to the brand. Zumba Fitness thus offers us a window into how racial stereotypes become naturalized and then normalized within an allegedly postracial society. This aspect of Zumba Fitness is not unique. Instead, it reflects what other scholars have noted is a trend within our popular culture to simultaneously celebrate racial difference and dismiss systemic racism.[3]

Uncovering this contradiction within Zumba Fitness demonstrates that people of any racial group can participate in upholding neoliberal and postracial ideologies. Latinx people are not immune from promoting the problematic ideas associated with tropicalized Latinness. Instead, some actually stand to benefit from them. Zumba Fitness similarly reveals that not all people of color experience the same thing. Afro-Latinx and African American instructors contend with an additional set of racialized assumptions tied to their Blackness. This not only results from long-standing stereotypes about Black communities in US society more generally, but also from the continuous distancing of tropicalized Latinness from Blackness despite its borrowing from many Afro-Latinx movements, sounds, and traditions. Zumba Fitness's emphasis on the body furthers these distinctions.

I have focused my analysis on the circulation of these hegemonic ideas within Zumba Fitness because I wanted to show how they manifest in everyday spaces. In many ways, the cultural work of tropicalized Latinness is obscured precisely because it is so ordinary. It is in the sounds, the two-steps, the hand gestures, and the hip swivels that happen every day in Zumba Fitness. Zumba instructors play a critical role in the dissemination of these ideologies. They take great care to learn their craft in order to be effective instructors for their students and to be able to make a profit in this difficult industry. But, for many, their reliance on the Zumba Home Office for their information sometimes makes them accomplices in the promotion of these racial stereotypes, even if they do so without realizing it.

And yet, I have also highlighted the ways that individual instructors negotiate what they learn in relation to their own experiences as they prepare to teach their Zumba Fitness classes. Not all instructors buy into everything that Zumba Fitness tells them about a given dance, music, or group of people. Their critiques addressed a wide variety of issues, from the company's business model to its declaration of authenticity to its selection of innocuous charitable causes. And their experiences show how difficult it is to create alternative spaces within these seemingly all-encompassing neoliberal and postracial ideologies.

Nevertheless, spaces of difference do emerge. They happen in spaces like my former class in the Brazilian church, where students and instructors diverged from some of the normative Zumba Fitness styles rooted in tropicalized Latinness, instead using their own cultural backgrounds to orient their classes. They happen when instructors like Morgan or Kathy use their Zumba Fitness classes as platforms to shed light on current events, or when instructors like Miriam, Rebecca, Leah, or Amanda encourage their students to try new things that might introduce them to new cultures they maybe otherwise would not have encountered.

They happen when instructors like Julia, Erin, or Angela invest time and money into learning more about the dance practices they teach in order to feel that they are doing these cultural traditions justice. They happen when instructors like Stephanie and Vicki hope to offer not only exercise but also emotional support. And they happen when all of these instructors create community with one another or try to cultivate it for their students. As Kathy mentioned to me, the hope is that as instructors they might make a difference to one person, which might then cause a ripple effect, however small, that could introduce new ideas to other people.

For me, Rony Gratereaut's bomba and plena routine on the Zumba Cruise was both fascinating and moving. I saw the pride he evoked in many other students in the class, who expressed sheer joy waving flags and singing along during his routine. I knew that not everyone would understand his cultural references, and some might even interpret them in problematic ways. Still, I felt my own sense of joy and comfort participating in that space. And I think that this is the promise of Zumba Fitness for many people. The Zumba Home Office's emphasis on monitoring instructors' payments of their dues rather than the content of their classes has enabled the creation of diverse, local Zumba scenes. I am certain that researchers in other places will encounter more alternative spaces within Zumba Fitness. I hear about them often from friends in other parts of the country whose experiences differ quite a bit from my own. Still, I have focused this book primarily on the ways that Zumba Fitness circulates hegemonic ideologies and stereotypes of tropicalized Latinness because it was important to me to outline how this happens in order to counter it. Systemic racism works because ideologies like neoliberalism or postracialism render it invisible. It also works because of its ordinariness. By centering the infiltration of tropicalized Latinness within the everyday space of the gym, I hope to have contributed, at least a little, to unmasking how neoliberal and postracial discourses operate in order to help identify spaces of possibility for dismantling them. Even though Zumba Fitness is a microcosm of these problems at work, I still think it can be one of these spaces of possibility. So I'll lace up my sneakers, grab my water, and get to work.

NOTES

~~~

WARM-UP

1 HIIT refers to "high-intensity interval training," characterized by intense spurts of exercise followed by short recovery periods.

2 See, e.g., Delextrat et al., "An 8-Week Exercise Intervention"; Lee et al., "Affective Change with Variations"; Viana et al., "Anxiolytic Effects of a Single Session."

3 Throughout this book, I use *rhythms* to refer to these genres in keeping with Zumba's vocabulary. However, as I mentioned previously, I recognize that these are all actual genres of music that incorporate various rhythms.

4 Throughout this book, I use the term *Latinx* to refer to people and cultural practices of Latin American descent within the United States (except when directly quoting other authors who use other terms). Proponents of the term *Latinx* argue that it is more inclusive of gender, sexuality, and race. I also see *Latinx* as a uniquely US-based construction that speaks to the particular experiences of people of Latin American descent within the United States. This makes the term especially useful for this project since I am primarily focused on interrogating the various meanings and representations of Latinness and Latinidad in Zumba Fitness scenes within the United States.

5 Pérez and Greenwood-Robinson, *Zumba*, 46.

6 I pieced together this story from multiple accounts of Zumba Fitness's founding. Of particular relevance are Pérez and Greenwood-Robinson's book *Zumba: Ditch the Workout, Join the Party!*, and an in-depth interview with Beto Pérez and Alberto Perlman on the NPR podcast *How I Built This*. See Guy Raz, "Zumba: Beto Pérez and Alberto Perlman," December 4, 2017, in *How I Built This*, produced by Rund Abdelfatah, podcast, 42:32, https://www.npr.org/2017/12/04/567747778/zumba-beto-perez-alberto-perlman.

7 When I began this research in 2016, the Zumba Fitness official website claimed to have over 200,000 classes in 180 countries. At the time of this writing in 2022, however, those statistics have been removed. This could be for many reasons—declining popularity, a shifting marketing focus, or a host of other issues. Nevertheless, it is undeniable that Zumba Fitness is a global fitness phenomenon.

8 Leigh Buchanan, "Zumba Fitness: Company of the Year," *Inc.*, December 4, 2012, https://www.inc.com/magazine/201212/leigh-buchanan/zumba-fitness-company-of-the-year-2012.html.

9 Nancy Dahlberg, "How Zumba Still Rocks the Fitness World," *Miami Herald*, August 26, 2018, https://www.miamiherald.com/latest-news/article217263095.html.

10 For an overview of these arguments, see Carey, "Citizenship."

11 LeBesco, "Fat."

12 McKenzie, *Getting Physical*.

13 McKenzie, *Getting Physical*, 38.

14 McKenzie, *Getting Physical*.

15 McKenzie, *Getting Physical*, 123.

16 Dworkin and Wachs, *Body Panic*; McKenzie, *Getting Physical*.

17 Dworkin and Wachs, *Body Panic*, 35.

18 Smith Maguire, *Fit for Consumption*, 20.

19 McKenzie, *Getting Physical*, 164.

20 Woitas, "'Exercise Teaches You the Pleasure of Discipline'"; McKenzie, *Getting Physical*, 164–65.

21 McKenzie, *Getting Physical*, 145.

22 For a critique of the "welfare queen" stereotype, see P. Collins, *Black Feminist Thought*, 78–81.

23 Hernandez, *Aesthetics of Excess*, 9–11.

24 Ferrell, "'White Man's Burden,'" 260.

25 Firth, "Healthy Choices and Heavy Burdens"; Greenhalgh and Carney, "Bad Biocitizens?"; Minkoff-Zern and Carney, "Latino Im/Migrants, 'Dietary Health' and Social Exclusion"; Thompson, "Neoliberalism, Soul Food, and the Weight of Black Women."

26 Boero, "Fat Kids, Working Moms, and the 'Epidemic of Obesity,'" 116.

27 Minkoff-Zern and Carney, "Latino Im/Migrants, 'Dietary Health' and Social Exclusion," 471.

28 For instance, Molina shows how public health programs in Los Angeles at the turn of the twentieth century targeted Chinese, Japanese, and Mexican immigrant groups and promoted good health and hygiene as crucial for citizenship. See Molina, *Fit to Be Citizens?*

29 Ramírez, *Assimilation*, 12.

30 Ramírez, *Assimilation*, 72.

31 Zanker and Gard, "Fatness, Fitness, and the Moral Universe," 49.

32 California's Proposition 187 blocked undocumented immigrants from accessing public services. Although it was ultimately declared unconstitutional, Prop 187 reflected the growing anti-immigrant sentiment of the 1990s. The Illegal Immigration Reform and Immigrant Responsibility Act of 1996 was federal legislation that significantly criminalized undocumented immigration, militarized the US-Mexico

border, and limited immigration to those who could prove they would not become a public charge. For more information, see Menjívar, "Illegality"; and Paik, *Bans, Walls, Raids, Sanctuary.*

33 Amaya, *Citizenship Excess*; Bebout, *Whiteness on the Border.*

34 For analysis of the immigrant marches, see Chavez, *Latino Threat.*

35 Bebout, *Whiteness on the Border*; Chavez, *Latino Threat.*

36 Chavez, *Latino Threat*, 3.

37 Bebout, *Whiteness on the Border.*

38 For more on the Latin boom, see Cepeda, *Musical ImagiNation.*

39 Cepeda, *Musical ImagiNation*, 58.

40 Rivera-Rideau, "Reinventing Enrique Iglesias."

41 Santa Ana, *Brown Tide Rising.*

42 Perry, *Cultural Politics of U.S. Immigration*, 185, 189.

43 Amaya, *Citizenship Excess*, 162.

44 Dávila, *Latino Spin.*

45 I use pseudonyms for all of the Zumba instructors whom I interviewed except for public figures (e.g., Zumba International Presenters) who agreed to the use of their names.

46 Zack Guzman, "How Zumba's Founders Turned a Video Made on the Beach with a Handycam into a Global Phenomenon," CNBC, last updated July 24, 2018, https://www.cnbc.com/2018/07/19/how-zumba -exercise-class-went-from-an-idea-to-global-phenomenon.html.

47 For an overview of how scholars approach the concept of Latinidad, see Aparicio, "Latinidad/es."

48 Mora, *Making Hispanics.*

49 Dávila, *Latinos, Inc.*

50 Aparicio, *Negotiating Latinidad*, 31.

51 Herrera, *Latin Numbers*, 13.

52 Molina-Guzmán, *Dangerous Curves*, 9.

53 Aparicio and Chávez-Silverman, *Tropicalizations*, 8.

54 Aparicio and Chávez Silverman, *Tropicalizations*, 8.

55 Maldonado-Torres, "Sovereignty."

56 Aparicio and Chávez-Silverman, *Tropicalizations*; Herrera, *Latin Numbers*; Sandoval-Sánchez, *José, Can You See?*; Dávila, *Latinos, Inc.*; Báez, *In Search of Belonging.*

57 Dahlberg, "How Zumba Still Rocks the Fitness World."

58 "Becky G at the XII Zumba Fitness-Concert," Zumba, August 12, 2019, YouTube video, 0:56, youtube.com/watch?v=q7TqP8LxwpU.

59 Melamed, "Spirit of Neoliberalism."

60 hooks, *Black Looks.*

61 Other scholars who have researched comparable fitness programs have encountered similar restrictions. For example, Devon Powers and DM Greenwell note that the "proprietary, litigious nature" of

the CrossFit and Bikram Yoga brands that they study required that they use a combination of ethnography and outside resources like "journalism, trade books, Internet resources" to analyze these fitness brands. See Powers and Greenwell, "Branded Fitness," 524.

62 I finished my research just before the COVID-19 pandemic hit. Like everything else, Zumba Fitness classes shut down. However, as I detail later in the book, the Zumba Home Office allowed instructors to teach online. This meant that I could continue taking classes. It also enabled me to take classes with Zumba International Presenters who live in other states and to attend special master classes that Zumba International Presenters opened to the public. Although I maintained my own Zumba Fitness practice throughout this research, I collected all of the ethnographic and interview data for this project prior to the pandemic.

63 Ramírez, *Assimilation*, 15.

64 Zumba International Presenters are instructors, most of whom have climbed the Zumba ranks, who often serve as the face of the brand with features in advertisements, videos, and the like.

CHAPTER 1. SELLING AUTHENTICITY

1 "Zumba Fitness World Party Video Game US Commercial," November 27, 2013, YouTube video, 0:30, https://www.youtube.com/watch?v=bRsoDAK35HI.

2 "Zumba Fitness World Party—Nintendo Wii," Amazon.com listing, accessed March 23, 2023, https://www.amazon.com/Zumba-Fitness-World-Party-Nintendo-Wii/dp/B00DJYK8XS/.

3 It is worth pointing out that this distinction between exotic tropical others and modern whiteness is also evident in the video game itself. The segments about Los Angeles and Europe focus primarily on technique and training, while the segments on Brazil, the Caribbean, Puerto Rico, and Hawai'i all emphasize feeling, inherent rhythm, and tradition. This distinction further reinforces the dichotomy between the modern Global North and the tropicalized Global South. It also mirrors similar discourses in other dance scenes like ballroom wherein European-derived dances are often thought of as more technical and refined than Latin ones.

4 Miller, *Playable Bodies*, 63.

5 Miller, *Playable Bodies*, 64.

6 Miller, *Playable Bodies*, 75, 166.

7 Miller, *Playable Bodies*, 1.

8 Daniel Nye Griffiths, "Marketing Zumba Fitness: Selling Games without Gamers," *Forbes*, February 23, 2012, https://www.forbes.com

/sites/danielnyegriffiths/2012/02/23/zumba-fitness-game-marketing/#3b2dd14d31c8.

9   Dávila, *Latinx Art*, 15.

10   Dorr, *On Site, in Sound*; Feld, "Sweet Lullaby"; Guilbault, "On Redefining the 'Local.'"

11   Sánchez Prado, "Diana Kennedy, Rick Bayless and the Imagination."

12   Dávila, *Latinx Art*.

13   Pérez and Greenwood-Robinson, *Zumba*, 68.

14   Godreau, *Scripts of Blackness*.

15   Garcia, *Listening for Africa*, 9.

16   Kheshti, *Modernity's Ear*, 56.

17   Garcia, *Listening for Africa*, 264.

18   Pérez and Greenwood-Robinson, *Zumba*, 73.

19   Pérez and Greenwood-Robinson, *Zumba*, 68.

20   For more about the transnational circulations and transformations of merengue, cumbia, reggaetón, and other popular Latin music genres, see Pacini Hernandez, *Oye Como Va!* For more specific information on cumbia, see Fernández L'Hoeste and Vila, *Cumbia!*; and Fernández L'Hoeste, "All Cumbias, the Cumbia." For more specific information about merengue, see also Austerlitz, "Local and International Trends." For more information about reggaetón, please see Rivera, Marshall, and Hernandez, *Reggaeton*; and Rivera-Rideau, *Remixing Reggaetón*. Finally, for more information about salsa, see Waxer, *Situating Salsa*; and Flores, *Salsa Rising*.

21   Pérez and Greenwood-Robinson, *Zumba*, 69.

22   Pérez and Greenwood-Robinson, *Zumba*, 71.

23   Pérez and Greenwood-Robinson, *Zumba*, 69.

24   For an overview of the debates about salsa's origins, see Berríos-Miranda, "Is Salsa a Musical Genre?"

25   Flores, *Salsa Rising*; Valentín-Escobar, "El Hombre que Respira Debajo del Agua."

26   Pérez and Greenwood-Robinson, *Zumba*, 69.

27   There are several other problems with this statement. For example, Puerto Ricans are all US citizens. Although they often share many aspects of the immigrant experience, particularly around adjusting to new cultural and linguistic norms, they technically are not immigrants due to their citizenship status. The periodization in this statement is also a little off; although the debate about origins makes the time period in which salsa developed tricky to discern, I think it is generally acknowledged that the heyday for New York Puerto Rican salsa was actually more in the 1970s than the 1950s.

28   Cepeda, *Musical ImagiNation*; Pacini Hernandez, "Name Game."

29 Zumba Fitness, "Grammy Award-Winning Singer, Songwriter, and Multi-Platinum Artist Meghan Trainor Teams with Zumba to Promote Latest Single 'No Excuses' and Empower Women Everywhere," PR Newswire, March 5, 2018, https://www.prnewswire.com/news-releases/grammy-award-winning-singer-songwriter-and-multi-platinum-artist-meghan-trainor-teams-with-zumba-to-promote-latest-single-no-excuses-and-empower-women-everywhere-300608147.html.

30 Latin music is, of course, made up of several different genres of music. However, I call it one genre here because that is how it was reported. For more, see Jeff Benjamin, "Latin Music Is Now More Popular Than Country and EDM in America," *Forbes*, January 4, 2019, https://www.forbes.com/sites/jeffbenjamin/2019/01/04/latin-music-in-2018-album-song-sales-consumption-buzzangle-report/?sh=2051f07d5add.

31 Leila Cobo, "Body Rock: Is Zumba the Next Music Platform?," *Billboard*, June 22, 2012, https://www.billboard.com/articles//1093057/body-rock-is-zumba-the-next-music-platform.

32 Zumba Fitness, "Zumba Fitness Launches Inventive Music Platform; Dances to a New Song from International Superstar Pitbull," PR Newswire, June 9, 2011, https://www.prnewswire.com/news-releases/zumba-fitness-launches-inventive-music-platform-dances-to-a-new-song-from-international-superstar-pitbull-123542509.html.

33 Leila Cobo, "The Big Don Data," *Billboard*, April 28, 2012, 14+.

34 Quoted in Cobo, "Body Rock."

35 Cobo, "Body Rock."

36 Cobo, "Body Rock."

37 For data on Daddy Yankee's performance on the *Billboard* Latin Rhythm Airplay chart, see "Daddy Yankee," *Billboard*, accessed July 25, 2023, https://www.billboard.com/artist/daddy-yankee/chart-history/lra/. For information on Daddy Yankee's status as the first Latin artist to reach number one on Spotify, see "Daddy Yankee Is First Latin Artist to Hit No. 1 on Spotify," *Billboard*, July 9, 2017, https://www.billboard.com/music/latin/daddy-yankee-spotify-first-latin-artist-no-1-7858042/.

38 Quoted in Gail Gaden Spencer, "Zumba Bulks Up Latin Stars' Fan Base," *Washington Post*, August 24, 2013.

39 "Daddy Yankee and Zumba Announce Global Partnership in Support of Artist's New Single 'Hula Hoop,'" *Z-Life*, March 3, 2017, https://web.archive.org/web/20171108121316/https://zlife.zumba.com/daddy-yankee-zumba-announce-global-partnership-support-artists-new-single-hula-hoop/.

40 Pérez and Greenwood-Robinson, *Zumba*, 71.

41 For more about the development of reggae en español, see Rivera, Marshall, and Pacini Hernandez, *Reggaeton*, 99–109.

42 Pérez and Greenwood-Robinson, *Zumba*, 71.

43 For example, see "Daddy Yankee and Zumba Announce Global Partnership."

44 Julia's reference to "African" rhythm here homogenizes music and dance practices across continental Africa despite referencing Angolan kizomba. Her language reflects the broader trend of people in the Global North homogenizing African cultures but also Zumba Fitness's definition of "African" as one of its rhythms at the time of this interview. Given the popularity of Afrobeat and other pop styles from western African countries like Nigeria, in particular, the new list of workshops for the 2023 Zumba Convention include sessions that center specifically on dance traditions from Ghana and South Africa. However, the convention also includes the session "African Workout: Enter the Jungle" that many instructors I met with had taken in the early 2010s. See "ZinCon," accessed March 8, 2023, https://convention.zumba.com/sessions/flavors.

45 Master Classes are special Zumba Fitness classes that are open to the public. They are often taught by a guest, such as a popular Zumba International Presenter, or a group of instructors who do not normally work together. Master Classes also usually cost more than typical Zumba classes; over the course of my research I paid between twenty and fifty dollars to attend Master Classes around New England. In many ways, Master Classes are akin to a concert. In fact, depending on the venue, up to a few hundred people might attend a Master Class by a particularly famous Zumba Presenter.

46 Fiol-Matta, "Pop Latinidad."

47 I never had the opportunity to attend a Jam Session or see notes that instructors brought home from them. Still, given that this contradiction around authenticity in Zumba Fitness is a general pattern, it is not surprising to me that some instructors would have these experiences in Jam Sessions.

48 In the past, Zumba Fitness would post the titles of all of their Flavor Sessions online, and they were publicly accessible. At the start of this research around 2015 and 2016, I noticed other flavor sessions about dancehall, soca, Motown, Bollywood, and more. Unfortunately, over the past few years, Zumba Fitness restricted access to the convention program to those with a ZIN account. The names of workshops I list here come from the interviews I conducted with Zumba Instructors. However, in preparation for the 2023 Convention, Zumba Fitness listed all of the possible Flavor Sessions online once again. It is notable that they have since removed names like Asian

Invasion and Mandarin Mayhem. Instead, they offer a new K-Pop session called "Superstar K." Nevertheless, they have kept the "Enter the Jungle" name for the "African" workshop, and added new names that similarly reproduce racial stereotypes such as "Mexican Fiesta 2.0" and "Cha Cha Fever." See "ZinCon," March 23, 2023, https://convention.zumba.com/sessions/flavors.

49 Hutchinson, *From Quebradita to Duranguense*; Simonett, *Banda*.

50 Hutchinson, "Breaking Borders / Quebrando Fronteras," 49.

51 Kun, "What Is an MC If He Can't Rap to Banda?"

CHAPTER 2. SELLING FIESTA

1 Guy Raz, "Zumba: Beto Pérez and Alberto Perlman," December 4, 2017, in *How I Built This*, produced by Rund Abdelfatah, podcast, 42:32, https://www.npr.org/2017/12/04/567747778/zumba-beto-perez-alberto-perlman.

2 Corona, "Cultural Locations of (U.S.) Latin Rock," 250.

3 Sandoval-Sánchez, *José, Can You See?*

4 Abreu, *Rhythms of Race*; Sandoval-Sánchez, *José, Can You See?*

5 Poey, *Cuban Women and Salsa.*

6 For more on the Latin boom, see Cepeda, *Musical ImagiNation*; Fiol-Matta, "Pop Latinidad."

7 Rivera-Rideau and Torres-Leschnik, "Colors and Flavors of My Puerto Rico."

8 For example, see Dávila, *Latinos, Inc.*; Goin, "Marginal Latinidad"; Rivera-Rideau, "Reinventing Enrique Iglesias."

9 Cocks, *Tropical Whites*, 5.

10 León, "Tropical Overexposure," 214.

11 Cocks, *Tropical Whites*, 19–22.

12 León, "Tropical Overexposure," 214. For a historical overview of the way that European writers described the Caribbean as a tropical landscape characterized by primitivity and "hedonism," see Sheller, "Natural Hedonism."

13 Cocks uses the idea of the "Southland" to describe the tropics. In her study, US places like Florida and Southern California become part of this "Southland" because of their reputations as warm-weather vacation spots characterized by beaches and sunshine. Similarly, León's analysis centers Miami as a place that represents the tropics within US boundaries. In this book, I argue that Zumba Fitness constructs the tropics as a place that exists outside of the United States in ways that further the company's attachment to foreignness as a marker of authenticity.

14 Sandoval-Sánchez, *José, Can You See?*, 23.

15 Sandoval-Sánchez, *José, Can You See?*, 24.

16 Sandoval-Sánchez, *José, Can You See?*, 59.

17 Rivera-Rideau, "Reinventing Enrique Iglesias."

18 Poey, *Cuban Women and Salsa*, 87.

19 Cepeda, *Musical ImagiNation*.

20 Sandoval-Sánchez, *José, Can You See?*, 28.

21 Forman, *'Hood Comes First*, 51.

22 Rivera-Rideau, *Remixing Reggaetón*.

23 For examples in the food industry, see Gaytán, "From Sombreros to Sincronizadas"; and Pilcher, *Planet Taco*. For fine arts, see Dávila, *Latinx Art*.

24 Bosse, "Whiteness and the Performance of Race." See also McMains, "'Hot' Latin Dance."

25 García, *Salsa Crossings*.

26 Dormani, "So You Think You Can Salsa."

27 Desmond, "Embodying Difference," 50.

28 Stoever, *Sonic Color Line*, 7.

29 Stoever, *Sonic Color Line*, 13. Roshanak Kheshti similarly argues that world music consumers have an "aural imaginary" that enables them to imagine a racialized foreign other through their listening practices. See Kheshti, *Modernity's Ear*.

30 Corona, "Cultural Locations of (U.S.) Latin Rock." For analysis of the role of sound in imagining the Caribbean, particularly in the tourism industry, see Guilbault and Rommen, *Sounds of Vacation*.

31 Bosse, "Whiteness and the Performance of Race," 33; McMains, "Hot' Latin Dance," 483.

32 McMains, "'Hot' Latin Dance," 484.

33 Susan Perez, "Zumba Home Office Employee Spotlight: Melanie Canevaro," *Z-Life*, July 12, 2016, archived November 9, 2020, at Archive .org, https://web.archive.org/web/20201109235045/https://zlife.zumba .com/zumba-home-office-employee-spotlight-melanie-canevaro/.

34 Nancy Dahlberg, "How Zumba Still Rocks the Fitness World," *Miami Herald*, August 26, 2018. It is also worth pointing out that Perlman mentioned to NPR that the COVID-19 pandemic only strengthened the company's clothing brand given consumers' overall interest in comfortable workout gear during the pandemic. See Guy Raz, "How I Built Resilience: Alberto Perlman of Zumba," August 6, 2020, produced by Candice Lim, podcast, 20:33, https://www.npr.org/2020/08 /05/899285867/how-i-built-resilience-alberto-perlman-of-zumba.

35 Quoted in Vivian Giang, "How Zumba Became the Largest Fitness Brand in the World," *Business Insider*, December 31, 2012, https://www .businessinsider.com/how-zumba-became-the-largest-fitness-brand -in-the-world-2012-12.

36 Stoever, *Sonic Color Line*, 13.

37 Stoever, *Sonic Color Line*, 12.

38 Barbara Gonzalez, "AirBnb Tourist Calls Dominican NYC Neigh-borhood 'Loud' and 'Uneducated,' Gets Slammed on Reddit," *Latina*, August 9, 2016, archived February 16, 2017, at Archive.org, https://web.archive.org/web/20170216011934/http://www.latina.com /lifestyle/our-issues/tourist-calls-dominican-neighborhood-loud -slammed-reddit.

39 Stoever-Ackerman, "Splicing the Sonic Color-Line."

40 Hernandez, *Aesthetics of Excess*, 12.

41 Hernandez, *Aesthetics of Excess*.

42 Casillas, Ferrada, and Hinojos, "Accent on *Modern Family*."

43 For analysis of this issue, see Hernandez, *Aesthetics of Excess*; Molina-Guzmán, *Dangerous Curves*, 23–49.

44 Tim Clark, "Tweets (and More) of the Week: Why Are We Looking at Sotomayor's Nails?," *Forbes*, December 24, 2009, https://www.forbes .com/2009/12/24/sonia-sotomayor-justice-latina-forbes-woman-style -red-nail-polish.html#3818ed5164d5; Marci Robin, "Why It Matters That Alexandria Ocasio-Cortez Wore Hoops to Her Swearing-In Ceremony," *Allure*, January 5, 2019, https://www.allure.com/story /alexandria-ocasio-cortez-red-lipstick-hoops-swearing-in-sonia -sotomayor-nail-polish; Roberta Gorin-Paracka, "Rep. Alexandria Ocasio-Cortez Explains Why She Wore Red Lipstick and Gold Hoop Earrings to Swearing-In Ceremony," *Teen Vogue*, January 5, 2019, https://www.teenvogue.com/story/alexandria-ocasio-cortez-red -lipstick-gold-hoop-earrings-swearing-in-ceremony.

45 Londoño, *Abstract Barrios*, 97.

46 Hernandez, *Aesthetics of Excess*, 18.

47 Hernandez, *Aesthetics of Excess*, 9.

48 Quoted in Susan Perez, "Ready to Get Wild? Your New Jungle-Inspired Zumba Wear Is Waiting," *Z-Life*, April 25, 2017, archived November 12, 2020, at Archive.org, https://web.archive.org/web /20201112032640/https://zlife.zumba.com/ready-get-wild-new-jungle -inspired-zumba-wear-waiting/.

49 In an interesting twist, Lopez incorporated "Let's Get Loud" into a rendition of patriotic songs ("This Land Is Your Land" and "Amer-ica the Beautiful") at President Joe Biden's 2021 inauguration just after reciting a portion of the Pledge of Allegiance in Spanish. This event followed her 2020 Super Bowl halftime show in which analysts claimed her performance of "Let's Get Loud" was a political rallying cry against the unlawful imprisonment of unaccompanied Latin American immigrant minors during the Trump administration.

However, at the time of the Zumba Wear collection (2017), the song was not generally recognized as a political anthem.

50 For more on the butt as a symbol of Latina hypersexuality (including as it pertains to Jennifer Lopez), see Barrera, "Hottentot 2000"; Beltrán, "Hollywood Latina Body"; Durham and Báez, "Tail of Two Women"; Molina-Guzmán and Valdivia, "Brain, Brow, and Booty"; and Negrón-Muntaner, *Boricua Pop*, 228–46.

51 DJ MAM'S OFFICIAL, "DJ MAM'S—Fiesta Buena (Feat Luis Guisao & Soldat Jahman & Special Guest Beto Perez) [OFFICIEL]," October 10, 2012, YouTube video, 3:12, https://www.youtube.com/watch?v=7QZ7KEa-qjM.

52 For more on stereotypes of Latinx people in the media, see Ramirez Berg, *Latino Images in Film*; Molina-Guzmán, *Dangerous Curves*.

53 Chavez, *Latino Threat*.

54 Aparicio and Chávez-Silverman, *Tropicalizations*, 10

55 For example, see Bosse, "Whiteness and the Performance of Race"; García, *Salsa Crossings*.

56 Dworkin and Wachs, *Body Panic*.

57 Park, "Psy-Zing Up."

58 For analysis of Shakira's crossover, see Cepeda, *Musical ImagiNation*.

59 For analysis of Beyoncé and the politics of respectability, see Amin, "Girl Power, Real Politics"; Durham, "Check on It"; and Griffin, "At Last . . . ?"

60 Nieri and Hughes, "All about Having Fun."

61 Gaunt, "Is Twerking African?," 312, 316.

62 Gaunt, "Is Twerking African?"; Pérez, "Ontology of Twerk." It is important to point out that Gaunt and Pérez are both skeptical of moves to trace twerking's origins directly to specific dance practices in continental Africa. Pérez argues that doing so reproduces problematic assumptions about Africa as a site of past tradition, and that such moves also aim to situate twerking within dominant tropes of respectability. Still, both Gaunt and Pérez argue that understanding twerking in relation to larger diasporic dance practices offers opportunities to consider African diasporic connections in more nuanced and productive ways.

63 Gaunt, "YouTube, Twerking and You."

64 Rivera-Rideau, *Remixing Reggaetón*, 137.

65 For analysis of how hip-hop and Black masculinity circulate in the mainstream, see Jeffries, *Thug Life*.

66 Rita Moreno is a Puerto Rican actress perhaps best known for her role as Anita in the 1961 film *West Side Story*. Some critics have argued that the figure of Anita furthered stereotypes of the Latina

spitfire in US popular culture; for example, see Sandoval-Sánchez, *José, Can You See?*

67 McMains, "'Hot' Latin Dance," 486–87.

CHAPTER 3. SELLING FUN

1 GroupX refers to group fitness classes in a gym or health club.
2 Smith Maguire, *Fit for Consumption*; McKenzie, *Getting Physical*.
3 hooks, *Black Looks*, 26.
4 Nieri and Hughes, "All about Having Fun."
5 Seal et al., "Fear of Judgement," 385.
6 McKenzie, *Getting Physical*, 167. See also Woitas, "'Exercise Teaches You the Pleasure of Discipline.'"
7 Smith Maguire, *Fit for Consumption*, 140, 143.
8 Smith Maguire, *Fit for Consumption*, 143.
9 Dworkin and Wachs, *Body Panic*; Smith Maguire, *Fit for Consumption*.
10 Dawson, "CrossFit: Fitness Cult or Reinventive Institution?"; Musselman, "Training for the 'Unknown and Unknowable.'"
11 James and Gill, "Neoliberalism and the Communicative Labor of CrossFit," 716. See also Dawson, "CrossFit"; Powers and Greenwell, "Branded Fitness."
12 James and Gill, "Neoliberalism and the Communicative Labor of CrossFit"; Musselman, "Training for the 'Unknown and Unknowable.'"
13 Danielle Freeman, "The Secret Sexual History of the Barre Workout," *Cut*, January 19, 2018, https://www.thecut.com/2018/01/barre -workout-sexual-history.html.
14 Markula and Clark, "Ballet-Inspired Workouts."
15 Markula and Clark, "Ballet-Inspired Workouts," 68.
16 Markula and Clark, "Ballet-Inspired Workouts," 59.
17 Nieri and Hughes, "Zumba Instructor Strategies," 9.
18 Nieri and Hughes, "All about Having Fun," 139; Nieri and Hughes, "Zumba Instructor Strategies," 10.
19 Nieri and Hughes "All about Having Fun."
20 For example, see Viana et al., "Anxiolytic Effects"; Delextrat et al., "8-Week Exercise Intervention."
21 Brandi Neal, "The Best Workout for Anxiety Isn't What You Think," *Bustle*, July 6, 2018, bustle.com/p/the-best-workout-for-anxiety-isnt -what-youd-think-9684630.
22 Jacquelyn Brummond, "Dancing through My Anxiety," *Z-Life*, March 16, 2016, archived October 3, 2022, at Archive.org, https://web .archive.org/web/20221003053047/https://zlife.zumba.com/dancing -through-my-anxiety/.

23 Jessica Smith, "5 Ways to Burn More Fat in Zumba Class," *Shape*, February 7, 2012, archived May 13, 2021, at Archive.org, https://web.archive.org/web/20210513072501/https://www.shape.com/fitness/tips/5-ways-burn-more-fat-zumba-class.

24 Zumba PR, "What Happens to Your Brain When You Dance?," *Z-Life*, September 3, 2015, archived October 3, 2022, at Archive.org, https://web.archive.org/web/20221003053843/https://zlife.zumba.com/story/what-happens-to-your-brain-when-you-dance/.

25 Lau, *New Age Capitalism*.

26 For a critique of the assumption that African diasporic music is primitive, see Garcia, *Listening for Africa*.

27 Desmond, "Embodying Difference," 41.

28 Bosse, "Whiteness and the Performance of Race."

29 Yahoo Finance, "Global Dance Fitness Phenomenon Zumba Launches First Multimedia Campaign 'Let It Move You,'" September 18, 2014, https://finance.yahoo.com/news/global-dance-fitness-phenomenon-zumba-130000101.html.

30 Yahoo Finance, "Global Dance Fitness."

31 Yahoo Finance, "Global Dance Fitness."

32 For an analysis of this rhetoric, see Santa Ana, *Brown Tide Rising*.

33 View the commercial at Seguidos por Sherlock, "ZUMBA—Let It Move You," September 23, 2014, YouTube video, 1:30, https://www.youtube.com/watch?v=pWqsziP2LMQ.

34 Yahoo Finance, "Global Dance Fitness"; "Zumba's 'Let It Move You' Campaign Spreads Dance Movement Everywhere," *Fitness Gaming*, November 15, 2014, https://www.fitnessgaming.com/news/events-and-fun/zumba-let-it-move-you.html

35 Bebout, *Whiteness on the Border*.

36 Carlye Wisel, "Crazy Happy Zumba," *Racked*, May 31, 2016, https://www.racked.com/2016/3/31/11333100/zumba-cruise.

37 See, e.g., Delextrat et al., "8-Week Exercise Intervention"; Viana et al., "Anxiolytic Effects"; Donath et al., "Effects of Zumba Training"; Vendramin et al., "Health Benefits of Zumba Fitness Training"; Krishnan et al., "Zumba Dance Improves Health"; Sternlicht, Frisch, and Sumida, "Zumba Fitness Workouts."

38 See Zumba, "Zumba Stories: Smiling on the Outside, Trapped Inside," April 15, 2015, YouTube, 3:39, https://www.youtube.com/watch?v=Yqq7Tnj508Q; and *Z-Life*, "Smiling on the Outside, Trapped Inside," April 15, 2015, archived April 3, 2017, at Archive.org, https://web.archive.org/web/20170403002810/https://zlife.zumba.com/smiling-on-the-outside-trapped-inside/.

39 "Check Out These Incredible Before and After Photos," *Z-Life*, May, 21, 2018, archived December 2, 2022, at Archive.org, https://web

.archive.org/web/20221202023449/https://zlife.zumba.com/check
-incredible-photos/.

40 Jane Chertoff, "How to Use Zumba for Weight Loss," *Healthline*,
April 30, 2019, https://www.healthline.com/health/fitness-exercise
/zumba-for-weight-loss; Markham Heid, "Why Zumba Is Insanely
Good Exercise," *Time*, March 9, 2017, https://time.com/4696746
/zumba-workout-dance-aerobics/; Faith Watson, "Benefits of Zumba
Workouts," *Livestrong*, January 19, 2018, https://www.livestrong.com
/article/68324-zumba-workout-benefits/.

41 "Interview with Gina Grant—Fitness Guru and Education Specialist
for Zumba," *Smartlife*, April 8, 2019, http://www.bindugopalrao.com
/interview-with-gina-grant-fitness-guru-and-education-specialist-for
-zumba/.

42 Dworkin and Wachs, *Body Panic*, 74.

43 Dworkin and Wachs, *Body Panic*, 96. See also L. Collins, "Working
Out the Contradictions."

44 Dworkin and Wachs, *Body Panic*, 56. See also L. Collins, "Working
Out the Contradictions," 93.

45 For example, many Black women who are International Presenters
like US Americans Gina Grant and Loretta Bates, or Colombian
Heidy Torres have light complexions. Many other women presenters embody the so-called Latin look dominant in both English- and
Spanish-language media, such as Dominican-Americans Jeimy
Bueno and Cat Medina, or even Turkish fitness star Ecem Özam. It is
notable that there are more dark-complexioned men in the Zumba
International Presenter ranks, including Mauritian fitness star Ri-
cardo Marmitte, Colombians Wally Díaz and Armando Salcedo, US
American Dahrio Wonder, and Puerto Rican Rony Gratereaut. Still,
all of these men, along with other male International Presenters like
Mauricio Camargo, Jonathan Benoit, and Steve Boedt, share with
Pérez the ideal fitness male body.

46 For more on the global dynamics of colorism, see Nakano Glenn,
Shades of Difference.

47 Powers and Greenwell, "Branded Fitness."

48 Smith Maguire, *Fit for Consumption*, 165.

49 Smith Maguire, *Fit for Consumption*, 176.

50 Nieri and Hughes, "Zumba Instructor Strategies," 10.

51 Nieri and Hughes, "Zumba Instructor Strategies," 10.

52 Nieri and Hughes, "Zumba Instructor Strategies."

53 "Your Happy Place," Zumba Fitness, archived June 9, 2023, at Archive
.org, https://web.archive.org/web/20230609151516/https://www
.zumba.dance/happy.

1   For example, see Gretchen Reynolds, "Is It Safe to Go Back to the Gym?," *New York Times*, updated July 16, 2021, https://www.nytimes .com/2020/05/13/well/move/coronavirus-gym-safety.html; Tara Parker-Pope and Gretchen Reynolds, "Is It Safe to Go Back to Group Exercise Class at the Gym?," *New York Times*, updated August 25, 2021, https://www.nytimes.com/2021/03/22/well/move/exercise -classes-gym-coronavirus-covid.html; Alexis Benveniste, "The $94 Billion Fitness Industry Is Reinventing Itself as COVID-19 Spreads," CNN Business, updated April 1, 2020, https://www.cnn.com/2020/04 /01/business/fitness-studios-coronavirus/index.html.

2   "Coronavirus: South Korean Sect Identified as Hotbed," BBC, February 20, 2020, https://www.bbc.com/news/world-asia-51572137.

3   Jang, Han, and Rhee, "Cluster of Coronavirus Disease Associated with Fitness Dance Classes."

4   Gretchen Reynolds, "What's the Future of Group Exercise Classes?," *New York Times*, updated August 17, 2020, https://www.nytimes.com /2020/06/03/well/coronavirus-gym-exercise-classes-group-fitness.html.

5   Jang, Han, and Rhee, "Cluster of Coronavirus Disease Associated with Fitness Dance Classes," 1919.

6   Benveniste, "The $94 Billion Fitness Industry"; Nathaniel Meyersohn, "Gyms Are Reopening but Virtual Fitness Classes Aren't Going Anywhere," CNN, May 27, 2021, https://www.cnn.com/2021/05 /27/business/virtual-fitness-classes/index.html.

7   Guy Raz, "How I Built Resilience: Alberto Perlman of Zumba," produced by Candice Lim, podcast, minute 2:40 of 20:33, August 6, 2020, https://www.npr.org/2020/08/05/899285867/how-i-built-resilience -alberto-perlman-of-zumba.

8   Many Zumba Fitness instructors had already started using Zoom to teach their courses by the time the company rolled out ZIN Studio. In January 2021, the company added a Zoom Add-On that would give instructors access to premium Zoom functions at a discounted price. Instructors pay an additional $7.50 per month to access the Zoom Add-On. See "Zumba Zoom Add-On FAQs," *Zumba Fitness*, accessed December 9, 2021, https://www.zumba.com/en-US/faq/zoom-studio.

9   At the time of this writing, ZIN Studio remains free, although the Zumba Home Office states on their website that as the pandemic evolves, they will reassess and eventually charge instructors for the service. See "Zumba Zoom Add-On FAQs," https://www.zumba.com /en-US/faq/zin-studio.

10 Raz, "How I Built Resilience," minute 7:30.

11 Raz, "How I Built Resilience," minute 5:37.

12 Raz, "How I Built Resilience," minutes 6:10 and 6:28.

13 Raz, "How I Built Resilience," minute 2:50.

14 Guy Raz, "Zumba: Beto Pérez and Alberto Perlman," December 4, 2017, in *How I Built This*, produced by Rund Abdelfatah, podcast, minute 25:15 of 42:32, https://www.npr.org/2017/12/04/567747778 /zumba-beto-perez-alberto-perlman.

15 Ashley Weatherford, "An Interview with the Founder of Zumba, by My Mom," *Cut*, April 5, 2016, https://www.thecut.com/2016/04/i -asked-my-mom-to-interview-zumba-ceo-shake.html.

16 For a critical analysis of this rhetoric as it pertains to Puerto Rican and Black women, see Briggs, "*La Vida*, Moynihan, and Other Libels."

17 Chavez, *The Latino Threat*, 45.

18 Figueroa et al., "Community-Level Factors Associated with Racial and Ethnic Disparities."

19 Dávila, *Latino Spin*.

20 Lima, *Being Brown*.

21 Lima, *Being Brown*, 47.

22 Ramírez, *Assimilation*, 12.

23 Ramírez, *Assimilation*.

24 Ramírez, *Assimilation*, 82.

25 Ramírez, *Assimilation*, 143.

26 Lima, *Being Brown*; Ramírez, *Assimilation*.

27 Lima, *Being Brown*, 70. See also Perry, *Cultural Politics of US Immigration*.

28 Perry, *Cultural Politics of US Immigration*, 185.

29 Perry, *Cultural Politics of US Immigration*, 178–79.

30 Chris Morris, "5 Self-Made Hispanic Immigrant Millionaires," CNBC, updated June 12, 2017, https://www.cnbc.com/2017/06/12/5-self-made -hispanic-us-immigrant-millionaires.html.

31 Pérez and Greenwood-Robinson, *Zumba*, 27.

32 Pérez and Greenwood-Robinson, *Zumba*, 28.

33 Pérez and Greenwood-Robinson, *Zumba*, 28.

34 Pérez and Greenwood-Robinson, *Zumba*, 29.

35 Pérez and Greenwood-Robinson, *Zumba*, 30.

36 Pérez and Greenwood-Robinson, *Zumba*, 30–31, 34–35.

37 Pérez and Greenwood-Robinson, *Zumba*, 35.

38 Pérez and Greenwood-Robinson, *Zumba*, 35.

39 Pérez and Greenwood-Robinson, *Zumba*, 36–37.

40 Pérez and Greenwood-Robinson, *Zumba*, 39–41.

41 Pérez and Greenwood-Robinson, *Zumba*, 43.

42 For example, see K. Aleisha Fetters, "Meet the Man behind the Dance-Cardio Craze That Changed the Fitness Industry," *Women's Health*, October 20, 2015, https://www.womenshealthmag.com/fitness /a19955263/meet-the-man-behind-the-dance-cardio-craze-that -changed-the-fitness-industry/; Luana Ferreira, "How a Missing Tape

Launched a Global Craze," BBC, August 12, 2019, https://www.bbc
.com/news/business-49111612.

43 Fetters, "Meet the Man behind the Dance-Cardio Craze that
Changed the Fitness Industry."

44 Ferreira, "How a Missing Tape Launched a Global Craze."

45 Beto Pérez, "The Moment I Realized That I—and Zumba—Had
Achieved the American Dream," PopSugar, September 28, 2017,
https://www.popsugar.com/latina/Beto-Perez-Hispanic-Heritage
-Month-Essay-43993418.

46 Pérez, "Moment I Realized."

47 Pérez, "Moment I Realized."

48 Rank, "Random Factor."

49 Dávila, *Latino Spin*, 48–49; Dávila, *Latinos, Inc.*, 95.

50 Dávila, *Latinos, Inc.*, 98–99.

51 Ramírez, *Assimilation*.

52 Zumba, "Zumba Stories: Nour Jabri," October 19, 2017, YouTube
video, 3:43, https://www.youtube.com/watch?v=kTj0b71oupA&t=1s.

53 Zumba, "Zumba Story: 'I Am Myself When I Teach Zumba'—Jhon
Gonzalez," October 12, 2018, YouTube video, 2:41, https://www
.youtube.com/watch?v=6PloS2E8HTM.

54 Zumba, "Zumba Story: 'I Am Myself When I Teach Zumba,'"
minute 0:55.

55 Zumba, "Meet 5 Zumba Choreographers," April 24, 2017, YouTube
video, 2:45, https://www.youtube.com/watch?v=rNqWZAdt8PY. See
minute 1:37.

56 Zumba, "Zumba Story: 'I Am Myself When I Teach Zumba,'" minute 2:15.

57 Zumba, "Zumba Story: Rony Gratereaut," January 22, 2018, YouTube
video, 3:14, https://www.youtube.com/watch?v=ZDbdn2oyeH0.

58 For more information about racial segregation and the criminaliza-
tion of public housing in Puerto Rico, see Dinzey-Flores, *Locked In,
Locked Out*; LeBrón, *Policing Life and Death*; Rivera-Rideau, *Remixing
Reggaetón*, 21–53.

59 Zumba, "Zumba Story: Rony Gratereaut," minute 1:00.

60 Zumba, "Zumba Story: Rony Gratereaut," minute 0:18.

61 Zumba, "Zumba Story: Rony Gratereaut," minute 2:32.

62 Zumba, "Zumba Story: Rony Gratereaut," minute 2:52.

63 Ramírez, *Assimilation*, 87–90.

64 Zumba, "Zumba Stories: Henry Cedeño," June 7, 2017, YouTube
video, 2:40, https://www.youtube.com/watch?v=gn1_ToVl5p0.

65 Zumba, "Meet 5 Zumba Choreographers," minute 1:23.

66 Zumba, "Josette Tkacik's Zumba Story," May 11, 2016, YouTube
video, 2:43, https://www.youtube.com/watch?v=Ehc-LpKCLzA. See
minute 0:32.

67 Zumba, "Zumba Story: Maggie Engels," November 21, 2016, YouTube video, 2:51, https://www.youtube.com/watch?v=3eOEv9LmjFg. See minute 0:06.

68 Zumba, "Zumba Story: Maggie Engels," minute 0:16

69 Zumba, "Zumba Story: Maggie Engels," minute 1:12.

70 Zumba, "Zumba Story: Maggie Engels," minute 1:44.

71 Zumba, "Josette Tkacik's Zumba Story," minute 1:04.

72 Zumba, "Josette Tkacik's Zumba Story," minute 2:05. Based on the similarities between Josette's story and the one that Perlman told NPR about the California instructor, I assume that these are the same person, but I cannot be certain. Perlman never names the instructor specifically. However, Tkacik's success is such an anomaly that it seems very possible that he could be referring to her.

73 Zumba Fitness, "How to Become a Zumba Instructor," accessed March 4, 2022, https://www.zumba.com/en-US/become-a-zumba -instructor.

74 Zumba Fitness, "Stop Party Crashers," accessed March 19, 2023, stop-partycrashers.com.

75 The Nia Technique blends mindfulness, yoga, strength training, and aerobic exercise. Although the Nia Technique website claims that it is "NOT your ordinary 'dance fitness' workout," many people I have met in different dance-fitness settings have described it as such. Bol- lyX is a "Bollywood-inspired dance-fitness program that combines dynamic choreography with the hottest music from around the world" but centers primarily on Bollywood and Bhangra from India. For more information on the Nia Technique, see "About," www.nianow .com/about-nia, accessed July 26, 2023. For more information about BollyX, see "About," www.bollyx.com/about, accessed July 26, 2023.

CHAPTER 5. SELLING LOVE

1 For more about Hurricane María and its aftermath, see Bonilla and LeBrón, *Aftershocks of Disaster*.

2 "Zumba Nation, Our Hearts Are with You," *Z-Life*, September 19, 2017, archived September 27, 2022, at Archive.org, https://web.archive .org/web/20220927141929/https://zlife.zumba.com/zumba-nation -hearts/.

3 "Zumba Nation, Our Hearts Are with You."

4 Zumba Fitness, "FAQs: ZIN-Hosted Zumba Events," accessed March 25, 2023, https://www.zumba.com/en-US/faq/events.

5 See Spread Love, accessed March 19, 2023, polospreadslove.com.

6 Banet-Weiser, *Authentic^{TM}*, 25; Mukherjee and Banet-Weiser, *Commodity Activism*.

7   See Mukherjee and Banet-Weiser, *Commodity Activism*; Orgad and Gill, *Confidence Culture*.

8   King, "Civic Fitness."

9   Mukherjee, Banet-Weiser, and Gray, *Racism Postrace*, 5.

10 Bonilla-Silva, *Racism without Racists*.

11 Melamed, "Spirit of Neoliberalism," 1.

12 Melamed, "Spirit of Neoliberalism."

13 Mukherjee, "Antiracism Limited," 50.

14 For a wide range of examples of the intersections of postracial ideology and US media and popular culture, see Mukherjee, Banet-Weiser, and Gray, *Racism Postrace*.

15 Gray, "Race after Race," 25.

16 Mukherjee and Banet-Weiser, *Commodity Activism*, 9.

17 Mukherjee and Banet-Weiser, *Commodity Activism*, 11.

18 Banet-Weiser, *Authentic*™, 4.

19 Banet-Weiser, *Authentic*™.

20 Powers and Greenwell, "Branded Fitness," 524.

21 Powers and Greenwell, "Branded Fitness," 527.

22 Please note that these statistics pertain to the year 2012. See "Zumba Fitness Introduces Zumba Love Fundraising Platform Supporting Charitable Causes throughout the World," PR Newswire, August 1, 2012, https://www.prnewswire.com/news-releases/zumba-fitness -introduces-zumba-love-fundraising-platform-supporting-charitable -causes-throughout-the-world-164569496.html.

23 See Zumba, "FAQs: ZIN-Hosted Zumba Events."

24 Zumba, "Zumba Love, Philanthropic Platform," YouTube video, 0:54, August 19, 2022, https://www.youtube.com/watch?v =Cz7pgfng2eo.

25 Zumba Fitness, "The World's Largest Dance-Fitness Charity Initiative Turns Party in Pink Zumbathon Campaign into Global Movement," PR Newswire, October 5, 2011, https://www.prnewswire.com /news-releases/the-worlds-largest-dance-fitness-charity-initiative -turns-party-in-pink-zumbathon-campaign-into-global-movement -131133573.html.

26 Zumba, "Dance 'Til You Feel Better! Zumba Party in Pink 2015," August 18, 2015, YouTube video, 2:00, https://www.youtube.com/watch ?v=LYMlTFmrPwo.

27 Zumba, "Jocelyn's Persistence Saved Her Life—Zumba Stories," October 16, 2015, YouTube video, 2:47, https://www.youtube.com/watch?v =ROCa3hbLGsw.

28 Banet-Weiser, *Authentic*™, 144.

29 Banet-Weiser, *Authentic*™, 148.

30 King, "Civic Fitness," 200.

31 It is possible that some individual Zumba Fitness instructors did, in fact, promote these causes. Here, I refer to the Zumba Home Office and the broader Zumba Fitness corporation.

32 "Our Mission: How Zumba Love Is Making a Difference in 2021," *Z-Life*, January 26, 2021, archived September 27, 2022, at Archive.org, https://web.archive.org/web/20220927142423/https://zlife.zumba .com/mission-zumba-love-making-difference-2021/.

33 Zumba, "Zumba Love, Philanthropic Platform," August 19, 2022, YouTube video, 0:54 minutes, https://www.youtube.com/watch?v =Cz7pgfng2eo.

34 King, "Civic Fitness," 215.

35 Orgad and Gill, *Confidence Culture*, 84.

36 Orgad and Gill, *Confidence Culture*, 11.

37 It is worth noting that the products and messages that Orgad and Gill analyze target upper and upper-middle-class white women while simultaneously celebrating racial difference and visible diversity. But not all self-care discourses are the same. Orgad and Gill primarily analyze self-care in the context of hegemonic confidence culture that centers individual attitudes and confidence as the key to neoliberal success. However, alternative discourses of self-care circulate in other communities as a method of survival, such as in Black feminist invocations of self-care as a way to carry on in the face of systemic racism and sexism.

38 Orgad and Gill, *Confidence Culture*, 54.

39 Orgad and Gill, *Confidence Culture*, 41. Emphasis in original.

40 Chris Wright, "Radamel Falcao, James Rodriguez, and Yerry Mina Star in Colombian Music Vid," ESPN, April 23, 2018, https://www.espn .com/soccer/blog/the-toe-poke/65/post/3468976/radamel-falcao -james-rodriguez-and-yerry-mina-star-in-colombia-music-vid.

41 "New HOT Track: Gianluca Vacchi ft. Sebastián Yatra—Love," *Z-Life*, June 10, 2018, archived October 2, 2022, at Archive.org, https://web .archive.org/web/20221002154238/https://zlife.zumba.com/new-hot -track-gianluca-vacchi-ft-sebastian-yatra-love/.

42 Zumba, "Zumba Kids," accessed March 25, 2023, https://www.zumba .com/en-US/party/classes/class-kids.

43 "Dance with Your Kids This September (Choreography)," *Z-Life*, September 1, 2016, archived October 4, 2022, at Archive.org, https:// web.archive.org/web/20221004042053/http://zlife.zumba.com/dance -kids-september-choreography/.

44 Zumba, "Spread Love—Rony Gratereaut and the Zumba Kids," September 1, 2016, YouTube video, 3:18, https://www.youtube.com/watch ?v=ry_3hK0PVUM.

45 "Dreamers" refers to recipients of Deferred Action for Childhood Arrivals (DACA), a program enacted during the Obama administration. It offered people under thirty years old who arrived undocumented in the United States before they were sixteen and who had lived in the United States since 2007 temporary relief from deportation and the ability to receive work permits. At the time of my interview with Kathy in 2017, the Trump administration announced that it would repeal DACA. Since then, DACA has gone through several iterations and legal challenges.

46 Banet-Weiser, *Authentic™*.

47 For more on decolonial love, see Figueroa-Vázquez, *Decolonial Diasporas*.

48 Orgad and Gill, *Confidence Culture*, 43.

49 Brough, "'Fair Vanity'"; Orgad and Gill, *Confidence Culture*, 125–42.

50 Comella, "Changing the World One Orgasm at a Time," 243.

COOLDOWN

1 See chapter 2, which includes Angela's recollection of her experiences in "Puerto Rican Flow" at a Zumba Convention.

2 Aparicio and Chávez-Silverman, *Tropicalizations*, 8, 11. They also note that sometimes Latinx and Latin American cultural workers also engage in "re-tropicalization" that critiques forms of hegemonic tropicalization.

3 Mukherjee, Banet-Weiser, and Gray, *Racism Postrace*.

BIBLIOGRAPHY

~~~~

Abreu, Christina D. *Rhythms of Race: Cuban Musicians and the Making of Latino New York City and Miami, 1940–1960*. Chapel Hill: University of North Carolina Press, 2015.

Amaya, Hector. *Citizenship Excess: Latinos/as, Media, and the Nation*. New York: New York University Press, 2013.

Amin, Takiyah Nur. "Girl Power, Real Politics: Dis/Respectability, Post-Raciality, and the Politics of Inclusion." In *Oxford Handbook of Dance and the Popular Screen*, edited by Melissa Blanco Borelli, 255–67. New York: Oxford University Press, 2014.

Aparicio, Frances R. "Latinidad/es." In *Keywords for Latina/o Studies*, edited by Deborah R. Vargas, Lawrence La Fountain-Stokes, and Nancy Raquel Mirabal, 113–17. New York: New York University Press, 2017.

Aparicio, Frances R. *Negotiating Latinidad: Intralatina/o Lives in Chicago*. Urbana: University of Illinois Press, 2019.

Aparicio, Frances R., and Susana Chávez-Silverman, eds. *Tropicalizations: Transcultural Representations of Latinidad*. Hanover, NH: University Press of New England, 1997.

Austerlitz, Paul. "Local and International Trends in Dominican Merengue." *World of Music* 35, no. 2 (1993): 70–89.

Báez, Jillian M. *In Search of Belonging: Latinas, Media, and Citizenship*. Urbana: University of Illinois Press, 2018.

Banet-Weiser, Sarah. *Authentic^{TM}: The Politics of Ambivalence in a Brand Culture*. New York: New York University Press, 2012.

Barrera, Magdalena. "Hottentot 2000: Jennifer Lopez and Her Butt." In *Sexualities in History: A Reader*, edited by Kim M. Phillips and Barry Reay, 407–20. New York: Routledge, 2000.

Bebout, Lee. *Whiteness on the Border: Mapping the US Racial Imagination in Brown and White*. New York: New York University Press, 2016.

Beltrán, Mary. "The Hollywood Latina Body as a Site of Social Struggle: Media Constructions of Stardom and Jennifer Lopez's 'Cross-over Butt.'" *Quarterly Review of Film and Video* 19, no. 1 (2002): 71–86. https://doi.org/10.1080/10509200214823.

Berríos-Miranda, Marisol. "Is Salsa a Musical Genre?" In *Situating Salsa: Global Markets and Local Meanings in Latin Music*, edited by Lise Waxer, 23–50. New York: Routledge, 2002.

Boero, Natalie. "Fat Kids, Working Moms, and the 'Epidemic of Obesity': Race, Class, and Mother-Blame." In *The Fat Studies Reader*, edited by Esther Rothblum and Sondra Solovay, 113–19. New York: New York University Press, 2009.

Bonilla, Yarimar, and Marisol LeBrón, eds. *Aftershocks of Disaster: Puerto Rico before and after the Storm*. Chicago: Haymarket, 2019.

Bonilla-Silva, Eduardo. *Racism without Racists: Color-Blind Racism and the Persistence of Racial Inequality in America*. 4th ed. Lanham, MD: Rowman and Littlefield, 2014.

Bosse, Joanna. "Whiteness and the Performance of Race in American Ballroom Dance." *Journal of American Folklore* 120, no. 475 (2007): 19–47.

Briggs, Laura. "*La Vida*, Moynihan, and Other Libels: Migration, Social Science, and the Making of the Puerto Rican Welfare Queen." *Centro Journal* 14, no. 1 (2002): 75–101. https://www.redalyc.org/pdf/377/37711290004.pdf.

Brough, Melissa M. "'Fair Vanity': The Visual Culture of Humanitarianism in the Age of Commodity Activism." In *Commodity Activism: Cultural Resistance in Neoliberal Times*, edited by Roopali Mukherjee and Sarah Banet-Weiser, 174–94. New York: New York University Press, 2012.

Carey, Allison. "Citizenship." In *Keywords for Disability Studies*, edited by Rachel Adams, Benjamin Reiss, and David Serlin, 37–39. New York: New York University Press, 2015.

Casillas, Dolores Inés, Juan Sebastian Ferrada, and Sara Veronica Hinojos. "The Accent on *Modern Family*: Listening to Representations of the Latina Vocal Body." *Aztlán: Journal of Chicano Studies* 43, no. 1 (2018): 61–87. https://doi.org/10.1525/azt.2018.43.1.61.

Cepeda, María Elena. *Musical ImagiNation: U.S.-Colombian Identity and the Latin Music Boom*. New York: New York University Press, 2010.

Chavez, Leo R. *The Latino Threat: Constructing Immigrants, Citizens, and the Nation*. 2nd ed. Stanford, CA: Stanford University Press, 2013.

Cocks, Catherine. *Tropical Whites: The Rise of the Tourist South in the Americas*. Philadelphia: University of Pennsylvania Press, 2013.

Collins, Leslea Haravon. "Working Out the Contradictions: Feminism and Aerobics." *Journal of Sport and Social Issues* 26, no. 1 (2002): 85–109. https://doi.org/10.1177/0193723502261006.

Collins, Patricia Hill. *Black Feminist Thought: Knowledge, Consciousness, and the Politics of Empowerment*. 2nd ed. New York: Routledge, 2009.

Comella, Lynn. "Changing the World One Orgasm at a Time: Sex Positive Retail Activism." In *Commodity Activism: Cultural Resistance in Neoliberal Times*, edited by Roopali Mukherjee and Sarah Banet-Weiser, 240–53. New York: New York University Press.

Corona, Ignacio. "The Cultural Locations of (U.S.) Latin Rock." In *The Routledge Companion to Latina/o Media Studies*, edited by Dolores Inés Casillas and María Elena Cepeda, 241–58. New York: Routledge, 2017.

Dávila, Arlene M. *Latino Spin: Public Image and the Whitewashing of Race*. New York: New York University Press, 2008.

Dávila, Arlene M. *Latinos, Inc.: The Marketing and Making of a People*. 2nd ed. Berkeley: University of California Press, 2012.

Dávila, Arlene M. *Latinx Art: Artists, Markets, Politics*. Durham, NC: Duke University Press, 2020.

Dawson, Marcelle C. "CrossFit: Fitness Cult or Reinventive Institution?" *International Review for the Sociology of Sport* 52, no. 3 (May 2017): 361–79. https://doi.org/10.1177/1012690215591793.

Delextrat, Anne A., Sarah Warner, Sarah Graham, and Emma Neupert. "An 8-Week Exercise Intervention Based on Zumba Improves Aerobic Fitness and Psychological Well-Being in Healthy Women." *Journal of Physical Activity and Health* 13, no. 2 (2016): 131–39. https://doi.org/10.1123/jpah.2014-0535.

Desmond, Jane C. "Embodying Difference: Issues in Dance and Cultural Studies." In *Everynight Life: Culture and Dance in Latina/o America*, edited by Celeste Frasier Delgado and José Esteban Muñoz, 33–64. Durham, NC: Duke University Press, 1997.

Dinzey-Flores, Zaire Zenit. *Locked In, Locked Out: Gated Communities in a Puerto Rican City*. Philadelphia: University of Pennsylvania Press, 2013.

Donath, Lars, Ralf Roth, Yannick Hohn, Lukas Zahner, and Oliver Faude. "The Effects of Zumba Training on Cardiovascular and Neuromuscular Function in Female College Students." *European Journal of Sport Science* 14, no. 6 (2014): 569–77. https://doi.org/10.1080/17461391.2013.866168.

Dormani, Carmela Muzio. "So You Think You Can Salsa: Performing Latinness on Reality Dance Television." *Journal of Popular Culture* 53, no. 3 (2020): 720–38. https://doi.org/10.1111/jpcu.12929.

Dorr, Kirstie A. *On Site, in Sound: Performance Geographies in América Latina*. Durham, NC: Duke University Press, 2018.

Durham, Aisha. "Check on It: Beyoncé, Southern Booty, and Black Femininities in Music Video." *Feminist Media Studies* 12, no. 1 (2012): 35–49. https://doi.org/10.1080/14680777.2011.558346.

Durham, Aisha, and Jillian M. Báez. "A Tail of Two Women: Exploring the Contours of Difference in Popular Culture." In *Curriculum and the Cultural Body*, edited by Stephanie Springgay and Debra Freedman, 131–45. New York: Peter Lang, 2007.

Dworkin, Shari L., and Faye Linda Wachs. *Body Panic: Gender, Health, and the Selling of Fitness*. New York: New York University Press, 2009.

Feld, Steven. "A Sweet Lullaby for World Music." *Public Culture* 12, no. 1 (2000): 145–71. https://doi.org/10.1215/08992363-12-1-145.

Fernández L'Hoeste, Héctor. "All Cumbias, the Cumbia: The Latin Americanization of a Tropical Genre." In *Imagining Our Americas: Toward a Trans-*

national Frame, edited by Sandhya Shukla and Heidi Tinsman, 338–64. Durham, NC: Duke University Press, 2007.

Fernández L'Hoeste, Héctor, and Pablo Vila, eds. *Cumbia! Scenes of a Migrant Latin American Music Genre*. Durham, NC: Duke University Press, 2013.

Ferrell, Amy. "'The White Man's Burden': Female Sexuality, Tourist Postcards, and the Place of the Fat Woman in Early 20th-Century U.S. Culture." In *Fat Studies Reader*, edited by Esther Rothblum and Sondra Solovay, 256–62. New York: New York University Press, 2009.

Figueroa, José, Rishi K. Wadhera, Dennis Lee, Robert W. Yeh, and Benjamin D. Sommers. "Community-Level Factors Associated with Racial and Ethnic Disparities in COVID-19 Rates in Massachusetts." *Health Affairs* 39, no. 11 (2020): 1984–92. https://doi.org/10.1377/hlthaff.2020.01040.

Figueroa-Vázquez, Yomaira C. *Decolonial Diasporas: Radical Mapping of Afro-Atlantic Literature*. Chicago: Northwestern University Press, 2020.

Fiol-Matta, Licia. "Pop Latinidad: Puerto Ricans in the Latin Explosion, 1999." *Centro Journal* 14, no. 1 (2002): 27–51.

Firth, Jeanne. "Healthy Choices and Heavy Burdens: Race, Citizenship and Gender in the 'Obesity Epidemic.'" *Journal of International Women's Studies* 13, no. 2 (2012): 33–50. https://vc.bridgew.edu/jiws/vol13/iss2/4.

Flores, Juan. *Salsa Rising: New York Latin Music of the Sixties Generation*. New York: Oxford University Press, 2016.

Forman, Murray. *The 'Hood Comes First: Race, Space, and Place in Rap and Hip-Hop*. Middletown, CT: Wesleyan University Press, 2002.

García, Cindy. *Salsa Crossings: Dancing Latinidad in Los Angeles*. Durham, NC: Duke University Press, 2013.

Garcia, David F. *Listening for Africa: Freedom, Modernity, and the Logic of Black Music's African Origins*. Durham, NC: Duke University Press, 2017.

Gaunt, Kyra D. "Is Twerking African?" In *The Routledge Companion to Black Women's Cultural Histories*, edited by Janell Hobson, 310–20. New York: Routledge, 2021.

Gaunt, Kyra D. "YouTube, Twerking and You: Context Collapse and the Handheld Co-presence of Black Girls and Miley Cyrus." *Journal of Popular Music Studies* 27, no. 3 (2015): 244–73. https://doi.org/10.1111/jpms.12130.

Gaytán, Marie Sarita. "From Sombreros to Sincronizadas: Authenticity, Ethnicity, and the Mexican Restaurant Industry." *Journal of Contemporary Ethnography* 37, no. 3 (2008): 314–41. https://doi.org/10.1177/0891241607309621.

Godreau, Isar. *Scripts of Blackness: Race, Cultural Nationalism, and U.S. Colonialism in Puerto Rico*. Urbana: University of Illinois Press, 2015.

Goin, Keara K. "Marginal Latinidad: Afro-Latinas and US Film." *Latino Studies* 14, no. 3 (2016): 344–63. https://doi.org/10.1057/s41276-016-0006-2.

Gray, Herman. "Race after Race." In *Racism Postrace*, edited by Roopali Mukherjee, Sarah Banet-Weiser, and Herman Gray, 23–36. Durham, NC: Duke University Press, 2019.

Greenhalgh, Susan, and Megan Carney. "Bad Biocitizens? Latinos and the US 'Obesity Epidemic.'" *Human Organization* 73, no. 3 (2014): 267–76. https://doi.org/10.17730/humo.73.3.w53hh1t413038240.

Griffin, Farah Jasmine. "At Last . . . ? Michelle Obama, Beyoncé, Race and History." *Daedalus* 140, no. 1 (2011): 131–41. https://doi.org/10.1162/DAED_a_00065.

Guilbault, Jocelyne. "On Redefining the 'Local' through World Music." *World of Music* 35, no. 2 (1993): 33–47. https://www.jstor.org/stable/43615565.

Guilbault, Jocelyne, and Timothy Rommen, eds. *Sounds of Vacation: Political Economies of Caribbean Tourism*. Durham, NC: Duke University Press, 2019.

Hernandez, Jillian. *Aesthetics of Excess: The Art and Politics of Black and Latina Embodiment*. Durham, NC: Duke University Press, 2020.

Herrera, Brian Eugenio. *Latin Numbers: Playing Latino in Twentieth-Century U.S. Popular Performance*. Ann Arbor: University of Michigan Press, 2015.

hooks, bell. *Black Looks: Race and Representation*. Boston: South End, 1992.

Hutchinson, Sydney. "Breaking Borders / Quebrando Fronteras: Dancing in the Borderscape." In *Transnational Encounters: Music and Performance at the U.S.-Mexico Border*, edited by Alejandro Madrid, 41–66. New York: Oxford University Press, 2007.

Hutchinson, Sydney. *From Quebradita to Duranguense: Dance in Mexican American Youth Culture*. Tucson: University of Arizona Press, 2007.

James, Eric P., and Rebecca Gill. "Neoliberalism and the Communicative Labor of CrossFit." *Communication and Sport* 6, no. 6 (2018): 703–27. https://doi.org/10.1177/2167479517737036.

Jang, Sukbin, Si Hyun Han, and Ji-Young Rhee. "Cluster of Coronavirus Disease Associated with Fitness Dance Classes, South Korea." *Emerging Infectious Diseases* 26, no. 8 (2020): 1917–20. https://doi.org/10.3201/eid2608.200633.

Jeffries, Michael P. *Thug Life: Race, Gender, and the Meaning of Hip-Hop*. Chicago: University of Chicago Press, 2011.

Kheshti, Roshanak. *Modernity's Ear: Listening to Race and Gender in World Music*. New York: New York University Press, 2015.

King, Samantha. "Civic Fitness: The Body Politics of Commodity Activism." In *Commodity Activism: Cultural Resistance in Neoliberal Times*, edited by Roopali Mukherjee and Sarah Banet-Weiser, 199–218. New York: New York University Press, 2012.

Krishnan, Sridevi, Theresa N. Tokar, Mallory M. Boylan, Kent Griffin, Du Feng, Linda Mcmurry, Christina Esperat, and Jamie A. Cooper. "Zumba Dance Improves Health in Overweight/Obese or Type 2 Diabetic Women." *American Journal of Health Behavior* 39, no. 1 (January 2015): 109–20. https://doi.org/10.5993/AJHB.39.1.12.

Kun, Josh. "What Is an MC If He Can't Rap to Banda? Making Music in Nuevo L.A." *American Quarterly* 56, no. 3 (2004): 741–58. https://doi.org/10.1353/aq.2004.0036.

Lau, Kimberly J. *New Age Capitalism: Making Money East of Eden.* Philadelphia: University of Pennsylvania Press, 2000.

LeBesco, Kathleen. "Fat." In *Keywords for Disability Studies*, edited by Rachel Adams, Benjamin Reiss, and David Serlin, 84–85. New York: New York University Press, 2015.

LeBrón, Marisol. *Policing Life and Death: Race, Violence, and Resistance in Puerto Rico.* Berkeley: University of California Press, 2019.

Lee, Junglyeon, Jinhan Park, Yujin Kim, and Minjung Woo. "Affective Change with Variations in Zumba Fitness Intensity as Measured by a Smartwatch." *Perceptual and Motor Skills* 128, no. 5 (2021): 2255–78. https://doi.org/10.1177/00315125211022700.

León, Juan. "Tropical Overexposure: Miami's 'Sophisticated Tropics' and the Balsero." In *Tropicalizations: Transcultural Representations of Latinidad*, edited by Frances R. Aparicio and Susana Chávez-Silverman, 213–28. Hanover, NH: University Press of New England, 1997.

Lima, Lázaro. *Being Brown: Sonia Sotomayor and the Latino Question.* Berkeley: University of California Press, 2019.

Londoño, Johana. *Abstract Barrios: The Crises of Latinx Visibility in Cities.* Durham, NC: Duke University Press, 2020.

Maldonado-Torres, Nelson. "Sovereignty." In *Keywords for Latina/o Studies*, edited by Deborah R. Vargas, Lawrence La Fountain-Stokes, and Nancy Raquel Mirabal, 204–8. New York: New York University Press, 2017.

Markula, Pirkko, and Marianne I. Clark. "Ballet-Inspired Workouts: Intersections of Ballet and Fitness." In *The Evolving Feminine Ballet Body*, edited by Prikko Markula and Marianne I. Clark, 49–72. Edmonton: University of Alberta Press, 2018.

McKenzie, Shelly. *Getting Physical: The Rise of Fitness Culture in America.* Lawrence: University Press of Kansas, 2016.

McMains, Juliet. "'Hot' Latin Dance: Ethnic Identity and Stereotype." In *Oxford Handbook of Dance and Ethnicity*, edited by Anthony Shay and Barbara Sellers-Young, 480–500. New York: Oxford University Press, 2016.

Melamed, Jodi. "The Spirit of Neoliberalism: From Racial Liberalism to Neoliberal Multiculturalism." *Social Text* 24, no. 4 (89) (2006): 1–24. https://doi.org/10.1215/01642472-2006-009.

Menjívar, Cecilia. "Illegality." In *Keywords for Latina/o Studies*, edited by Deborah R. Vargas, Nancy Raquel Mirabal, and Lawrence La Fountain-Stokes, 93–96. New York: New York University Press, 2017.

Miller, Kiri. *Playable Bodies: Dance Games and Intimate Media.* New York: Oxford University Press, 2017.

Minkoff-Zern, Laura-Anne, and Megan A. Carney. "Latino Im/Migrants, 'Dietary Health' and Social Exclusion: A Critical Examination of Nutrition Interventions in California." *Food, Culture and Society* 18, no. 3 (2015): 463–80. https://doi.org/10.1080/15528014.2015.1043108.

Molina, Natalia. *Fit to Be Citizens? Public Health and Race in Los Angeles, 1879–1939*. Berkeley: University of California Press, 2006.

Molina-Guzmán, Isabel. *Dangerous Curves: Latina Bodies in the Media*. New York: New York University Press, 2010.

Molina-Guzmán, Isabel, and Angharad N. Valdivia. "Brain, Brow, and Booty: Latina Iconicity in U.S. Popular Culture." *Communication Review* 7, no. 2 (2004): 205–21.

Mora, G. Cristina. *Making Hispanics: How Activists, Bureaucrats, and Media Constructed a New American*. Chicago: University of Chicago Press, 2014.

Mukherjee, Roopali. "Antiracism Limited: A Pre-history of Post-race." *Cultural Studies* 30, no. 1 (2016): 47–77. https://doi.org/10.1080/09502386.2014.935455.

Mukherjee, Roopali, and Sarah Banet-Weiser, eds. *Commodity Activism: Cultural Resistance in Neoliberal Times*. New York: New York University Press, 2012.

Mukherjee, Roopali, Sarah Banet-Weiser, and Herman Gray, eds. *Racism Postrace*. Durham, NC: Duke University Press, 2019.

Musselman, Cody. "Training for the 'Unknown and Unknowable': CrossFit and Evangelical Temporality." *Religions* 10, no. 11 (2019): 624. https://doi.org/10.3390/rel10110624.

Nakano Glenn, Evelyn, ed. *Shades of Difference: Why Skin Color Matters*. Stanford, CA: Stanford University Press, 2009.

Negrón-Muntaner, Frances. *Boricua Pop: Puerto Ricans and American Culture from West Side Story to Jennifer Lopez*. New York: New York University Press, 2004.

Nieri, Tanya, and Elizabeth Hughes. "All about Having Fun: Women's Experience of Zumba Fitness." *Sociology of Sport Journal* 33, no. 2 (2016): 135–45. https://doi.org/10.1123/ssj.2015-0071.

Nieri, Tanya, and Elizabeth Hughes. "Zumba Instructor Strategies: Constraining or Liberating for Women Participants?" *Leisure Sciences*, February 10, 2021, 1–18. https://doi.org/10.1080/01490400.2021.1881669.

Orgad, Shani, and Rosalind Gill. *Confidence Culture*. Durham, NC: Duke University Press, 2022.

Pacini Hernandez, Deborah. "The Name Game: Locating Latinas/os, Latins, and Latin Americans in the US Popular Music Landscape." In *A Companion to Latina/o Studies*, edited by Juan Flores and Renato Rosaldo, 49–59. Malden, MA: Blackwell, 2007.

Pacini Hernandez, Deborah. *Oye Como Va! Hybridity and Identity in Latino Popular Music*. Philadelphia: Temple University Press, 2010.

Paik, A. Naomi. *Bans, Walls, Raids, Sanctuary: Understanding U.S. Immigration for the Twenty-First Century*. Berkeley: University of California Press, 2020.

Park, Michael K. "Psy-Zing Up the Mainstreaming of 'Gangnam Style': Embracing Asian Masculinity as Neo-Minstrelsy?" *Journal of Communication Inquiry* 39, no. 3 (2015): 195–212. https://doi.org/10.1177/0196859915575068.

Pérez, Beto, and Maggie Greenwood-Robinson. *Zumba: Ditch the Workout, Join the Party! The Zumba Weight Loss Program*. New York: Wellness Central, 2009.

Pérez, Elizabeth. "The Ontology of Twerk: From 'Sexy' Black Movement Style to Afro-Diasporic Sacred Dance." *African and Black Diaspora: An International Journal* 9, no. 1 (2016): 16–31. https://doi.org/10.1080/17528631.2015.1055650.

Perry, Leah. *The Cultural Politics of U.S. Immigration: Gender, Race, and Media*. New York: New York University Press, 2016.

Pilcher, Jeffrey M. *Planet Taco: A Global History of Mexican Food*. New York: Oxford University Press, 2012.

Poey, Delia. *Cuban Women and Salsa: To the Beat of Their Own Drum*. New York: Palgrave Macmillan, 2014.

Powers, Devon, and DM Greenwell. "Branded Fitness: Exercise and Promotional Culture." *Journal of Consumer Culture* 17, no. 3 (2017): 523–41. https://doi.org/10.1177/1469540515623606.

Ramírez, Catherine Sue. *Assimilation: An Alternative History*. Berkeley: University of California Press, 2020.

Ramirez Berg, Charles. *Latino Images in Film: Stereotypes, Subversion and Resistance*. Austin: University of Texas Press, 2002.

Rank, Mark R. "The Random Factor: Chance, Luck, and the American Dream." In *The Routledge Handbook of the American Dream*, vol. 1, edited by Robert Hauhart and Mitja Sardoc, 123–32. New York: Routledge, 2021.

Rivera, Raquel Z., Wayne Marshall, and Deborah Pacini Hernandez, eds. *Reggaeton*. Durham, NC: Duke University Press, 2009.

Rivera-Rideau, Petra R. "Reinventing Enrique Iglesias: Constructing Latino Whiteness in the Latin Urban Scene." *Latino Studies* 17, no. 4 (2019): 467–83. https://doi.org/10.1057/s41276-019-00210-1.

Rivera-Rideau, Petra R. *Remixing Reggaetón: The Cultural Politics of Race in Puerto Rico*. Durham, NC: Duke University Press, 2015.

Rivera-Rideau, Petra, and Jericko Torres-Leschnik. "'The Colors and Flavors of My Puerto Rico': Mapping Despacito's Crossovers." *Journal of Popular Music Studies* 31, no. 1 (2019): 87–108. https://doi.org/10.1525/jpms.2019.311009.

Sánchez Prado, Ignacio M. "Diana Kennedy, Rick Bayless and the Imagination of 'Authentic' Mexican Food." *Bulletin of Spanish Studies* 97, no. 4 (2020): 567–92. https://doi.org/10.1080/14753820.2020.1699330.

Sandoval-Sánchez, Alberto. *José, Can You See? Latinos on and off Broadway.* Madison: University of Wisconsin Press, 1999.

Santa Ana, Otto. *Brown Tide Rising: Metaphors of Latinos in Contemporary American Public Discourse.* Austin: University of Texas Press, 2002.

Seal, Emma, Matthew Nicholson, Nicola McNeil, Arthur Stukas, Paul O'Halloran, and Erica Randle. "Fear of Judgement and Women's Physical (In)Activity Experiences." *International Review for the Sociology of Sport* 57, no. 3 (2022): 381–400. https://doi.org/10.1177/10126902211016631.

Sheller, Mimi. "Natural Hedonism: The Invention of Caribbean Islands as Tropical Playgrounds." In *Tourism in the Caribbean: Trends, Development, Prospects*, edited by David Timothy Duval, 23–38. New York: Routledge, 2004.

Simonett, Helena. *Banda: Mexican Musical Life across Borders.* Middletown, CT: Wesleyan University Press, 2001.

Smith Maguire, Jennifer. *Fit for Consumption: Sociology and the Business of Fitness.* London: Routledge, 2014.

Sternlicht, Eric, Frank Frisch, and Ken D. Sumida. "Zumba Fitness Workouts: Are They an Appropriate Alternative to Running or Cycling?" *Sport Sciences for Health* 9, no. 3 (December 2013): 155–59. https://doi.org/10.1007/s11332-013-0155-8.

Stoever, Jennifer Lynn. *The Sonic Color Line: Race and the Cultural Politics of Listening.* New York: New York University Press, 2016.

Stoever-Ackerman, Jennifer. "Splicing the Sonic Color-Line: Tony Schwartz Remixes Postwar Nueva York." *Social Text* 28, no. 1 (102) (2010): 59–85. https://doi.org/10.1215/01642472-2009-060.

Thompson, Cheryl. "Neoliberalism, Soul Food, and the Weight of Black Women." *Feminist Media Studies* 15, no. 5 (2015): 794–812. https://doi.org/10.1080/14680777.2014.1003390.

Valentín-Escobar, Wilson A. "El Hombre que Respira Debajo del Agua: Trans-Boricua Memories, Identities, and Nationalisms Performed through the Death of Héctor Lavoe." In *Situating Salsa: Global Markets and Local Meanings in Latin Music*, edited by Lise Waxer, 161–86. New York: Routledge, 2002.

Vendramin, Barbara, Marco Bergamin, Stefano Gobbo, Lucia Cugusi, Federica Duregon, Valentina Bullo, Marco Zaccaria, Daniel Neunhaeuserer, and Andrea Ermolao. "Health Benefits of Zumba Fitness Training: A Systematic Review." *PM&R* 8, no. 12 (December 2016): 1181–200. https://doi.org/10.1016/j.pmrj.2016.06.010.

Viana, Ricardo Borges, Claudia Lima Alves, Carlos Alexandre Vieira, Rodrigo Luiz Vancini, Mario Hebling Campos, Paulo Gentil, Marília Santos Andrade, and Claudio Andre Barbosa de Lira. "Anxiolytic Effects of a Single Session of the Exergame Zumba Fitness on Healthy Young Women." *Games for Health Journal* 6, no. 6 (2017): 365–70. https://doi.org/10.1089/g4h.2017.0085.

Waxer, Lise, ed. *Situating Salsa: Global Markets and Local Meanings in Latin Popular Music*. New York: Routledge, 2002.

Woitas, Melanie. "'Exercise Teaches You the Pleasure of Discipline': The Female Body in Jane Fonda's Aerobics Videos." *Historical Social Research* 43, no. 2 (2018): 148–64. https://doi.org/10.12759/hsr.43.2018.2.148-164.

Zanker, Cathy, and Michael Gard. "Fatness, Fitness, and the Moral Universe of Sport and Physical Activity." *Sociology of Sport Journal* 25, no. 1 (2008): 48–65. https://doi.org/10.1123/ssj.25.1.48.

INDEX

Page numbers followed by *f* refer to figures.

ship and, 25; civic rights and, 123; fun and, 101; Latino Threat Narrative and, 11, 185–86; salsa and, 36; tropicalized Latinness and, 18, 58, 184–86

Latinx populations, 8, 11–12, 19, 26, 124, 133; urban, 62; US, 67

Latinx stars, 9, 124

Lavoe, Hector, 180, 183

León, Juan, 60–61, 196n13

"Let It Move You" campaign, 89, 97–100

Lopez, Jennifer, 12, 57, 69, 77, 124, 128, 198n49, 199n50

love, 23–26, 126, 158–59, 164–68, 170, 173–76, 178–79, 185–86; decolonial, 209n47; in general, 160; self-love, 152, 162–63; selling, 149, 151–55, 161, 179

McKenzie, Shelly, 6, 91

McMains, Juliet, 64, 197n24

mambo, 34, 61, 84

marketing, 1–2, 14, 20, 22, 105, 181, 189n7; American dream and, 121, 127; authenticity and, 31, 37, 44; branding and, 154; campaigns, 114–15; of ethnic difference, 5; fiesta and, 84; fun and, 91; health and fitness, 163; instructors and, 4, 111, 119, 138, 146; multilevel, 20, 142, 147; strategy, 149; of video games, 30

Marmitte, Ricardo, 49, 202n45

Martin, Kass, 27, 103

Martin, Ricky, 11, 47–48, 57–58

masculinity, 74; Black, 80, 199n65

media, 21, 89, 98; Black and Latina women in, 82; "Despacito" and, 57; discourses, 6; English-language, 13; Latinx hypersexuality in, 71; Latinx people in, 199n52; mainstream, 10–12, 17; popular, 18, 127; postracial ideology and, 207n14; Puerto Rican migration and, 66; social, 20, 41, 136, 138, 156; Spanish-language, 16, 41, 58, 202n45

memes, 2, 20–21, 24, 73–77

merengue, 1–3, 32, 35, 39, 83, 86, 108, 112, 165, 193n20; marches, 180

meritocracy, 5, 137, 179

Mexico, 32, 51; US border with, 10–12, 50, 52, 130, 190–91n32

Miami, 3, 19, 25, 37, 64, 69, 126–29, 180; tropics and, 196n13

Miranda, Carmen, 57–58

modernity, 23, 31, 175; hegemonic discourses of, 37; US, 17; Western, 56, 94, 96, 115

morality, 6–7, 91–92; of modern Western subjects, 101; of modern white subjects, 61

Mukherjee, Roopali, 152, 207n7, 207n14

multiculturalism, 149, 152, 167; neoliberal, 19, 25, 152–53

Murphy, Kaitlyn, 133–34

music, 1, 3–4, 14–15, 23, 28, 31–40, 42, 44–48, 50, 55, 67, 81, 87–88, 94, 102, 112, 126, 170, 177, 187, 189n3; African, 195n44, 201n26; BollyX and, 206n75; Caribbean, 82; country, 172; fiesta and, 56, 66; Latin American, 34, 36; Latinx, 18; Let It Move You campaign and, 97–98, 100–101; license, 117; loud, 66; Puerto Rican, 47–48, 180; Spanish Caribbean, 63; tropicalized Latinness and, 63; videos, 57, 71, 74–75, 157, 164, 167f; world, 32, 40, 197n29; Zumba-produced, 20, 52–53, 119, 139, 166, 171, 174–75. *See also* Afropop; bachata; Bollywood; Brazilian funk; cumbia; dancehall; flamenco; hip-hop; kizomba; Latin music; mambo; merengue; plena; popular music; reggaetón; salsa; samba; soca; Zumba formula

music industry, 54; Latin, 11, 36, 42, 61; world, 32

national origin, 15–16, 31, 96, 137

neoliberalism, 5, 24, 122–24, 162, 174–75; American dream and, 147; racism and, 188

New England, 2, 21, 120, 195n45

Newsome, Bree, 160, 175

Nia Technique, 143, 206n75

Nieri, Tanya, 77, 89, 94, 113

Obama, Barack, 153; administration of, 209n45

obesity, 8–9; childhood, 8, 157, 160, 166–67; epidemic, 7–8

Orgad, Shani, 162–63, 166, 174, 208n37

Orlando, Florida, 48, 111, 131–32, 139

otherness, 12, 25, 124; of Latinness, 88, 153; racial/racialized, 17, 66–67, 89, 120

participants, 26, 30, 38, 54, 90, 92–93, 117, 149, 181, 183; branded fitness and, 154; COVID-19 and, 116; fiesta and, 24; fun and, 115; Latinness and, 18; philanthropy and, 161; physical health and, 102, 107; tropicalized Latinness and, 64, 73, 77, 88, 96; women, 95

Party in Pink, 157, 159, 161

patriotism, 165; CrossFit and, 92, 154; fitness and, 6

Perlman, Alberto, 3–4, 41–42, 97, 117, 119–20, 127, 145–46, 197n34, 206n72; on inclusivity, 19; Zumba Fitness's business model and, 14, 55; Zumba Wear and, 64–65

Perlman, Raquel, 3, 129

Pérez, Alberto "Beto," 3, 9, 23, 25, 27–28, 33, 41, 55, 71, 103–4, 120, 125, 128–32, 137–38, 145–46, 157, 189n6, 202n45; classes taught by, 101; *Zumba Ditch the Workout, Join the Party! The Zumba Weight Loss Program*, 23, 32, 34–36, 44, 51, 87, 125–27

Pérez, Elizabeth, 78–79, 199n62

perreo, 79, 83

Perry, Leah, 12, 124, 204n27

Pitbull (Armando Christian Pérez), 37–38, 40, 43, 48

physical activity, 9, 90, 159

physical fitness, 6, 9, 107, 149, 151; education, 88, 110

plena, 33, 47–48, 180–81, 188

Polo Spreads Love organization, 149, 150f

popular culture, 22, 71; Latinx, 186; Latinx populations in, 124; postracial ideologies and, 153, 207n14; US, 9, 56, 172, 200n66

popular/pop music, 11, 18, 23, 43–44, 56, 86, 93, 184; African, 195n44 (*see also* Afropop); Asian, 48–49; authenticity and, 67; contemporary, 37; global, 40, 48; Latin, 37; Latina women in, 71; US, 15, 34, 37–38, 40, 77, 79, 175

postracialism, 5, 24, 26, 122–24, 149, 151–53, 174, 188

Powers, Devon, 154, 191–92n61

primitivity, 24, 31, 35, 123; the Caribbean and, 196n12; Latin American, 23; tropicalized Latinness and, 100

Proposition 187, 9, 51, 190n32

Psy, 74–75, 76f

Puerto Rico, 18, 33–34, 47, 124, 131–32, 148–49, 174–75, 180–81, 182f, 192n3, 205n58. *See also* bomba; Daddy Yankee; Hurricane María; plena; reggaetón; salsa

quebradita, 2, 50–52

Quintanilla, Selena, 12, 124

race, 3, 63, 74, 96, 131, 166, 178; American dream and, 137, 147; assimilation and, 123; authenticity and, 54; fun and, 88; Latinidad and, 16; Latinx and, 189n4; loudness and, 66; love and, 186; relations and, 151–52; sexuality and, 24; in the United States, 26

racial difference, 17, 19, 133, 167, 172, 186; love and, 162–63, 165, 171; postracialism and, 151–53; racism and, 124; white women and, 208n37

racial hierarchies, 5, 17, 23–24, 73, 101, 162; American dream and, 124; fun and, 97; global, 37; hegemonic, 172; mind-body divide and, 115; modern, 31, 34, 72

racial segregation, 152, 205n58

racism, 82, 120, 124, 137, 178; antiracism, 152–54; authenticity and, 31; diversity and, 163; Latin music industry and, 61; love and, 168; structural, 19, 25, 133, 172. *See also* postracialism; systemic racism

Ramírez, Catherine, 8, 25, 123, 129, 133

Reagan administration, 6–7